ROBERT HAGIN'S experience in first
understanding, and then successfully
applying, the new science of investing
parallels the development of this book.
In 1961, while studying under an IBM
research fellowship, he became one of
the pioneers in using computers and
advanced research techniques to ex-
pose the stock market's myths and
secrets. He has taught graduate-level
courses at both UCLA's Graduate
School of Business and the University
of Pennsylvania's Wharton School of Finance.

CHRIS MADER is an Assistant Professor at the Wharton School of Finance.
He has co-authored with Dr. Hagin a
book entitled *Information Systems:
Technology, Economics, Applications.*

what today's investor should know about
THE NEW SCIENCE OF INVESTING

what today's investor
should know about
THE NEW SCIENCE
OF INVESTING

ROBERT HAGIN

Director of Marketing Support
duPont Walston, Incorporated

with

Chris Mader

Assistant Professor
Wharton School of Finance and Commerce
University of Pennsylvania

1973

DOW JONES-IRWIN, INC.   *Homewood, Illinois 60430*

First Printing, November 1973

ISBN 0-87094-064-3
Library of Congress Catalog Card No. 73-87367

Printed in the United States of America

To all investors,

but especially those who lost money
in the bear markets of the last
decade

Dow Jones Industrial Average, 1961–73

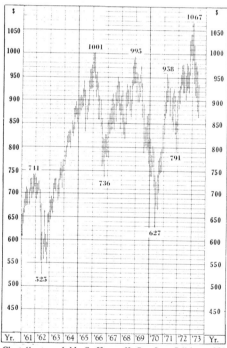

Chart Courtesy of M. C. Horsey & Co., Inc., Salisbury, Md.
21801

Preface

Historically, there have been two types of investment books. Most offer advice with scant factual support. Other books, and the learned journals, contain a wealth of information, but typically leave the reader without practical suggestions. This book is different. It offers practical advice based on factual information. The facts have been gleaned from hundreds of scientific research studies, conducted by both university researchers and investment professionals. The conclusions drawn from these studies furnish a disturbing contrast to the practices of most individual, as well as many professional, investors. Clearly, most investors have not kept pace with the explosive growth of investment knowledge, and obsolete techniques of asset management abound.

Ironically, *the new science of investing* was born in a decade during which repeated bear markets and poor asset management inflicted catastrophic losses on many investors. The sight of once lush portfolios drained of value, coupled with the financial failure of many inadequately capitalized and poorly managed brokerage firms, have prompted many investors to leave the market. Many of these investors have now blindly placed their investable funds into presumably safe havens offering relatively unattractive yields and no appreciation possibility—and no escape from the steady erosion of inflation. If continued, this "head-in-the-sand" approach to investing may destroy the financial security and independence of millions of American families. To counter this disturbing trend, this book provides the knowledge and direction you need to invest profitably while *protecting your assets*.

The advice in this work has been distilled from the two largely separable worlds of theory and practice. The resultant investing strategies can be understood and applied by the general public. They combine what is *known* about investing, and what is *practiced,* into successful asset management techniques. The book begins by condensing *into an easily understandable form* the essential content of an advanced investments course at one of the nation's leading business schools. This scientific knowledge is then balanced against the practical mechanics of the investment business. The book is written for today's investor. No special knowledge or required educational level is assumed—only an interest in building and protecting a prosperous future through modern investment management.

What Today's Investor Should Know About The New Science of Investing is organized around three ingredients of a successful investing strategy: planning what needs to be done; understanding how to do it; and finally, doing it. The five introductory chapters guide you toward the development of an overall personal financial plan and introduce concepts that will help you understand and appreciate modern investment science. The first major portion of the book—Understanding the New Science—explains what we really know about how to, and how *not* to, invest. The second major portion—Applying the New Science to Personal Investing—translates what should, and should not, be done into an easily understood and easily applied investment strategy.

It is impossible to acknowledge each of the hundreds of people who have contributed to this book. Special thanks should go to my coauthor, Professor Chris Mader of the Wharton School of Finance, who, as an outstanding student, and then as a colleague, and always as a close friend, has made a significant contribution to the ideas presented here.

At the risk of detracting from those who are not mentioned, I would like to acknowledge the inspiration and guidance of Ross Perot of Electronic Data Systems, Morton Meyerson of duPont Glore Forgan, Inc., and Robert Dunwoody of duPont Walston Incorporated. Through the commitment of such men, an investment services industry dedicated to meeting the unique needs of each individual, without generating needless commission dollars, will become a reality.

My personal thanks to Frederick Hampton and Erich Weissenberger who edited the manuscript, Janet Egbert, who checked the bibliographic references, and Pearl Coggeshall, who typed the myriad drafts. And finally, an especial thanks to my friends and acquaintances in the several cities where the book was written. Their repeated investment mistakes were the stimulus for this book.

The authors welcome the reader's comments, criticisms, and inquiries. Every effort will be made to draft an individual reply to such letters. Correspondence should be addressed to:

> DR. ROBERT L. HAGIN
> P. O. Box 199
> Wall Street Station
> New York, New York   10005

> or

> DR. S. CHRIS MADER
> Wharton School
> Philadelphia, Pennsylvania 19174

Contents

Part II
APPLYING THE NEW SCIENCE TO PERSONAL INVESTING

A.   Knowing What to Expect

B.   Balancing Performance and Risk

C.   Analyzing Alternative Investment Instruments

an introductory essay

The Working American—
An Economic Miracle

by H. ROSS PEROT

The most valuable resource in the American economic system is the working American. The working American makes our country the world's largest market for goods and services. The working American is the backbone of our tax system. The working American creates business growth, business profits, and business taxes. The working American, by investing, also helps create his own job and jobs for others. Collectively, the working Americans are the world's largest financial institution, without whose investment capital our national needs cannot be met. In short, the working American is an economic miracle, supporting his family and bearing the burdens of his city, his state, and his nation.

Unfortunately, the working American has been poorly served by the investment community. In Wall Street's myopic world of picking hot stocks, passing along tips and reading the market's tea leaves, the industry has often lost sight of its primary purpose—to channel the investable funds of the working American into profitable investments. This lack of interest in the small investor, coupled with the financial collapse or forced merger of more than one hundred brokerage firms over the past few years, has driven many working Americans away from Wall Street.

As an industry, the investment profession can, and must, adopt several policies to aid the efficient flow of funds from the working American to the economy that his investments make possible. The first policy is *honesty!* In my experience, successful businesses and successful people have one characteristic that stands out—honesty. *What Today's In-*

vestor Should Know About the New Science of Investing is an honest book about investing. It is not based on stories, tips, or gimmicks. It is not a get-rich-quick scheme. It is an honest look at what everyone should know about investing.

In the years ahead our increased understanding and application of *The New Science of Investing* will dramatically change the investment business as we know it today. Only now is the investment community beginning to bring this new science to each individual investor. A new and revitalized investment industry that is responsible and responsive to the needs of individual investors is, however, scant comfort to the citizen whose hard-earned investable funds are drained away by ever-growing taxes.

In view of this fact, I believe that the working American needs a tax break. America's working families need a government policy that encourages and permits them to accumulate a stake—to accumulate capital—so that they can possess a meaningful share of the growth and gain of this economy.

For our system to be successful, each American willing to work must have a job available to him. Jobs can never be taken for granted. During our lifetimes, we have seen men and women looking for jobs that did not exist. We have seen defeat and despair on the faces of those who could not provide for their families. None of us wants to see that again.

It is only as a working American that the average American can continue to be our most important resource. Our national objectives must assure that the working American continues to have a job—and the better his job, the larger a customer he becomes, while the United States continues to grow as the collective customer. As our population expands we must see that his children have jobs. We must make the words "Made in USA" the symbol of excellence at a competitive price. We can do it. We must do it. The question is how do we do it?

We must take the long-term steps necessary to regenerate our economy's competitive position. It is imperative that we invest hundreds of billions of dollars to modernize and expand our industrial capability in order to allow the working American, with his high standard of living, to compete effectively with his counterparts around the world. This is going to take money—more money than we have ever raised before in our country. It is this massive new investment which will protect the jobs we have and create future ones. During this same period, we must also launch and complete a very expensive search for new energy sources.

We must expand our public utility and transportation systems. We must create a fluid and economical system for financial transactions. Dramatic improvements must be made in our cities. The list of requirements is endless.

What mechanism will we use to raise this money? The United States capital market is without question the finest in the world. Ask any businessmen from any other country. There is only one Wall Street. It is a great resource for achieving our national goals. Simply stated, it is an alternative to oppressive taxes. However, we must strengthen this capital market to meet the urgent demands of the coming years.

We can think of the New York Stock Exchange and the other securities markets simply as scoreboards reflecting corporate performance. In a prosperous economy, as a company grows in size and profits, the price of its stock tends to rise. It is a winning company. It pays more taxes and tends to create new jobs, with each new worker being a new taxpayer. If every company were a winning company, we would not be preoccupied with raising more taxes, finding more jobs, and competing internationally.

There is one unique characteristic about these scoreboards, though— the scores can go down as well as up. There are those in this country who assume that, no matter what conditions prevail, the scoreboards will always reflect good corporate performance. *The fact is that these scoreboards also reflect the willingness of people to invest in America's businesses.*

In plain talk, these stock exchange scoreboards could conceivably flicker or even go out if the capital markets are badly enough abused. I have seen the scoreboards flicker. I invested 65 million dollars to keep the scoreboard lights burning at a time of crisis. The fact that I took a risk of this size is the strongest evidence I can give you of my conviction that we must keep the financial springs flowing in this country without interruption.

The flow of capital in the United States can be compared to the Mississippi River. Looking at this great river, it is inconceivable that it could ever dry up. Flowing into it are springs, creeks, small rivers, and other tributaries. However, by simply clogging these springs and damming the tributaries, even the Mississippi River could become a ditch. If we clog our financial springs in the same fashion, our capital market could also become a lifeless ditch just when it should be at full flow.

The working American is the key to a smooth-flowing supply of investment capital. The millions of individual investors in this country are like the springs that build the Mississippi River. We must make investing an attractive option to the working American. Only this collective financial institution has enough money to finance the work that must be done.

Our financial springs must provide the money to create the plants, the jobs, the new transit systems, urban improvements, and so forth. Yet, some are proposing that we raise capital gains taxes. This would clog the financial springs. Why? Because today's working American has an option about investing his money! If there is no economic advantage to investing in our capital system, he will not choose to do so. Our capital rivers would then begin to drop—just when we need them full to the banks.

The capital gains tax proposal I have made to Congress would stimulate these financial springs and make our markets more liquid. Most important, I know through my own experience that getting started is the hardest part of the American economic system. This proposal will allow people who work and save to get started—and get ahead.

My capital gains tax proposal is simple. The millions of citizens who work, pay taxes, save money, and dream that their children will have a better opportunity are the financial backbone of this country. Only they can save and invest enough for the huge capital expansion necessary to make and keep the United States competitive. Therefore, *I have proposed to Congress that every American be given the opportunity to accumulate $100,000 in capital gains—tax free.* This is meant to encourage the working American who is trying to accumulate the stake in life that all families want and need. Indeed, our principal economic competitors—the Germans and the Japanese—already impose no capital gains taxes and subsidize businesses to create jobs.

An economic miracle will take place if this proposal materializes. We will build a whole new base of substantial taxpayers. Once these taxpayers cross the $100,000 threshold, I propose that they be taxed in the same way all other capital gains taxes are handled. In addition to building a new tax base of substantial individuals in this country, we will reap further benefits from the many new jobs created by these investments.

What does all this mean to the typical American worker? It means a great deal. Maybe he doesn't want to invest. In all probability, however, his retirement income is tied to stock values. Profit-sharing funds are also invested in securities. Damage the capital market in this country and stock prices will drop. An investment in any security is worth only what someone will pay for it. Keeping industry strong and the market liquid protects the worker's job and protects the value of his personal and pension funds.

I know I speak for the average American when I say he considers it very important that his children have an opportunity to achieve goals and dreams beyond his own grasp. I am sure you are wondering what sort of capital gains tax I would propose for persons in my category. I will leave that to your judgment. It would be self-serving for me to discuss this, although I will say that I certainly expect to pay my fair share.

It is fundamentally important to give the man who is trying to get started a chance to get ahead. We can best do this by allowing him to invest and reinvest in our country's future—the businesses that provide the jobs. As these jobs grow, he will grow. As he grows, the tax base grows. As that happens, the United States becomes stronger.

A current catchphrase is, "Money made by money should be taxed like money made by men." But, this statement equates two totally different types of money—income money and investment money. In addition, it assumes that "money will be made by money" and that a job will exist to allow "money to be made by men." The capital rivers may not always flow nor always be profitable. The financial scoreboards may flicker and go out if the financial springs dry up.

I believe some of the greatest wisdom in our country comes from everyday people. Recently, a construction worker handed me an envelope. He said, "I am from the mountains of West Virginia. We have a saying you will like." Scrawled in pencil were these words, "There ain't many hunters, but everybody wants the meat." The hunters—as its workers and taxpayers—make this country great. Our challenge is to develop as many hunters as possible to balance the taxpayer who produces more than he uses with the tax user who cannot produce as much as he needs. In every possible way, we must increase the proportion of those who can and will build the tax base.

If we are to raise the capital requirements for our future, the working American must be given opportunity through our tax laws to become a participating capitalist. I propose that he be given a proper incentive to share in capital gains through investing and that the investment community provide him with the knowledge and service to succeed in that endeavor. *The New Science of Investing* will help you understand and apply modern investing knowledge. With this knowledge the working American can share in the fruits of our capitalistic system through his earnings *and* his investment returns—and the words "Made in USA" will become the hallmark of excellence and economic efficiency.

introduction

chapter
1
Successful Investing

Investing and speculation originated with Mesopotamian merchants in the third millennium B.C. Since then, millions of intelligent men and women have spent billions of hours searching for profitable investing strategies. What, then, can this book offer investors that is either new or useful? Quite simply, this book offers you a readable explanation of the startling *new science of investing* and tells you how to apply this science for personal profit.

In the last ten years, computerized investment studies have opened new vistas of understanding. This research effort has been so intense that, in the last decade, we have more than doubled our knowledge of how to invest. Researchers have developed, refined and tested concepts like the random-walk model, the efficient capital market theory, and beta coefficients, to name a few. Unfortunately, many investors, as well as some market professionals, assume that these concepts are difficult to understand and apply. To correct this common misconception, this book condenses and explains the new science of investing in everyday language and distills the conclusions into easily applied investment strategies.

There are two paradoxes in the way most people approach investing. First, while most investors rank financial success and security among their most sought after goals, they pursue this goal with a mixture of hasty and haphazard guesswork and wishful thinking. Second, in the tireless, often fanatic, search for investment *news,* new investment *knowledge* is often overlooked.

Paradox 1: Despite Its Importance, Investing Is Often Haphazard

While financial security is a dominant concern of most American families, relatively few people plan and execute a reasoned approach to investing. Most investors want to own shares of well-managed companies. A recognized feature of such organizations is that they measure their performance against realistic goals and objectives. Presumably, no one would knowingly buy stock in a company that did not weigh its performance against explicit short- and long-range goals. Yet, while investors seek this kind of company, few of them properly plan and manage their own investments around well-defined goals.

The failure of most families to achieve financial security through well-planned and well-managed investing can be traced to a combination of

- fragmented asset management, and
- irrational decision making.

A typical family has a checking account at a convenient commercial bank. It also very likely has a savings account, either at the same bank or at a savings and loan association. The mortgage, if there is one, is often made with yet another institution. Life insurance coverage is probably obtained through a combination of a long-standing policy and the employer's group plan. Retirement income, one of the most haphazardly handled and least understood parts of personal wealth, is somehow to be derived, when needed, from Social Security and retirement funds. The will, if there is one, probably leaves everything to the spouse with no consideration of confiscatory taxes. Upon this fragmented foundation, the typical family erects a *potpourri* of investments: savings bonds, mutual fund shares, stocks, and so forth. Once a year, they pull everything together just long enough to figure out their income tax, and then forget about it for another year. This is fragmented asset management!

Fragmented asset management is the result of looking at each of your assets—such as real estate, insurance, savings, and investments—individually, rather than as part of a total structure. With fragmented asset management the important interrelationships among assets are overlooked. Investment decisions are reached without evaluating tax implications. Insurance commitments are made without carefully considering the ultimate value and disposition of current assets, estate tax implications, and so on.

The failure of most people to view their assets as part of one closely related structure, designed *in toto* to meet specified objectives, is largely the result of a fragmented financial services industry. For a variety of reasons, we have historically bought stock from stock brokers, insurance from insurance agents, banked at banks, and borrowed from lending institutions. This fragmentation of the financial services industry has led the industry's customers into making irrational financial decisions.

Such irrational choices manifest themselves in the public's tendency

- to select investments compatable with their needs and goals, and
- to engage in unplanned, impulse buying and selling.

Most people buy stock because they hope it will go up in value. Few fully consider how high the stock can reasonably be expected to rise, over what period of time, and how these hopes relate to their needs and objectives. Few weigh the risks associated with different classes of investment instruments: speculative stocks, securities of seasoned blue-chip companies, corporate bonds, warrants, puts, calls, and so forth. The result is that most investors buy one product—stock—without ascertaining how much the investment is supposed to return, how soon, the downside risk, and how it relates to other investments.

These irrational purchases result largely from impulse buying. When the market is pushing new highs, and everyone is talking about their profits, there is an emotional urge to "jump on the bandwagon." When the market has sagged, and people see stocks selling at fractions of their recent highs, there is an emotional urge to "buy the bargains." In between, there is a mixture of hope and fear. When you are in the market, you hope it will go higher, but are afraid it will go lower. When you are out of the market, you hope it will go lower so you can buy at the level where you wish you had bought, but you are afraid it will go higher before you make up your mind. This endless hope-fear-hope cycle is the result of impulse buying.

The solution to the related problems of fragmented asset management and irrational decision making is to make all investment decisions in terms of the

- composite structure of *all* your assets, and
- your personal financial objectives.

The easiest way to analyze your financial asset structure is to imagine a triangle that is divided into four layers, as shown in Figure 1–1. The bottom layer represents your foundation assets. The assets in the founda-

FIGURE 1–1
Asset Triangle

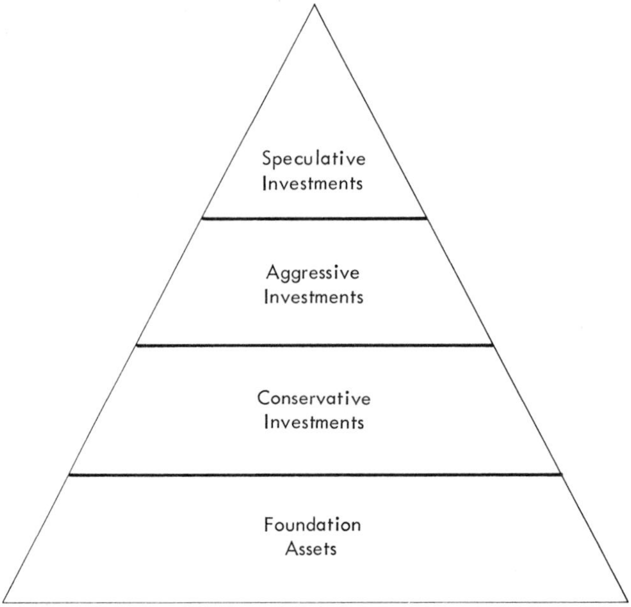

tion layer, such as equity in your home, provide the basis for your current standard of living. Other foundation assets, such as bank savings, insurance, Social Security and retirement benefits, protect you and your family against short- and long-term contingencies.

The next layer of the asset triangle, which we call conservative investments, represents low-risk investments with long-term objectives. These include mutual funds with histories of good, stable performance, blue-chip common stocks, high-grade bonds, and so forth. The third layer of the asset triangle represents aggressive investments. This layer includes good-quality investments with shorter-term performance goals but a somewhat higher degree of risk. The top layer of the asset triangle represents speculative investments, such as high-risk new issues and historically volatile performers. Viewed in this way, your otherwise fragmented financial assets form a composite structure designed to meet your personal needs and objectives.

Successful investing begins with establishing realistic goals that balance your financial resources against your present and future needs. A procedure for translating your financial requirements into specific investment objectives is presented in the following two chapters. Once overall goals are established, you need to determine the proportion of your investments to be allocated to each layer of the asset triangle. Then, to eliminate confusion and temptation in investment selection you must, in turn, specify the performance objectives and risks for each layer of the triangle so that you pick the combination of instruments that will enable you to attain your financial goals. When your asset triangle is so structured, and the role of each asset is clearly earmarked, the first paradox of managing your financial future with irrational, reflex-response decisions disappears.

Paradox 2: The New Investment Knowledge Is Not Widely Known

Most people like to keep up-to-date on their investments. They buy newspapers with closing stock prices and routinely turn to the financial pages to see how they are doing. Paradoxically, few of these readers who follow the latest price movements are up-to-date on the *significance* and *usefulness* of the information they are reading. They do not know how to translate this latest news into a meaningful investment strategy. What would you do, for example, if your favorite stock increased in price, on higher volume, over each of the past five trading days? Modern research which we are going to examine will indicate what you *should* do with such news.

In addition to keeping up with the news, many investors search feverishly for companies that are steeped in science or the pursuit of innovative concepts. Yet, ironically, in their quest for an undiscovered IBM, Polaroid, Syntex, or Xerox, these same people are unfamiliar with the latest scientific knowledge concerning an important part of their own business—their personal investing.

In fairness to most investors, this knowledge has not been generally available to the public. The mathematical rigor of well-done, stock market research puts it beyond the understanding of most investors—and many investment professionals. The very fact that these studies are conducted by objective researchers and reported according to the highest standards of professional and academic excellence renders them, on the one hand, undeniably true to the informed, and on the other hand, unreadable to most investors. In the deluge of current information and new concepts, little of this startling new knowledge has filtered forward to individual investors. As a result, many of those who keep abreast of the latest market information are using out-of-date investment know-how and are unknowingly basing their future prosperity on investment techniques *now shown to be worthless!*

This serious lag between scientific discovery and widespread practical implementation has three main causes. First, it is difficult to accept facts if they are counter to our intuition. Psychologically, we rely on intuition in the face of uncertainty. Yet, as we will demonstrate shortly, intuition is not enough in today's competitive securities markets.

Secondly, investors generally have not absorbed the new knowledge because its significance and meaning have not been adequately interpreted for them. Indeed, university researchers are remiss in that they frequently couch important findings in scientific jargon. This communications gap between researcher and investor is colorfully depicted by "Adam Smith" (in reality George Goodman, formerly editor of *Institutional Investor* magazine) in his best seller *The Money Game* as follows, ". . . no random-walk theoretician has managed to write a complete paper in English yet, and most Wall Streeters cannot read those little Greek symbols lying on their sides inside the square-root symbols." [**156**, p. 159] *

Some contend that a third influence slowing dissemination of the new investment knowledge stems from the structure of Wall Street itself. Since your broker earns a commission when he executes transactions for you, it follows that he needs reasons for you to buy and sell. Similarly, investment advisers clearly must advise. Much of the modern research, however, casts doubt on the popular rationale and techniques some brokers and advisers use in stock selection. Hence, it is sometimes asserted that Wall Street has little incentive to drop a theory which generates trading volume.

Whatever the cause, be it your psychological resistance, poor communication due to academe's arcane rhetoric, or Wall Street's reluctance to promote investor knowledge, the purpose of Part I—Understanding the New Science—is to acquaint you with the meaning and significance of the latest investing knowledge.

Part II—Applying the New Science to Personal Investing—guides the reader toward attaining personal investment goals through various combinations of investment strategies. These strategies are tailored to the particular needs and desires of the individual, depending on his goals, wealth, desired risk, and so forth.

All investors rely on Wall Street professionals for varying degrees of

---

* Boldface numbers refer to Bibliography at back of book.

information and advice. This distinction between *information* and *advice* is important. Most brokers relay significant news to their clients. Thus, the role of a broker or investment manager as a "news monitor" is an important one. Still, his more important job is drawing inferences from such information and suggesting investment action. Here, modern research has revealed many *dos* and *don'ts* that will help you accurately assess the meaning and significance of investment news.

What Price Advice?

Investors also need to weigh carefully the costs and benefits of professional money management. *All* investors who buy and sell stock, either directly or indirectly through bank trusts, professionally managed accounts, or mutual funds, pay brokerage commissions. In return for these commissions, brokerage firms provide their customers, be they individuals or financial institutions, with a free "bundle" of services. When an investor elects to hire a professional money manager, through a mutual fund, bank trust account, or other financial institution, he adds an *avoidable* expense. These people pay twice for advisory services—once as a "free" service unavoidably bundled in their commissions, and again in their avoidable management fees. The services of the professional money manager are a good buy only if the performance differential between professionally managed and broker-advised portfolios is sufficient to offset the extra management fees.

In this context, all investors need to assess for themselves such disquieting facts as Senator Thomas McIntyre's historic demonstration before the Senate Banking Committee. By merely buying and holding a group of stocks selected through the random throwing of darts at a newspaper listing of securities on the New York Stock Exchange, McIntyre showed that he would have outperformed almost all mutual funds! Or, consider the exhaustive research on mutual fund performance by Professors Friend, Blume, and Crockett in 1970, which concluded that ". . . random portfolios of New York Stock Exchange stocks with equal investment in each stock performed on the average better over the period [January 1960 through June 1968] than did mutual funds in the same risk class." [**55**, p. 56]

Does this evidence mean that your nest egg would be better managed by a child with a handful of darts? This question, and many others, are answered in the following chapters. Besides preparing you to evaluate your own or another's asset management, this book will help you define and attain your investment objectives through the asset triangle that is best suited to your particular needs. What are your investment alternatives? How much should you allocate to insurance, stocks, bonds, mutual funds, and so forth? What kinds of stocks, bonds, or mutual funds? How do you decide? These questions are answered by the emerging new science of investing.

In summary, this book provides you with the knowledge and procedures for profitable investing. The introductory chapters lay the foundation for the book in terms of personal financial objectives and a conceptual understanding of what is to follow. Part I explains what we have learned, but not applied, from the emerging science of investing. Specifically, we will analyze the merits and demerits of the so-called "technical" and "fundamental" approaches to investing, as well as caution you about misleading market folklore.

Part II tells you how to use this new knowledge to tailor a personal investing plan to your individual needs. We will explore the problem of performance versus risk, and will examine the role various investment instruments—stocks, bonds, mutual funds, and so on—play in your investment plans. Most importantly, Part II guides you in formulating an investing strategy suited to your personal objectives.

We are going to examine—and occasionally put to rest—some of the time-honored investment theories. As experienced investors know, the *don't*s of investing can be as important as the *do*s. For successful results, you must first learn to base your decisions on an overall plan compatible with your personal needs and desires, and to avoid the common and costly mistakes many investors make by trusting their intuition.

chapter
2
Investing by Objectives

Nearly everyone is concerned about money, but few people carefully plan their financial future. As an example, most of us spend more time working on, or worrying about, our income tax than our personal financial plan. All too frequently, vital decisions on investments and major family expenditures are made without considering their impact on subsequent stages of one's *financial lifeline*. In broad terms, your financial lifeline predicts your accumulation and dispersal of wealth throughout your lifetime. It involves three interrelated issues: the destination, the road map, and the vehicles.

The important first step of successful investing is to set realistic objectives. The second, and commonly overlooked, step is to use these objectives as specific milestones that act as a road map to guide and monitor investment performance. Too often, bad investment decisions, or good ones turned sour, are not corrected because they are not measured against well-defined performance milestones. The third and final step is to select the combination of insurance and investment vehicles which will carry you to your financial destination.

This chapter is designed for those who, while pursuing their own businesses and careers, have neglected the "business" of their own economic future. Most individuals have vague investment objectives and financial goals. Hence, before we tackle the major subject of "how to make money by investing," you must first decide *how much you want to make.*

The old adage "it takes money to make money" is true. You cannot profit from investments, if you do not *invest!* More specifically, if you can define your objectives, it is possible to predict quite accurately how much you should be setting aside each year to attain them. *How much*

11

you invest can be as crucial as *how well* you invest. Thus, before discussing The New Science of Investing, we will first answer two key questions.

- How much insurance should you have?
- How much of your current income should you invest?

The Responsibility Is Yours

Neither managers, generals, nor individuals can delegate responsibility. While you can delegate the authority to someone to act in your behalf, and you can make him responsible to you, such authorization does not relieve you of ultimate responsibility. This pervasive management principle, which was recognized for its *universalité* in 1916 by the French industrialist Henri Fayol, should not be overlooked by the modern investor. The responsibility for successfully attaining your financial objectives is, in the first and final analysis, yours. It is your responsibility to manage your finances like a well-run business. This means that you should *plan, organize, staff, direct,* and *control* your financial future.

Investment Performance

The goal of a well-run investment portfolio—like that of a well-run business—is planned growth. The growth of IBM to its position as the world's most valuable corporation (despite ongoing antitrust litigation) was not a happenstance. Rather, management made it happen.

By contrast, haphazard investing usually leads to volatile performance. The penalty for this can be illustrated by a sequence of investments by a hypothetical Mr. Adams: up 20 percent, up 40 percent, up 20 percent, down 50 percent. While Mr. Adams' performance might look acceptable, it is not. After the excitement of three good results, he is even after the fourth.[1] Also, changing the sequence of these gains and losses does not change the overall result. Unfortunately, such erratic performance is more than an exercise in percentages. Practically speaking, this happens to millions of investors!

---

[1] Overall performance *cannot* be measured by adding 20, 40, 20 and then subtracting 50 percent! The "return to GO and do not collect $200" result is derived from the period-to-period compounding. The "period" can be days, weeks, years, or any other interval. Using years, the period-to-period record is shown below:

Start	End of Year 1	End of Year 2	End of Year 3	End of Year 4
$100.00 (+20%) =	$120.00 (+40%) =	$168.00 (+20%) =	$201.60 (−50%) =	$100.80

The penalty for haphazard investing can be illustrated further by contrasting the three performance records shown in Table 2–1. Which investor has the most appreciation at the end of five years? As we have seen, Mr. Adams' performance is extremely volatile and he stands roughly even at the end of four years before making a comeback in the fifth year. Mr. Baker's performance shows exactly half the upside return of Mr. Adams' in the good years, but during the bad year his portfolio declines less than half that of Mr. Adams'. Mr. Clark, by contrast, plods along at 7 percent per year—hardly anything to dazzle the boys at the country club. The surprising fact is, however, that *the three investors have nearly identical overall returns*, but Mr. Clark also enjoys stability instead of being exposed to the risk of catastrophic loss.

TABLE 2–1
Comparison of Three Hypothetical Performance Records

Investor	Annual Percentage Gain or Loss				
	Year 1	*Year 2*	*Year 3*	*Year 4*	*Year 5*
Adams	+20	+40	+20	−50	+40
Baker.	+10	+20	+10	−20	+20
Clark	+ 7	+ 7	+ 7	+ 7	+ 7

Performance, and its realistic assessment, is discussed in later chapters. For now, the significance of Table 2–1 is that seemingly outstanding investment records which are interrupted by periodic sizable losses, over the long haul usually wind up average or below. Unfortunately, this "up four years out of five" performance record of many investors may not amount to successful investing. Investors with such bouncy portfolios should realize that one bad year can erase the heady performance of several good years. Unhappily, in the "good" years we must often tolerate the shortsighted braggadocio of haphazard, but lucky, investors. During "bad" years, the subject of investments is somehow ignored!

The brief comparison of returns from speculation versus those from conservative investing does not imply that one posture is better than the other. Both speculative and conservative investments have a place in most people's asset triangle. But it is essential to have an awareness of the proportions of each, and to scale the size of each layer of the triangle according to both the overall market outlook and your proclivity for risk. The lack of such perspective transforms investing into a combination of gambling and wishful thinking. Impulsive forays into the market are destined to produce losses. Unfortunately, many investors who are disheartened by such losses leave the market, never knowing that the way they played the game subjected them to inordinate and unnecessary risks.

Managing Your Investments

Investing by objectives, using a reasoned mixture of investment vehicles arrayed in an asset triangle according to their return and risk characteristics, with performance carefully monitored against milestones, is the surest road to financial success. Unfortunately, most personal investment programs are not managed within the context of a plan tailored to the individual's needs. Instead, decisions often originate in attempts to fit today's hot investment products to the customer, regardless of his unique requirements.

This obvious flaw in the way people manage their money stems from the understandable tendency of both investors and professionals to focus on the fun side of the job—the exciting concepts, the creative new products, the hot growth areas, and so forth. Facing such an array of seeming opportunities, it is difficult to remember to ask, "How does *that* relate to my investment objectives?" A physician, for example, recently asked this author for an opinion on AT&T warrants. I might as well have asked him, "Should I take penicillin or aspirin?" *Every investor, and every investment adviser, should not forget that one cannot recommend medicine before he judges what the patient requires—no matter how exciting or revolutionary the medicine may be!*

A suitably tailored plan is not enough. Success is rarely achieved by chance. Plans must be executed in a businesslike fashion by organizing, staffing, directing, and controlling the resources required to accomplish the plan. Organizing defines the authority-responsibility relationships among those carrying out the plan. Staffing involves selecting qualified people to implement the plan. Directing means leading and effecting the plan's implementation, while control audits the results. Let's look at these steps in terms of your personal responsibility as an investor.

First, you must *plan to invest!* Some people mistakenly assume that investing is something for "good times" or when one gets "a little bit ahead." Such an unplanned approach can spell fiscal disaster for you and your family. "Scarlett O'Hara investors" say, "I'll worry about that tomorrow," and spend all of their current income—and sometimes more—with scores of rationalizations about present needs. Yet, the harsh fact is that spending everything precludes the asset accumulation required to educate your children, purchase a vacation property, enter a personal business venture, assure a worry-free retirement, or fulfill whatever dreams you may have. "Scarlett O'Hara investors" forget one of *Gone With The Wind's* major themes—the struggle to retain Tara. It was Tara, Scarlett O'Hara's estate, that assured her financial tomorrow through war, death of husbands, and economic depression. Without investment, tomorrow *is* another day—for which you may not be ready.

If Your Goal Is $250,000 . . .

The benefits of early investment (although it is never too late) cannot be overemphasized. Suppose, for example, your goal is to have a quarter-of-a-million dollars at age 65. There are several ways to reach this goal. Assume your investments earn an after-tax rate of return of 7.5 percent each year. With that rate, Figure 2–1 shows three ways to arrive at your target of $250,000 at age 65.

FIGURE 2–1
Three Ways to Obtain $250,000 by Age 65

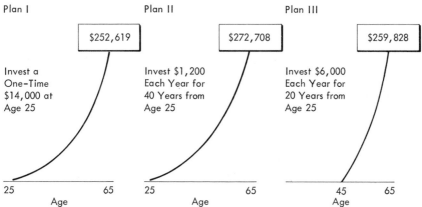

Plan I	Plan II	Plan III
$252,619	$272,708	$259,828
Invest a One-Time $14,000 at Age 25	Invest $1,200 Each Year for 40 Years from Age 25	Invest $6,000 Each Year for 20 Years from Age 25

25　　　　65　　25　　　　65　　　　45　　65
Age　　　　　　Age　　　　　　　Age

Note: Assumed after-tax rate of return is 7.5 percent each year.

Figure 2–1 confirms the maxim that it helps to be born rich. Under Plan 1, a one-time $14,000 investment that is allowed to compound for 40 years at an after-tax annual rate of return of 7.5 percent will grow to $252,619. Barring the good fortune of having $14,000 to invest at age 25, an alternative is to invest a certain sum each year. Plan II shows that investing $1,200 each year from age 25 to 65, with the same after-tax performance of 7.5 percent annually, will bring you $272,708 at age 65. The shorter the investment period, the greater the yearly commitment must be in order to reach the goal. The importance of investing early in life is emphasized by Plan III. If one does not start investing until age 45, it requires setting aside $6,000 per year to reach the goal of $250,000 by age 65.

One's ultimate asset position (say at age 65) depends on four factors:

- the initial investment amount,
- the annual additional investment,
- the annual after-tax rate of return, and
- the number of years over which the investment is allowed to compound (that is, until age 65).

Turning again to Figure 2–1, it should be noted that the after-tax rate of return—7.5 percent per year on the average—is approximately that obtained from holding a well-diversified portfolio of New York Stock Exchange (NYSE) stocks. These comparative charts show that the three plans provide roughly equivalent results. Whether it is possible to invest two years of your spouse's income before starting a family, or whether it is possible to start investing $100 a month at age 25, or $500 a month at age 45, are matters of personal preference. From an investment point of view, however, the conclusion is clear—*start investing as much as you can, as early as you can!*

More ebullient investors may feel that the assumption of an approximate historical after-tax rate of return of 7.5 percent is too conservative. Suppose performance can be improved to 12 percent annually after taxes. Figure 2–2 projects results of the three previous investment plans using

FIGURE 2–2
Improved Returns from Astute Investments

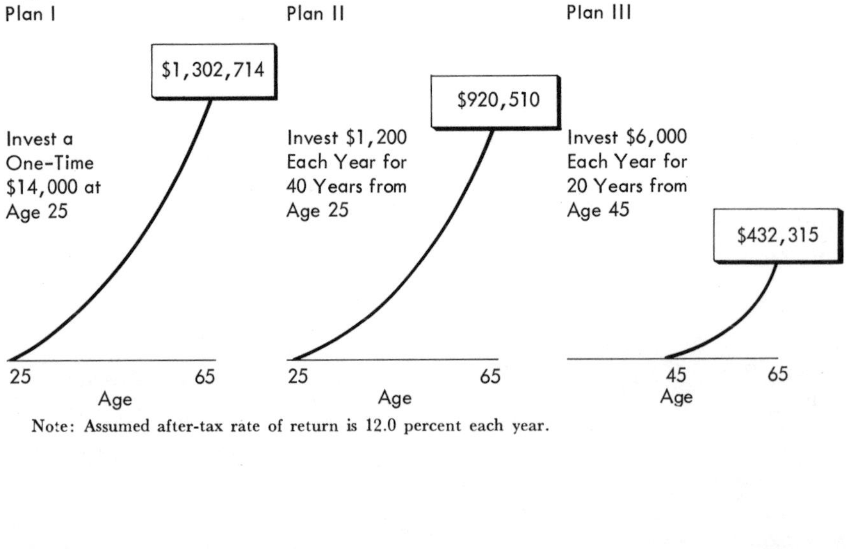

Plan I

Plan II

Plan III

$1,302,714

$920,510

Invest a
One-Time
$14,000 at
Age 25

Invest $1,200
Each Year for
40 Years from
Age 25

Invest $6,000
Each Year for
20 Years from
Age 45

$432,315

| 25 | 65 | 25 | 65 | 45 | 65 |

Age

Age

Age

Note: Assumed after-tax rate of return is 12.0 percent each year.

this superior rate of return. In each case, the totals are up dramatically. But the early investor (Plan I) gains the most—a mere $14,000 will grow to $1,302,714 in 40 years. Even the start-small-but-early investor (Plan II) more than doubles the performance of Plan III. Clearly, it pays to start investing as early as possible!

After Planning—Organize, Staff, Direct, and Control

Once you have set realistic financial goals and devised a plan for attaining them, you must organize your *income-spending-investing* pattern in accordance with this plan. Very personal priorities and decisions are required to assure the planned flow of investable funds. Again, however, the responsibility is yours, and new investment knowledge can only be applied when investable funds are made available.

Income in excess of spending is the only source of investable funds. This foreboding fact, coupled with the desire to live the good life and keep up with the neighbors, explains the failure of most to attain financial independence. In the classic words of Adam Smith, the famous 18th century economist, "Parsimony, and not industry, is the immediate cause of the increase of capital. But whatever industry might acquire, if parsimony did not save and store up, the capital would never be the greater" [**55**, p. 320]. To paraphrase this concept in modern English, "In the long run, the difference between those who become wealthy and all the rest is not the size of their income, but how much they invest!" That the value of parsimony is still recognized is confirmed by the motto of many Wharton School graduates: "Happiness cannot buy money!"

Remember,

- To attain a meaningful financial goal, you must invest.
- The more you invest, and the earlier you invest it, the larger your ultimate assets will become.
- The only source of investable funds is money which would otherwise go for current expenditures.

It is helpful to contrast two philosophies for providing these investable funds: a commonly accepted one that does not work and a simple one that does. The first begins with the premise that investable funds are what are "left over" after expenditures. But such an orientation is backward because it looks upon investing as "How much can I afford?" instead of viewing it as "What are my objectives and how will I attain them?" The flaw in this first philosophy is that our investing is continually forced to compete with our desire to consume, with the result that investing is too often postponed.

The second philosophy starts from the subtly different point of view that both insurance and investing fulfill imperative family objectives. Insurance is meant to guarantee the economic functioning of the family unit without its income provider. More likely, however, that provider will live, in which case investments must be the vehicle for reaching financial objectives. This consideration, plus the enormous advantage of investing as early as possible, dictates a simple, but sensible, approach to financial planning: *insure, invest, and spend the rest!*

This approach begins by estimating the cost of providing for your dependents in your absence, and by using this estimate as a bench mark for determining reasonable insurance against contingencies such as death, illness, or disability. The second step is to invest enough, soon enough, to make the attainment of your financial goals a reality. These two steps secure your financial future. How to spend the remaining income is a matter of personal preference. The important point in this approach is to prevent the flow of investable funds from continuously being funneled into such things as a new car, a swimming pool, a vacation, or what have you, at the expense of attaining the financial future most people profess to want more, but mistakenly think they can postpone.

Staff, Direct, and Control

Few people can, or should, determine their insurance and investment needs alone. Not since the Renaissance of the 1600s has one person been capable of being truly expert in all known areas. Today, there is almost infinitely more to know and life is much more complex. Estate planners, tax consultants, insurance specialists, investment counselors, and brokerage firms are available to aid investors in the myriad, specialized facets of financial planning. In response to this need for diversified services, and in reflection of the explosive growth of knowledge, the new science of investing encourages a *joindre ses forces* of experts who work on interrelated elements of one's financial lifeline. For instance, your last will and testament (and everyone should have one) has tax and insurance implications, and vice versa. Your age, in turn, bears on the urgency and terms of your will, your income-earning ability and its duration, insurance needs and costs, and investment risk preferences.

In this tangled milieu, one's annual tax return can become more than a necessary evil. It can also be used as an "annual financial checkup" that monitors your financial progress. This required annual accounting can pinpoint deviations from objectives that may dictate changes in the underlying investment plan. Thus, the concept of a financial lifeline helps you tie together the many aspects of financial planning, monitor your performance against measurable objectives, and routinely make the necessary adjustments to control it and keep it on track.

A new financial services industry is emerging. It is composed of companies that provide an ever-widening circle of personal financial planning services—trust and estate planning, tax assistance, insurance, investment counseling, brokerage, and so forth—each designed to mesh with the concept of managing your financial lifeline. Your personal financial planning and management can benefit from diverse skills and experienced professional assistance. This does not mean, however, that you can then divorce yourself from this task. In any organization, the staff must be both directed and controlled by management—you. The ultimate responsibility for the business of your personal investing rests with you. The next chapter explains your first responsibility: establishing your financial objectives.

chapter

3
Your Personal Financial Prospectus

A systematic review of one's investing status and objectives can be called a "Personal Financial Prospectus." Much like a security prospectus, which describes a company's current position and business objectives and plans, a Personal Financial Prospectus details your present financial status and aims, as well as the course of action you have designed to reach your goals.

A Personal Financial Prospectus, as shown pictorially in Figure 3–1, translates myriad vague goals and unanswered questions into realistic

FIGURE 3–1
Preparing a Personal Financial Prospectus

Salary increse...
When I retire...
Taxes
Something for the children...
Vacation...
Cost of living... College tuition...
Debts Could uncle help if...
Another child...
My equity in home...
Insurance
Debts...
Current bills... Past investment losses...
Possibility of unemployment...
Cost of living...
Mortgage
Inflation Vacation
If I only had the money I could..
I need a new...

• Financial need forecast

  • Financial lifeline
  • Present value of
    lifetime earnings
  • Insurance needs
  • Investment needs

• Current investable assets

• Investment objectives

investment objectives. Once your investment objectives are defined, *and not before,* you are prepared to move to the new science of investing and the knowledge necessary to:

- select the mix of investment instruments (stocks, bonds, mutual funds, etc.) which, in combination, form the asset triangle most likely to achieve your objectives,
- choose particular investment securities that will fulfill the risk-return expectations for each level of the triangle, and
- monitor the performance of your investment portfolio against your defined objectives.

Financial Need Forecast

A financial need forecast is a "best guess" estimate of what is likely to occur. This does not, however, destroy its usefulness. Once established, this projection provides important bench marks against which to measure your future income and investment performance. Knowing whether you are on target, or above or below your forecast, can be very useful. Furthermore, these projections will change when unforeseen events occur, such as the birth of triplets. Then your prospectus is a solid basis for replanning in light of new developments. A financial prospectus should not be dipped in bronze and forgotten. It deserves review, probably annually, and is modified as assumptions change.

Because of the complexities of pension and Social Security income, expenses for college tuition, financing a home, and so forth, forecasting detailed financial needs calls for specialized expertise and arduous calculations. For this reason, firms offer detailed, computerized forecasts that plug in childrens' ages and education plans, retirement ambitions, pension rights, potential inheritance, and in some cases almost "the day you trade the Cadillac for a three-wheel Schwinn." For now, this chapter develops ball-park estimates of your insurance and investing needs.

Financial Lifeline. Heads of households—whether single or with a family—have different financial responsibilities throughout the course of their financial lifeline. These responsibilities are typified in Figure 3–2. In addition to the need to provide income for current needs, a head-of-household's obligation to his family continues as long as there are surviving dependents. Thus, a Personal Financial Prospectus becomes a blueprint for meeting varying needs through all phases of the lifeline—with or without the head-of-household's earnings. This kind of protection is normally acquired through life insurance.

FIGURE 3–2
Phases and Extraordinary Needs in a Typical Financial Lifeline

Phase 1	Phase 2	Phase 3	Phase 4	Phase 5	Phase 6	Phase 7
Dependent upon family	Employed, single head-of-household	Marriage and parenthood	Growing children	Children's education	Countdown years	Retirement
Personal education expenses	Acquire personal property	Home and related assets	Growing expenses, vacations	Multiple tuitions	Buildup for retirement	Secure lifetime income and capital base

Both the number and characteristics of one's dependents influence the amount required by the household in his absence. A young couple with two small children, and burdened by the debts of household formation, have different insurance needs than a childless, high-salaried couple. In the former case, the economic impact of the husband's premature death would be severe, whereas a working wife is already self-sufficient and might easily remarry, especially if she is without children. As Professor John Bowyer of Washington University put it, ". . . the amount of life insurance a man carries should be in an inverse relationship to the relative attractiveness of his wife." [11, p. 27]

Present Value of Lifetime Earnings. One way to ascertain your dependents' needs in your absence is to calculate how much you are worth *alive.* The sum of your earnings between now and retirement determine the maximum economic loss your dependents would sustain by your premature death. The present value[1] of this lifetime stream of employment income can be estimated from:

- your current employment income,
- your expected growth in employment income,
- the number of working years until retirement, and
- an appropriate discount rate.

To simplify this calculation we have used data from the U.S. Bureau of the Census to approximate your probable lifetime earnings. For people

---

[1] The *present value* of money to be received in the future is less than the value of the same amount of money obtained now. Regardless of inflation considerations, money obtained today can earn interest and thereby grow to larger future amounts. Thus, the present value of $1.00 to be received in one year is only 94.3 cents today, when discounted at 6 percent per annum. Stated another way, if you invest 94.3 cents at 6 percent today, you will have $1.00 (before taxes) one year from now. Hence, the *present value* of future income is found by discounting the amounts expected to be earned in the future.

from ages 25 through 65, these representative earnings data have been discounted to their present value. The results, shown in Table 3–1, are based on:

- actual income growth experienced by male college graduates of various ages, as determined by the U.S. Bureau of the Census,
- an assumed retirement age of 65, and
- a discount rate of 6 percent per year.

Using Table 3–1, the present value of your lifetime earnings can be approximated by referring to your current age and income level. For example, if you are 25 years old and earning $10,000 annually, the discounted present value of your remaining income before retirement at age 65 is $252,620, assuming your income growth parallels that of the representative college graduate. A 42-year old currently earning $20,000 a year also has essentially this same present value of income if he works to age 65 and makes typical progress. Use Table 3–1 to approximate the current value of your remaining lifetime earnings. This figure provides a useful bench mark for evaluating your life insurance needs.

Insurance Needs.   Life or income insurance is designed to finance a dependent's consumption in the event the household head is unable to provide such support. Insurance sustains the financial lifeline without income from the insured. This need increases as the number of dependents rises, when a spouse becomes unable to support herself, and so on. But, regardless of these factors, the present value of your future earnings, estimated from Table 3–1, represents the *maximum economic loss* that your family would suffer if your income stopped today.

It is not necessary, *or prudent,* however, to insure yourself against this maximum potential loss. First of all, the purpose of life insurance is to make sure that your dependents are cared for in your absence. If you do not have any dependents, you do not need life insurance in excess of your estate expenses. Moreover, even if you have several dependents, not all of your future earnings would have been used to support your family. A significant percentage of this projected income would have been drained off by taxes, life insurance premiums, investments, and the portion that would have been consumed by you. Furthermore, sources of income other than earnings, such as dividends, interest, pensions, Social Security benefits, or the liquidation of assets, also offset the need for insurance.

Computer programs are available to analyze these factors and prescribe both the kind and amount of insurance best suited to individual

TABLE 3-1
Approximate Discounted Present Value of Remaining Lifetime Earnings

Current Age	Current Annual Income (from Employment)				
	$ 10,000	$ 15,000	$ 20,000	$ 30,000	$ 50,000
25	$252,620	$378,930	$505,240	$757,860	$1,263,100
26	236,610	354,915	473,220	709,830	1,183,050
27	223,160	334,740	446,320	669,480	1,115,800
28	211,660	317,490	423,320	634,980	1,058,300
29	201,650	302,475	403,300	604,950	1,008,250
30	192,790	289,185	385,580	578,370	963,950
31	184,820	277,230	369,640	554,460	924,100
32	177,580	266,370	355,160	532,740	887,900
33	170,930	256,395	341,860	512,790	854,650
34	164,790	247,185	329,580	494,370	823,950
35	159,060	238,590	318,120	477,180	795,300
36	153,680	230,520	307,360	461,040	768,400
37	148,600	222,900	297,200	445,800	743,000
38	143,780	215,670	287,560	431,340	718,900
39	139,160	208,740	278,320	417,480	695,800
40	134,730	202,095	269,460	404,190	673,650
41	130,440	195,660	260,880	391,320	652,200
42	126,260	189,390	252,520	378,780	631,300
43	122,150	183,225	244,300	366,450	610,750
44	118,090	177,135	236,180	354,270	590,450
45	114,050	171,075	228,100	342,150	570,250
46	109,990	164,985	219,980	329,970	549,950
47	105,920	158,880	211,840	317,760	529,600
48	101,790	152,685	203,580	305,370	508,950
49	97,570	146,355	195,140	292,710	487,850
50	93,270	139,905	186,540	279,810	466,350
51	88,840	133,260	177,680	266,520	444,200
52	84,300	126,450	168,600	252,900	421,500
53	79,600	119,400	159,200	238,800	398,000
54	74,720	112,080	149,440	224,160	373,600
55	69,640	104,460	139,280	208,920	348,200
56	64,330	96,495	128,660	192,990	321,650
57	58,750	88,125	117,500	176,250	293,750
58	55,790	83,685	111,580	167,370	278,950
59	47,200	70,800	94,400	141,600	236,000
60	40,640	60,960	81,280	121,920	203,200
61	33,650	50,475	67,300	100,950	168,250
62	26,170	39,255	52,340	78,510	130,850
63	18,130	27,195	36,260	54,390	90,650
64	9,430	14,145	18,860	28,290	47,150

Source: Table derived from Bureau of Census data in *Current Population Reports, Consumer Income, Annual Mean Income, Lifetime Income, and Educational Attainment of Men in The United States, For Selected Years, 1956 to 1966*, Series P-60, No. 56, August 14, 1968.

needs. While these computerized analyses are very helpful, there are certain decisions in the formulation of your insurance program that only you can make. First, in any such decision, your objectives should be kept clearly in mind. The primary objective of insurance is to safeguard against the unexpected loss of earnings. Many forms of insurance policies supply this protection, as well as an investment return (for example, the cash value buildup of a whole life policy). While both insurance and investment represent financial needs, the policy which provides the best insurance usually does not also provide the best investment.

This conflict is too often overlooked because the sale of insurance and the sale of other investment instruments have traditionally been handled by different groups of salesmen. From both an economic and a consumer-investor point of view, this is an artificial separation. A sound financial plan needs elements of both insurance and investment and not the conflicting interests of competing salesmen.

The evolving concept of a "one-stop financial supermarket" melds insurance-investment planning and products. One such product of the future is *variable life insurance*. The death benefit of such insurance fluctuates with the value of an underlying investment portfolio, but a minimum payout is still guaranteed. One indication of the potential demand for this product is the belief of Gordon Macklin, president of the National Association of Securities Dealers (NASD), that variable life policies will rival the current market for mutual funds.

Insurance is a complex subject, and a thorough analysis of it is helpful, but at the risk of incurring the wrath of the insurance industry, you can make a ball-park approximation of your insurance needs. If you have no dependent relatives or children needing support after your death, a strategy of *minimum* (burial expenses) insurance and maximum investment is appropriate. The other end of the spectrum of insurance need is typified by a young, large family without investment or pension income to help offset their insurance needs. After subtracting taxes, insurance premiums, savings, investments, and head-of-household consumption from such a family's current income, the remaining consumption by dependents might amount to 50 percent of the family's gross income, hinging mainly on family size.

The percentage of remaining lifetime earnings from Table 3–1 that should be protected by death-benefit insurance can be approximated from Figure 3–3. A person with no dependents has no need for insurance in excess of burial expenses. The addition of a spouse, or aged relative, does not impose a large insurance burden. The addition of successive

FIGURE 3–3
Approximate Percentage of Remaining Lifetime Earnings* That Should Be Protected by Death-Benefit Insurance
Percentage

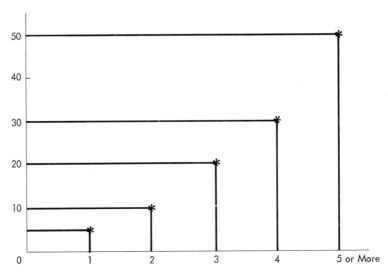

Number of Dependents (without Other Foreseeable Means of Support)
* From Table 3–1.

children, however, increases the need for insurance in *two* ways. First, the required child care can prevent a surviving wife from seeking employment, or if she is employed, the child-care costs can erode her income. Secondly, each new child incurs expenses. The suggestion of little need for additional insurance beyond that for a five-dependent family reflects the assumption that the older children can contribute to the family.

Investment Needs. The successful attainment of investment objectives is made much more likely through early and regular investing in a well-managed portfolio. As mentioned earlier, the analysis of alternative financial lifelines and insurance needs is greatly facilitated by utilizing computers. The more sophisticated of these computerized planning tools prepare a year-by-year forecast of your preretirement income, expenditures, and investments, culminating in your anticipated estate at retirement age.

As part of this forecasting process, your invested funds are adjusted by any extraordinary preretirement events, such as college tuitions or a vacation home. The basic forecast can then be used as a bench mark for comparison with your subsequent financial situation. Variations of such plans allow you to compare the actual and expected market value of your portfolio over the years. Such computerized analysis can accurately project the amount of annual investment required to cover a specified list of preretirement expenditures as well as to provide a retirement estate of, say, $250,000 at age 65.

Such detailed financial forecasts are clearly very helpful. As with insurance needs, however, it is possible to make an unaided approximation of how much a family should be investing. One such estimate is illustrated below:

1. Extraordinary preretirement expenditures (not financed from current earnings) :

Extraordinary Item	Years until Expenditure	Expenditure Amount
Son's college	10	$20,000
Daughter's college	15	$20,000

2. Desired retirement estate (in excess of pensions, etc.) :

Years until Retirement	Goal
25	$200,000

This goal can be balanced against the return you expect from your current investments in order to determine:

- The degree to which your current investments (the top three layers of your asset triangle) will fulfill your objectives, and
- The size and urgency of annual additions to the three investment layers of your asset triangle.

In matching your current investments against future expenditures, care should be taken to avoid the error of compounding funds you do not have. Suppose, for example, that you have current investments of $20,000. Our illustrative family would like to have $20,000 for their son's education in ten years. Table 3–2 shows the future value of a lump-sum investment. In ten years, with a 7.5 percent compounded annual after-tax return, your present investment will roughly double. Thus,

TABLE 3–2
Value of Each $1000 of Lump-Sum Investment
Compounded Annually at an After-Tax Return
of 7.5 Percent

Years Invested	Value of Investment
1	$ 1,075
2	1,156
3	1,242
4	1,336
5	1,436
–	–
–	–
–	–
10	2,061
15	2,959
20	4,247
25	6,098
30	8,755
35	12,569
40	18,044

$10,000 of the family's *current* holdings need to be earmarked for the son's education. (Note: this analysis also gives you valuable information about the risks you are willing to take with money designated for various planned extraordinary items.)

Suppose further that a younger daughter will be of college age in 15 years. You might reasonably expect the current value of your investments to triple by then. Assuming the $20,000 college cost is still valid after 15 years have passed, roughly another $7,000 of the family's *current* investments must be earmarked for their daughter's education. Suppose the father is 35 years old and expects to retire in 25 years, at age 60. Then the nonearmarked $3,000 in his current portfolio should grow about sixfold, according to Table 3–2, to over $18,000 by his retirement. Almost certainly, extra interim investments will be necessary.

To give an idea of the cumulating benefits of ongoing investment, Table 3–3 shows the final value of routinely investing $1,000 per year ($83.33 per month) over various numbers of years. Again, an after-tax rate of return of 7.5 percent annually is used for the projections. Table 3–3 shows that a person with 25 years until retirement can expect to augment his retirement nest egg by nearly $68,000 by routinely investing $1,000 each year. But if his retirement goals are higher, he must invest more! In the case of our illustrative family with virtually all of its current investments earmarked for the children's college educations, the goal of $200,000 at retirement requires a routine investment of $250 per month.

TABLE 3-3
Final Value of Each $100 per Year of Ongoing
Investment Compounded at an Annual After-
Tax Return of 7.5 Percent

Years until Goal	Value of Investment
1.	$ 1,000
2.	2,075
3.	3,231
4.	4,473
5.	5,808
10.	14,147
15.	26,118
20.	43,305
25.	67,978
30.	103,399
35.	154,252
40.	227,257

Current Investable Assets

Many investors, as well as investment advisers, make the mistake of rushing to look at the income statements and balance sheets of prospective investments before analyzing the comparable facts about the prospective investor. Every publicly owned company is required to prepare a certified annual report which summarizes its assets and income. By contrast, most investors—even those who carefully monitor their stocks in daily newspapers—lack comprehensive measures of their personal investment performance against realistic goals. Before deciding where you are going, and how you are going to get there, determine where you are *now* by assessing the amount of your investable funds.

In determining your current investable funds, it is important to separate the foundation layer of your asset triangle from the three investment layers. Individuals own property to fulfill a variety of requirements, including the need for living accommodations (houses, furniture, cars, and so forth), the desire for items that bring aesthetic appreciation and, in some instances, capital appreciation (art, antiques, jewelry, etc.), and the desire for pure investments. Foundation assets are rarely sold to finance the future. They make life more comfortable, while investments are designed to take care of the future. Your current investments should not be confused with your seldom sold foundation assets.

A careful valuation procedure is important, so that a large amount of personal property does not cloud the need for financial planning. More importantly, such a procedure forces evaluation of assets in relation to special events such as death or retirement contingencies. Say, for example, that Mr. and Mrs. Dow, a couple in their late 40s with two teen-age children, own a $100,000 house. What is its:

1. Current "foundation asset" value?
2. Net sale value if used to finance the children's education?
3. Net sale value in the event of Mr. Dow's death?
4. Net sales value at retirement age?

Looking at foundation-level assets in these terms forces one to think beyond the *current* value of the asset. Will the equity in the house be used to finance the children's education? Probably not. What will Mrs. Dow do with the house if her husband dies unexpectedly? If this occurs, she might *plan* to sell it and buy a $40,000 house. If this is part of their personal financial prospectus, they could reasonably put a planned liquidation value of $60,000 on the house in the event of Mr. Dow's death. Such a plan would free dollars for *investments*. What will they do with the house when they retire? If they keep it, its planned net sale value at retirement age would be zero, and so forth.

Investment Objectives

Finally, you now have enough information about your needs and means to determine sound, realistic investment objectives for *you*. Given the base of your financial lifeline and current investable assets, you can plan a course of action likely to lead to a satisfactory goal. But a meaningful goal must also be an attainable one. After insuring adequately, and assessing the long-term value of your current holdings, achieving your goal depends on two factors: (1) your ongoing investment amounts, and (2) your overall after-tax rate of return. You must make the commitment to provide the first. This book attempts to help you increase the second.

With your personal investment objectives decided, you have taken step one of successful investing. Step two is to use these objectives, and your plan for reaching them, as specific milestones which act as a road map to guide and monitor investment performance—replanning when necessary. The third and final step is to select the combination of vehicles that will carry you to your financial destination.

Summary

Let us briefly review the important points of the last two chapters, as they are crucial for your future financial success. Before investing, or even trying to improve results with the new science, gain an accurate perspective regarding your investment objectives. These depend on your financial lifeline—a composite of current and future income until retirement (or some other time)—coupled with your estimate of future needs for you and your dependents. After insuring, you must define your investment objectives and work out a realistic plan for attaining them. Your plan will depend on your current investable assets, the annual amounts you invest, the length of time before your goal, and the after-tax rate of return you achieve on your investments. The balance of this book will help you improve that final important variable—the rate of return on your investments!

chapter
4
Intuition Is Not Enough

Many people believe that successful money management is an *art,* not a science. This distinction characterizes the philosophical difference between the "old school" and the "new science of investing." A statement of the old school view that was recently given this author by a well known money manager went something like:

I have been managing O.P.M. [Other People's Money] since Tarzan was a boy. No one can tell me it is a science. It is an art. There are computers and all sorts of mathematical theories, but they do not make the market easier to understand. It is still personal intuition and the sensing of market patterns.

If, as an investor, you do not think the preceding quotation is alarming, consider what would happen if Wernher von Braun, the respected space scientist, were quoted as saying:

I conducted my first experiments with liquid-fuel rockets at Berlin-Ploetzesee in 1930. I have been managing rocket experiments ever since. No one can tell me it is a science. It is an art. There are computers and all sorts of mathematical theories, but they do not make rockets and space easier to understand. It is still personal intuition and the sensing of cosmic patterns.

Such a statement would probably stifle appropriations for space exploration within 24 hours. It seems remarkable, then, that similar statements by money managers do not immediately stop the flow of large sums of money to the institutions which espouse parallel beliefs.

The combined efforts of hundreds of researchers, augmented in recent years by modern computer technology, have substantially increased our understanding of the stock market. Yet, people who do not grasp the significance of the recent research, or who do not know how to apply it, will debate this point. On one side are the works of the many researchers and practitioners cited in this book which stand diametrically opposed to an intuitive approach to the stock market. The people who comprehend and apply this research contend that our understanding of the market is advancing every day. On the other side are people from the "old school" who believe that investing is an undefinable art. To such people, "personal intuition" is the cornerstone of the art of investing. But, in this decade, is intuition good enough?

Intuition

Suppose someone offered you an even-money bet that 2 of the next 25 people you meet will have the same birthday. You would quickly reason that, excluding leap year, there are 365 possible birthdays and, at most, only 25 days could be represented by 25 people. You might even calculate that 25 is only 6.8 percent of 365. Intuitively, it seems unlikely that 2 of these people would have been born on the same day. Would you take a bet that will double your money if no 2 people out of the next 25 you meet have the same birthday? Would you take the same bet for the next 50 people? The next 100? The next 180?

The answer is that you should not take any of the bets! Even with 25 randomly selected people, it is more likely than not that two of them have the same birthday.[1] This is counter to most people's intuition, but it is true. Yet, most people find this demonstration difficult to accept, and, in the face of uncertainty, they tend to trust their intuition. Furthermore, explanations of the logic underlying our birthday-bet discussion are usually given in the arcane language of combinatorial probability theory, which is difficult, if not impossible, for most people to understand.

---

[1] The birthday wager can be explained by noting that each person you meet has a *progressively better chance* of causing a birthday match. Some rather unintuitive results of the relevant mathematical calculation are summarized below:

Number of people	10	20	22	23	25	30	40	50
Likelihood of two matching birthdays (by percent)	12	41	48	51	59	71	89	97

Hence, with as few as 23 people it is a better than 50–50 bet that 2 will have matching birthdays. With 50 people, you have a 97 percent chance of having 2 with the same birthday. Unintuitive, but true.

This same failure to communicate marks much of the recent scientific stock market research. First, many of the findings contradict our intuition. Secondly, it is difficult for most investors, as well as many market professionals, to evaluate these discoveries because the underlying research relies heavily on mathematics and statistical inference beyond their understanding. The result is that most investors, and market professionals alike, are uncertain about the meaning and significance of this research, which in the years ahead is destined to alter dramatically investing as we know it today.

Later, you will see that examples of poor intuition are not limited to cocktail party bets. As in the case of the birthday wager situation, you can expect to find that much of the information in this book is contrary to your intuition, the age-old tenets of Wall Street, or both. Thus, to understand and use the new science of investing effectively, you should try to adopt the totally fresh viewpoint of the unindoctrinated. You should strive to set aside what you "know" about the stock market and take an objective look at what we have learned in the last decade. If you have difficulty doing this, you might consider taking your intuition and money to Las Vegas—where you will undoubtedly have more fun losing both. But in any event, whether you decide to go to Las Vegas or to invest your money, it will be helpful to look at the "laws of chance" that underlie our intuition about both gambling and the stock market.

Laws of Chance

The notion of "laws of chance" appears contradictory at first glance. On the one hand, "laws" implies predictability, and on the other hand, "chance" implies unpredictability. It is natural to expect laws to state that something will always happen in a certain way. For example, the law of gravity states that all objects, regardless of their weight, will fall toward the center of the earth with the same rate of acceleration. This law is readily accepted because it is invariant and can be easily demonstrated by experimentation.

Yet, even this basic law of physics was not accepted before Galileo's investigations in the early 1600s. Before this time, the accepted intuition of the "old school" had obscured the facts. Consider for example, the following quotation from a popular physics text:

Galileo's . . . work can be considered a turning point not merely in the history of physics but in the history of the natural sciences as well. Theretofore, people were attempting to philosophize laws of nature out of some vague, often meaningless "principles." They often drew perfectly logical conclusions from wrong premises and "derived" "natural laws" which were in contradiction to experience. Since no one made efforts to check these "laws" by experiment, they were accepted and dominated "scientific thought" for well over a millennium.

Aristotle's assertion that "bodies fall faster in proportion to their weight" provides a classic example of such "laws of nature." This statement is wrong, and Aristotle could have easily disproved it by trial. But the experimental method, which appears natural to us, evidently was not obvious to him or to most of his contemporaries and followers. Aristotle's contributions to science and philosophy are monumental in fields involving pure reasoning and observation. They are for the most part worthless or lacking in fields such as physics where the acquisition of knowledge must depend on experimentation. In fact, his [Aristotle's] authority in physics dominated thought for many centuries and materially blocked progress in this field. [**92**, pp. 16–17]

Galileo had the temerity to question the wisdom of Aristotle and, in so doing, changed the course of history. His experiments showed that, in opposition to popular belief, heavy objects do not fall more rapidly than light objects. In fact, unless impeded by air resistance, all objects fall to the earth equally fast regardless of their weight. What had been intuitively correct for generations of mankind, as a result of their observation of falling feathers and rocks, was *wrong!*

In the last ten years, many scholars have dared to question Wall Street's traditional "laws of nature." Armed with computers and the techniques of scientific inquiry, these researchers have sought to verify Wall Street's "laws." In so doing, they have challenged the intuitive shibboleths of the investment profession. The fact that many Wall Street practitioners see such research as heresy makes the parallel with Galileo complete. As students of history will recall, Galileo was condemned by the Inquisition for heresy—a sobering thought for this author!

Although the law of gravity long eluded our understanding, its truth can be verified through experimentation. Indeed, a feather and a rock were simultaneously dropped from the same height by an astronaut on the moon. As was televised to the world, with the absence of air resistance, both fell at the same speed.

The laws of chance, by contrast, are disturbing because they appear to vary. How can laws govern chance or random behavior? Laws of chance would seem to be lawless by definition! Fortunately for Las Vegas and Monte Carlo, events governed by laws of chance do not vary in a haphazard fashion. The behavior of such events can be specified quite precisely.

Many research studies explained in this book contrast the behavior of actual stock prices with the behavior of randomly selected stock prices (prices called out, as it were, by a croupier in charge of an appropriately designed roulette wheel). Much has been learned from these important investigations. Unfortunately, however, there are several reasons why the results of these studies are not widely understood. First, even a skilled statistician often has difficulty reading and comprehending the reports of these rigorous investigations. Secondly, it is difficult to accept something that we do not understand, especially if it does not match our intuition. Thirdly, many people suffer from what university professors call "symbol shock." For example, "Adam Smith" dramatized how frightening the language of the new science can appear by presenting the following mathematical quotation from William Steiger's chapter in *The Random Character of Stock Market Prices* "just to scare you."

. . . we have the sampling distribution function for $t_m(n)$[3.]

$$H(t) = P_r(t_{m,n} \leq t)$$

$$= 2 \sum_{j=1}^{\infty} \frac{1 - \left(\dfrac{N-2}{N^2}\right) 4J^2 t^2}{\left(\dfrac{1 + 4J^2 t^2}{N^2}\right)^{\frac{n+1}{2}}} + \frac{\left(\dfrac{N-2}{N^2}\right) 4J^2 V^2 - 1}{\left(\dfrac{1 + 4J^2 V^2}{N^2}\right)^{\frac{n+1}{2}}}$$

where

$$N = n - m \leq 2$$

and

$$V = \begin{cases} 1 & (N \text{ even}) \\ \sqrt{\dfrac{N}{N-1}} & (N \text{ odd}) \end{cases}$$

(Reference: [**24**, p. 255 and **156**, p. 149])

Indeed, scientific statements like the one above are "scary" if not understood. But similarly, the fact that von Braun's rocketry equations are also "scary" does not alter their validity! What really alarmed many readers is found on "Smith's" preceding page. Here he stated:

. . . Senator Thomas J. McIntyre, Democrat of New Hampshire and a member of the powerful Senate Banking Committee, brought his dart board in one day. Senator McIntyre had tacked the stock market page onto his dart board and thrown darts at it, and the portfolio picked by his darts outperformed almost all of the mutual funds. Senator McIntyre's darts thus supported the . . . testimony of Professors Paul Samuelson of MIT and Henry Wallich of Yale . . . [**156**, p. 148]

Now, what *really* scares you? *The portfolio picked by darts outperformed almost all of the mutual funds!* Should you be frightened by scientists' use of mathematical symbols, or by the serious evidence casting doubt on the ability of professionals who invest billions of dollars of your money through mutual funds, trusts, and pension and insurance funds? The answer should be obvious.

Before we continue, however, it would be wise to consider what you are, and are not, willing to believe—regardless of the evidence. You know, for example, that people lose and the house wins on the roulette tables in Las Vegas. Otherwise the wheels would not keep spinning night after night. Nonetheless, many people persist in believing that certain individuals, like lucky old "Aunt Sarah," can win at roulette. It may be true that Aunt Sarah *has* won at roulette. Winning in the past, unfortunately, does not improve the odds that Aunt Sarah, or anyone else, *will* win the next time.

No "system" can be devised to succeed against a fair roulette wheel. This does *not* mean that it is impossible to win at roulette. Rather, the odds are that you will lose. And, importantly, the longer you play, the more certain it becomes that you will lose! If no amount of evidence can make you *really* believe the preceding two sentences, then you are an incurable optimist. Yet, in spite of this awesome certainty of losing in the long run, some people like to play roulette. Las Vegas prospers even though its customers know the odds are against them.

A far more exciting game than roulette is the one the famous economist, John Maynard Keynes, referred to as "the game of professional investment." An intriguing aspect of this game for the 31 million shareholders playing it is the fact that, unlike in gambling, the odds of winning are overwhelmingly *in their favor!* Unhappily, this fact alone does not guarantee successful investing. The "game" of professional investing is played with myriad combinations of investment instruments and selection techniques. The informed player should know the "odds" of each.

The research examined in this book calculates these odds. It does not rely on "intuition" or what people "think" about the market. The conclusions distilled and reported here were derived from modern tools of scientific inquiry and statistical inference. The results are comprehensible to any investor. But, to appreciate the research more fully, it will be helpful to understand three related laws of chance that underpin many of the findings. The first law concerns random, or chance, occurrences. (In academic parlance, such events are said to be statistically independent.) The second law states that, while random events are not individually predictable, one can accurately predict the average of many such events (called the "expected value" by statisticians). The third law concerns the normal variance of events around this expected value. These important research tenets are introduced and illustrated in the next chapter. The reader who already grasps these concepts can skip to Chapter 6.

chapter

5

Independence, Means, and Variance

We can illustrate the concept of randomness, or statistical independence, by reviewing games of chance. Suppose someone asked you to bet on "heads" in a coin flip. This would be an even bet since "heads" and "tails" are equally likely. Half the time you would expect to win. Now, suppose you have just won two times in a row, that is, two consecutive heads have been tossed. What are your odds on the next bet? Are they still even?

Intuitively, a gambler knows that a sequence of three heads in a row does not occur very often. This is true. Yet, does this fact alter the odds of winning the next coin-toss bet? Similarly, a roulette player might observe two "blacks" in a row. How does he use this information for his next bet? The proper use of information of this kind—and, more importantly, how similar decisions arise in selecting stocks—comes from understanding what is, and is not, predictable about random events.

A random event is an occurrence whose outcome cannot be predicted from preceding events. Examples of random events are the result of a coin toss and the spin of a roulette wheel. For such events, the outcome of any single trial is determined by chance and is impossible to predict. For example, if you toss a fair coin it is impossible to know in advance whether that particular coin will fall heads or tails.

Let's return to the question of the gambler's odds once he has observed a run (a sequence of one kind of outcome). Gamblers often devise betting schemes based on run information. After observing a sequence of one result, say two consecutive coin-toss heads or two blacks in roulette, they adopt a particular betting strategy. Some gamblers infer that it

39

is not a good bet to expect still another head after two heads have been tossed. After all, they reason, everyone knows three heads in a row is a relatively rare occurrence. Conversely, other gamblers reason that the game is "running hot," and heads has a better than normal chance on the next toss. *These are both ridiculous betting systems!* Assuming that the coin or roulette wheel is fair and unbiased, both gambling systems are useless and will not lead to gambling success.

The futility of both betting systems will become clear if we analyze the game of coin tossing. Each toss has two possible outcomes: heads or tails. When heads occurs, tails cannot, and vice versa. The probability, or likelihood, that a fair coin will fall heads is said to be one half. This means that, *in the long run,* half of the outcomes are expected to be heads.

It is impossible to predict which outcome will occur on any particular toss, although one would expect half heads and half tails overall. Next, consider the possible results of two successive tosses. Four outcomes are possible from tossing a coin two times. These may be indicated by

$$HH, \quad HT, \quad TH, \quad TT$$

Here, HH means that a head was obtained on the first toss, and another head was obtained on the second toss; HT means a head followed by a tail, and so on. No other combinations of heads and tails are possible from two successive tosses. This situation is depicted in Figure 5–1.

The occurrence of two heads in a row is shown in the shaded area. Tossing heads twice is one of the four possible outcomes. Now assume that, having just tossed two heads, your friend says, "I'll bet you can't toss another head." What are your chances?

In games of chance such as roulette, dice, or coin tossing, the consecutive plays are called *independent* events. The coins, dice, or roulette wheels do not have memories. Having just been tossed two times, the coin does not "remember" which of the four possible sequences shown in Figure 5–1 has taken place. Whatever has gone on before cannot influence the coin. It remains a 50 percent chance that the next toss will be heads, and a 50 percent chance that it will be tails. After two heads in a row, the probability of heads on another fair coin toss is no more or less likely than it was on the preceding tosses—it's still an even bet. The information from the recent past is *useless* in predicting the next event.

FIGURE 5-1
The Four Possible Results from Tossing a Coin Twice

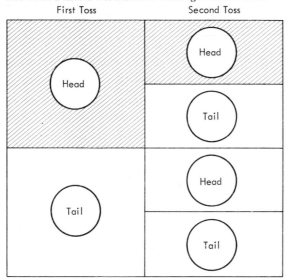

The Gambler's Fallacy: Part 1

Some gamblers have difficulty reconciling the fact that past information is useless with the additional fact that everyone "knows" three heads in a row is an unlikely occurrence. To resolve this point of confusion, let us expand our diagram from the four possible outcomes of tossing a coin twice to show the outcomes from tossing a coin three times. There are eight possible outcomes of a three-coin-toss event because each of the four possible outcomes from two tosses might be followed by either a head or a tail. A head following any of the four outcomes of two tosses produces:

HHH, HTH, THH, TTH

Similarly, the outcomes from two tosses might be followed by a tail on the third toss, producing four more possible outcomes of a triple-toss event:

HHT, HTT, THT, TTT

This produces eight possible outcomes from tossing a coin three times, as shown in Figure 5–2.

Now we can separate the *two questions* that produce the "gambler's

FIGURE 5–2
The Eight Possible Results from Tossing a Coin Three Times

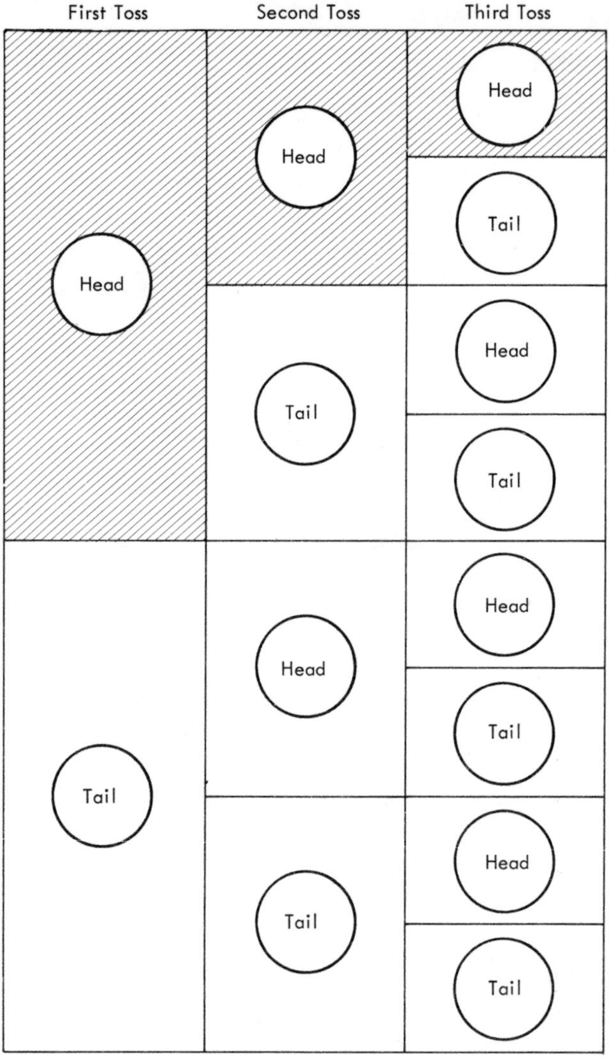

First Toss	Second Toss	Third Toss
		Head
	Head	
		Tail
Head		Head
	Tail	
		Tail
		Head
	Head	
		Tail
Tail		Head
	Tail	
		Tail

fallacy." First, we can ask what is the probability of tossing three heads in a row. Three heads in a row is one of eight equally likely possibilities. Therefore, the probability of three heads is said to be one eighth. This means that a large number of three-coin-toss events is *expected* to produce all heads about one eighth of the time.

The Gambler's Fallacy: Part 2

A second and quite different question is to ask what are the chances of tossing a single head after two heads have *already* been tossed. The difference between these two questions is subtle and has eluded some gamblers for years. It is generally known as the "gambler's fallacy." The chance of tossing a head after having just tossed two heads, or *any* number of heads with a "fair" coin, is unaltered—a head is still a 50–50 bet. Each coin toss is independent of every toss that has gone before. As Figure 5–2 indicates, even though two heads have *already* been tossed, the fact is that the two possible outcomes are equally likely on the *next* toss. While it is indeed true that three heads in a row is unusual (one in eight), getting a third head after two heads have already been flipped is not (one in two).

What is the point of this discussion? Simply this: If events are random, such as in coin tossing or roulette, *historical information cannot be used to predict subsequent events!* In later chapters we will raise, and answer, the question: Are day-to-day stock price changes "random" events? If they are, historical price information cannot be used to predict subsequent price movements!

Part of the new science of investing is that "you must know the odds before you play the game." In addition to randomness, or statistical independence, two important concepts for helping you assess these odds are expected values and variance. Essentially, these concepts boil down to knowing what to expect and knowing the chances of not getting what you expect.

Understanding Risk

In addition to knowing the expected odds, or expected *rate of return,* on stock market investing, we also want to know the risks. *Risk* can be defined as unpredictability, or the extent to which results do not match our expectations. The laws of chance govern these *variations* from expectations as well. This can be illustrated by extending our coin-tossing experiment to learn about risk and variance.

To illustrate risk, or variations from our expectations, the results of many three-coin-toss events are tabulated in the tables that follow. (In all honesty we did not toss coins thousands of times, but simulated the experiment on a computer). As explained earlier, we would *expect* each of the eight possible outcomes of a three-toss "event" to occur with equal likelihood and about one-eighth of the time.

The results of eight trials of our coin-tossing experiment are shown in Table 5–1. Notice that some of the possible outcomes did not occur

TABLE 5–1
Results of Eight Trials of a Three-Toss Experiment

Event	Expected Frequency	Actual Frequency	Percentage Difference
HHH.	1	1	0
HHT	1	0	−100
HTH	1	1	0
HTT	1	1	0
THH	1	0	−100
THT	1	2	+100
TTH	1	0	−100
TTT	1	3	+200
Totals	8	8	0

at all. But also notice that one outcome (TTT) occurred three times more often than we had "expected." With only eight trials of the three-toss experiment, such wide variations are *expected* to occur. In this case, the percentage difference between expected and *actual* results was as high as 200 percent.

Fortunately, statisticians understand the variability of such experimental results. Probability theory tells us what to expect from chance events, as well as the likely *variations* from these expectations. It also tells us that experimental results tend to coincide more closely with expectations the longer we run the experiment. Consequently, the percentage difference between what is expected and what actually happens tends to shrink the longer we "play the game."

The person unarmed with an awareness that actual results do vary *naturally* from expected results may look at Table 5–1 and see a different phenomenon than we have described. He might notice, for example, that the tail-tail-tail sequence has occurred three times. Does this mean that particular sequence is "running hot"? Or, does it mean that the tail-tail-tail sequences have been "used up"? Indeed, we have asserted that both notions are gamblers' fallacies.

To verify our point that the longer we play the game the closer our expected and actual outcomes will be, we can raise the number of three-toss trials. Results of 80 separate three-toss events are recorded in Table

5–2. The "percentage difference" column again is the difference between what was expected and what actually occurred.

TABLE 5–2
Results of 80 Trials of a Three-Toss Experiment

Event	Expected Frequency	Actual Frequency	Percentage Difference
HHH	10	9	−10
HHT	10	8	−20
HTH	10	14	+40
HTT	10	11	+10
THH	10	8	−20
THT	10	11	+10
TTH	10	8	−20
TTT	10	11	+10
Totals	80	80	0

The laws of chance state that, as the number of actual trials increases, the variations between the expected and actual frequencies will decrease. Indeed, the percentage difference figures in Table 5–2 are much smaller than before—dropping from a high of +200 percent to a high of +40 percent. Now the "hottest" sequence, with 14 occurrences, is head-tail-head. But this "information" is totally *useless*. We can safely bet on only one thing in this game: The longer we play, the closer the actual results will approach our statistical expectation. In no case can we use historical information to predict the result of the next toss.

Tables 5–3 and 5–4 show the results of more three-coin-toss trials.

TABLE 5–3
Results of 800 Trials of a Three-Toss Experiment

Event	Expected Frequency	Actual Frequency	Percentage Difference
HHH	100	99	−1
HHT	100	109	+9
HTH	100	107	+7
HTT	100	94	−6
THH	100	94	−6
THT	100	102	+2
TTH	100	99	−1
TTT	100	96	−4
Totals	800	800	0

TABLE 5–4
Results of 80,000 Trials

Event	Expected Frequency	Actual Frequency	Percentage Difference
HHH.	10,000	9,965	–.35
HHT	10,000	10,020	+.20
HTH	10,000	10,045	+.45
HTT	10,000	10,026	+.26
THH	10,000	9,995	–.05
THT	10,000	10,041	+.41
TTH	10,000	9,990	–.10
TTT	10,000	9,918	–.82
Totals	80,000	80,000	0

First, the results of 800 events are recorded, and then the outcome of 80,000 three-toss trials is tabulated. The percentage differences between expected and actual results become progressively smaller as the number of trials rises. With 80,000 trials recorded in Table 5–4, the outcome of this game is predicted within *less than 1 percent* even for the most deviate result.

Coin tossing is not big sport on Wall Street, or even in Las Vegas. But, in order to prepare better for the former, it is useful to consider what happens on the roulette tables of the latter. The American double-zero roulette table has 38 numbered compartments around its circumference. A little white ball is whirled around it and ultimately comes to rest. On a single-number bet, one wagers on any of the 38 possible outcomes. The payoff for a single-number roulette bet is 35 to 1. Thus, if a player wagered $1.00 and won, the croupier would return his $1.00 bet, plus the $35.00 he won.[1]

Laws of chance, which are based on probability theory, can reveal what to *expect* from a long series of chance events, but *not* what will actually *happen* on the next event. A bettor might place only one roulette bet and win on that particular turn of the wheel. In fact, probability theory tells us to expect this to happen once out of every 38 times. It is also possible to win twice in a row. Winning two single-number roulette bets is expected once in every 1444 (38 times 38) two-try sequences.

---

[1] Gambling parlance distinguishes between payoffs stated as *for* and *to*. In a 35 *for* 1 payoff, the casino keeps the wagered amount and pays the bettor $35.00 for each $1.00 wagered. In a 35 *to* 1 bet, *the winning bettor keeps his wager* and is paid $35.00 for each $1.00 gambled.

While no one can predict individual events, the more you play *the closer the total result will approach what is expected.*[2]

Unlike the immutable law of gravity, which accurately predicts *each* outcome, the laws of chance cannot predict the outcome of any *single* event. This does not, however, diminish their usefulness. Probability theory and statistical inference are the *sine qua non* of scientific inquiry. These tools, based on the laws of chance, allow scientists to specify quite precisely when groups of events are *not* happening in accordance with chance expectations.

Enterprising researchers have, for example, applied statistical inference to find roulette wheels that possessed mechanical biases. Many reasons might "explain" why no roulette wheel is perfect, such as warpage, miniscule cracks or bumps that alter the ball's path, metal imperfections, and rotational imbalances caused by wear. On the other hand, roulette wheels *are* precision instruments, and their owners cannot afford to have significant, detectable imperfections in their performance. A *fair wheel* will produce an *expected* advantage for the house on *every* spin. While countless roulette "systems" have been developed, if each play has an expected loss it is impossible to combine a series of such bets into a winning strategy. Any statistician or croupier will aver that conclusion!

Statistical techniques can be used to analyze the *deviations* from expectations in order to determine if, indeed, a wheel is "fair." Some readers may remember pictures of Albert Hibbs sipping milk at a Las Vegas roulette table, while his partner, Roy Walford, tabulated the frequency of various wins. By studying a wheel's performance for several days, Hibbs and Walford were able to detect nonrandom behavior patterns on certain wheels. Once they had established with a high degree of reliability that certain nonrandom events were happening, they were able to translate this nonchance behavior into a winning strategy. While in no case could they predict the "next event," they were able to say that, because of biases in the mechanical performance of the wheel, certain

---

[2] The house *expects* to lose one single-number bet out of each 38 and to pay $35 *to* $1. By taking in $37 from losing bettors while paying out $35 during these 38 bets, the house *expects* to win the difference of $2, or 5.26 percent (2/38), out of each $38 wagered. The only type of roulette bet where the house cannot *expect* to take 5.26 percent of bettors' money is the seldom-used five-way bet on 1–2–3–0–00 which pays 6 to 1. On this bet, the house expects to lose 5 out of 38 spins. Thus, it pays out $30 for five wins achieved on 38 different $1.00 bets. The bettors are expected to lose on the remaining 33 spins. The house wins $33 on these losing $1.00 bets and expects, therefore, to be ahead $3 for each $38 wagered. In this case, the house's expected return is 7.89 percent, making the five-way bet the player's worst on the table.

numbers occurred more often than would be expected if the wheel were mechanically perfect.

You may be asking yourself: What does coin flipping and roulette have to do with investing? Simply stated, understanding the difference between chance occurrences and predictable events will help you accept, despite your intuition, some important research results described in the following chapters. For example, some studies have begun by asking: How would stock prices move if the sequence of day-to-day price changes were completely independent of preceding price changes?

To find patterns in roulette wheel performance, one first assumes that the wheel's outcomes will be purely random, and then compares the actual performance against this bench mark. Similarly, in the coin-tossing example, we can *expect* some percentage difference between the anticipated and observed results. By hypothesizing that stock price changes occur randomly, they can be studied for deviations from random behavior. Then, by using the techniques of statistical inference, any discrepancies can be classified as *significant* or *chance* fluctuations. This approach permits the researcher to isolate any predictable patterns that might be useful for investment strategies. Armed with basic knowledge about statistical independence, expected values, and variance, we now turn to the new science of investing.

part I

understanding the new science

A THE TECHNICAL POINT OF VIEW

chapter

6

The Random What ? ? ?

The techniques used by stock market analysts can be broadly classified as either *fundamental* or *technical*. Fundamentalists attempt to predict stock price behavior from factors which are "fundamental" or internal to the company, its industry or the economy (for example, earnings, products, management, competition, consumer spending, etc.). A market fundamentalist might base a buy recommendation on the fact that a company has consistently shown year-to-year earnings increases and is in an industry that he believes will grow faster than the economy. Technicians, on the other hand, hold that all such fundamental factors are reflected in the market behavior of the stock. Thus, to a pure technician, all data of importance are internal to the stock market. Following this reasoning, technicians contend that future stock price movements can be predicted from diligent study of historical stock market information (for example, changes in stock prices and trading volume). A market technician might, therefore, base a buy recommendation on a pattern of recent price and volume changes.

Many security analysts rely on a combination of fundamental and technical information. In fact, a study guide used by brokers to prepare for securities examinations lists "both fundamental and technical" as the standard answer to the question, "Which kind of analysis should be used to select stocks." (See Loll [**105,** p. 110]) Despite the widespread acceptance of both analytical methods, however, there are differences of opinion regarding the usefulness and accuracy of fundamental and technical analysis. Research on the predictive ability of fundamentalists is reviewed in Chapters 10 through 13. The four chapters in this section focus on research that questions the credibility of technical analysis.

51

Stated in academic terms, this controversy involves what has become known as the *random-walk model*.[1]

This highly important "counter theory" to technical analysis has received much attention. In the last 75 years, numerous university researchers, financiers, and students of the stock market have devoted countless hours to developing and testing this model. Unfortunately, however, the random-walk literature has not been widely read. First, as we have discussed, people do not readily accept ideas counter to their intuition—particularly in money matters. The second and related reason for confusion over the random walk is that its meaning and significance lie hidden in scholarly journals. Even when discovered, these studies are unintelligible to most people. Certainly, academicians are guilty of pendantry for not explaining important research to the investment profession—much less to the investing public. Some segments of the investment community are likewise complacent for failing to assimilate these findings into their decision making. The sad result is that, today, the random-walk model is grossly misunderstood by the majority of practitioners and investors.

To give the reader a grasp of its significance, this chapter defines what is, and is not, meant by the random-walk model and examines its early history. Readers who have no interest in understanding technical analysis, or feel they already understand it, should ask themselves whether they think the following quotations are valid.

When a stock, or the market as a whole, has swung violently up or down, professionals look for a "technical rebound" or "technical reaction." That is, stocks tend to snap back, a third to two thirds of the way. If stocks have jumped, the quick trader sells to cash in on profits; if they've dropped, the "bargain hunters" rush in. Then, the stock may resume the original trend. In longer-range swings, there is a tendency for support or resistance to develop when the stock retraces half of the ground won, or lost, in the last move. [78, p. 45–46]

This is just a technical rally. [191, p. 5]

Analysts generally ascribed the surge to a technical correction sparked by bargain hunting after recent market weakness. [192, p. 27]

---

[1] Some authors, such as Lorie and Hamilton [107], refer to what has historically been called the "random-walk model" as "the 'weak form' of the efficient market hypothesis." Our use of the term "random walk" is synonomous with their definition of the "weak form of the efficient market hypothesis" a market in which historical price and volume changes cannot be used to predict either the direction or magnitude of subsequent price changes.

A brief flareup of volume during a price movement, *even though it does not appear on the chart to have interrupted the price trend,* often discloses a potent support or resistance area which later proves effective in checking a decline or a rally. [78, p. 46]

One of the first things to do before buying a security is to study its historic trading pattern. [65, p. 18]

A trendline helps to establish points at which stocks should be bought and sold. [144, p. 104]

Much of what is included within the rubric of technical analysis is based on the belief that studying historical price and volume movements can enable one to foretell the future. If you believe *any* of the foregoing statements is true, you should read Chapters 6 through 9 carefully. Remember, for successful investing reading the *news* can be misleading or confusing without the *knowledge* to interpret the news.

What the Random-Walk Model Is and Is Not!

The random-walk model (or, if you prefer, the weak form of the efficient market hypothesis) states that the pattern of recent changes in the price of a stock provides no useful information for predicting the next price movement. The random-walk model was once called the "drunkard's walk," and the parallel is apt. If you watch the pattern of a drunkard's steps you cannot forecast with any accuracy what his next step will be—either in size or direction. Similarly, the random-walk model asserts that knowing past price movements cannot assist you in predicting either the size or direction of the next price movement.

It is unfortunate that the word "random" has been used in connection with this description of stock prices. The *Merriam-Webster New Collegiate Dictionary* lists the following synonyms for random: haphazard, casual, and desultory. These words carry the implication of "happening by accident," "at the mercy of chance," "working without intention or purpose," and "ungoverned by a method or system." It should be emphasized that the random-walk model of stock behavior does *not* imply that changes in stock prices "just happen by accident" and are uncaused. Indeed, the forces of supply and demand culminating on the floor of the stock exchange cause price changes. In other words, the price levels are determined by the well-defined economics of a competitive marketplace. This is not a random or chance process. Nonetheless, it is a valid research bench mark to hypothesize that price changes in such competitive markets follow a random sequence. The movement of *actual* stock prices can then be compared against this model. If a researcher, having made such a comparison, cannot then discern repetitive price patterns, he must, by default, accept the random-walk model and conclude that stock price changes are not predictable from prior price information.

The random-walk issue boils down to one basic question: Is information on the historical price of a stock useful in predicting future price movement of that stock? Those who support the random-walk model answer this question with an emphatic "No!" But the biggest problem with the random-walk model is that, *intuitively,* it does not "seem" correct—just as *intuitively* it did not seem correct when Galileo said light objects will fall just as fast as heavy ones.

Professor Clive Granger, of England's University of Nottingham, has been studying the random-walk model for more than a decade. He recently wrote: "The opponents of the random-walk feel instinctively that there is something wrong with the model . . ." [60, p. 91] But, as we have seen, instinct or intuition can be a poor guide. Surprisingly, even though the random-walk model has been around for years, most investors have not examined and understood its meaning. Instead, they have been content to rely on instinct and intuition. This is not merely unwise—it is often dangerous.

Several areas of confusion befog understanding of the random-walk model. Some people erroneously confuse it with notions of "random portfolio selection." Indeed, certain important research does compare the performance of portfolios chosen by Wall Street professionals with the performance of portfolios picked randomly, such as by throwing darts. The random-walk model, however, is not connected with this research. Studies of randomly selected portfolios compare the behavior of "selected" stocks with that of "unselected" stocks. The random-walk studies, by contrast, examine the validity of selecting stocks based on their recent price performance.

Another point of confusion is that some people feel that if the random-walk model is valid, then all security analysis must be futile. This is not true. The model states only that predictions based solely on historical *price movements* are futile. This does not necessarily preclude the validity of predictive approaches based on *other* historical data.

Professor Granger has emphasized, for example, that "the question of whether or not future prices can be predicted using all the world's available information, such as earnings, dividends, expectations, indices of business confidence or even prices of other stocks, is a much wider

question than the one raised by the random-walk model." [**60**, p. 91]
In an attempt to clarify "What The Random-Walk Model Does NOT
Say," Professor Granger, in his article with the same title, discussed several quotations which misinterpret the true meaning of the model. One
of Granger's examples was the following remark by Henry Wallich, the
Yale economist and popular journalist: "The random-walk hypothesis
says little more than that the stock market is a competitive market."
[**171**, p. 161]

Granger has stressed that statements of this kind are not accurate.
[**60**, p. 92] The random-walk model states only that knowledge of yester-
day's, or last week's, or last month's price movements cannot help you
predict tomorrow's, or next week's, or next month's price movements.
The model only makes a statement of alleged fact. Such fact might be
explained by reasoning that the stock market is competitive, but the fact
should not be confused with a theory that might explain it. If past price
changes are devoid of predictive value, this hypothesis would be correct
regardless of the underlying cause of its validity.

Professor Granger notes that "Adam Smith" makes a similar mistake
when he states that:

The first premise of the random-walk is that the market—say the New
York Stock Exchange—is an "efficient" market, that is, a market where
numbers of rational, profit-maximizing investors are competing, with roughly equal access to information, in trying to predict the future course
of prices. [**156**, p. 149]

It should be reemphasized that notions of "efficient" and "competitive" markets are theoretical constructs seeking to explain why prices
behave as they do. The random-walk model only asserts how prices
change and not why.

Professor Granger notes another misinterpretation of the model by
the often controversial economist and presidential spokesman, Pierre Rinfret, who received much publicity for his widely quoted statement in
1969 that "there ain't going to be a recession." Rinfret has this to say
about the random-walk model:

The trouble with the Random-Walk Myth centers on the fact that,
on the one hand, it assumes a highly competitive, efficient stock-pricing
mechanism and, on the other hand, it denies the rewards to those "capable,"
"well-informed" experts who make this market what it is . . . [**142**, p.
166]

The random-walk model does not *assume* anything—it is a description of the way prices move. While "efficient" or "competitive" markets might *explain* what we observe, their existence, or lack thereof, does not alter the assertion of the random-walk model that price changes occur without trends or patterns. Also, the random-walk model does not deny the possibility of "experts" (or even lucky dart throwers) being able to achieve higher-than-average returns. It only says that historical price data are useless in this endeavor.

Whenever you hear of the "random walk" you should remember that:

1. The random-walk model has nothing to do with the market mechanisms that *determine* period-to-period price changes—it only describes alleged fact, not its cause.
2. A rising trend of stock prices is not inconsistent with the random-walk model.
3. The random-walk model is unaffected by the fact that prices of some stocks appreciate or depreciate more than the prices of others.
4. The validity of the random-walk model does not deny the possibility of superior investment performance from information *other than historical price data.* [cf. **12**, pp. 17–20]

The random-walk model asserts that you should not try to predict future price movements from historical price information! Now let's determine if this momentous assertion is true.

How It All Began

The random-walk model dates back to one of the first academic studies of speculative price behavior. In 1900, Louis Bachelier [4], a brilliant French mathematics student studying under the distinguished French mathematician H. Poincaré, formulated and tested the random-walk model of stock price behavior in his doctoral dissertation. Bachelier's dissertation is an amazing document even today. Not only did he discover one of the most significant phenomena in the history of the stock market—over 70 years ago—but his research was filled with other landmark contributions as well. In fact, the equation Bachelier used to describe the random walk was the same as the now-famous one "discovered" by Albert Einstein, five years later, to describe Brownian motion.[2]

---

[2] Named after Robert Brown, the Scottish botanist, Brownian motion is the name given to the random movement of microscopic particles that are suspended in liquids or gases. This movement, which was first observed by Brown, is caused by the

Bachelier's dissertation has significance in modern stock market research for two reasons. First, he provided an explicit statement of the random-walk model. Secondly, his tests of actual security prices corresponded closely to the random-walk model. This meant that the prices he studied did not move in meaningful trends, waves, or patterns. Thus, Bachelier showed that recent historical price data were useless for predicting future price changes. Either because Bachelier's work was so counter to intuition, or because it took an "Einstein" to understand it, his research findings fell into obscurity until they were rediscovered in 1960.[3]

An important lesson to learn from Bachelier's work is that a man with an intellect comparable to Einstein's could spend years studying the stock market, and could even develop a model that sparked intellectual excitement 60 years later, but could not also succeed in changing the investment behavior of his period. Apparently in 1900, as today, men of science quietly applauded the achievements of other men of science and made little effort to bridge the gap between theory and practice. There are lessons to learn from this history. Hopefully, we will learn them!

If one searches hard enough, there are other early instances where scholars raised the specter of doubt over those who use historical price data to predict price movements. The work of the Russian economist Eugen Slutsky [154], in 1927, is recognized as an independent rebirth of the random-walk. Slutsky, who was not aware of Bachelier's work, showed that randomly generated price changes look like actual stock-price changes and appear to exhibit cycles and other patterns. Unfortunately, ten years passed before Slutsky's work was translated into English in 1937, and even then, it did not spark the intellectual interest of either academicians or practitioners.

While market technicians proliferated during the boom preceding the 1929 stock market crash, there were no careful attempts to verify technical analysis during this period. After the 1929 debacle, virtually all enthusiasm for investment advice was dampened during Wall Street's

---

collision of such particles with the molecules that surround them and is of great interest to physicists. In 1905, Albert Einstein presented his renowned paper in which he "discovered" the mathematical equation that describes the Brownian motion phenomenon. Of all Einstein's work, he is said to have personally felt that this discovery was one of his greatest contributions. Yet, Einstein died not knowing that Bachelier, five years earlier, had discovered that the same equation could be used to describe the random behavior of stock prices!

[3] The first modern-day reference to Bachelier's work was published by Alexander [2] in 1961.

"era of disrepute." Investors had persistent memories of Black Tuesday, frightening stories of stock manipulation by investment pools, and many suicides. Nor could the public forget the corruption exemplified by Richard Whitney, scion of the wealthy Whitney family and ex-president of the New York Stock Exchange, who was convicted in criminal court for misusing company funds and sentenced to Sing Sing. Wall Street bore the stigma of these events for almost two decades during which the general public, and qualified researchers, had little to do with the market. In fact, only two research studies that made a material contribution to investing science were reported in the United States between 1930 and 1959.

In 1934, Holbrook Working [175] of Stanford University noted that speculative price patterns might be shown to be random by demonstrating that even artificially generated series of price changes form apparent trends and patterns. He later challenged ". . . a skilled and close student of prices to distinguish reliably which is the real and which is the artificial price series." [176, p. 1435] Working's studies, however, lacked both the mathematical rigor and empirical evidence needed to excite qualified researchers. Moreover, Bachelier's classic paper remained undiscovered. In spite of this early research by Bachelier, Slutsky, and Working, in the late 1930s no one seriously doubted the basic tenet of technical analysis: Stock prices move in discernible patterns.

In 1937, two distinguished researchers, Alfred Cowles and Herbert Jones [29] of the Cowles Commission (now Foundation) for Research in Economics, confirmed intuition supporting technical analysis by *erroneously* (according to their later admission) reporting that stock prices moved with predictable trends. These findings, which were withdrawn in 1960 after an error in the analysis was discovered, stood as damning evidence against the notion of the random-walk model for more than two decades. Unfortunately, the widespread belief in the United States that Cowles had put the random-walk theory to rest mistakenly turned would-be researchers away from the subject for the next 20 years.

While the seeds sown by early scholars lay dormant in the United States, Maurice Kendall [85] made significant advances in the study of the random-walk model. In 1953, at the London School of Economics, Kendall found, to his surprise, that price changes behaved almost as if they had been generated by a suitably designed roulette wheel. That is, each outcome was statistically independent of past history. Using periods of 1, 2, 4, 8, and 16 weeks, Kendall reported that when price changes were observed at fairly close intervals, the random changes from one price to the next were large enough to swamp any systematic patterns or trends which might have existed. He concluded that, ". . . there is no hope of being able to predict movements on the exchange for a week ahead without extraneous [that is, something besides price] information." [**85**, p. 16]

In contrast to the widely quoted (but later shown to be erroneous) research by Cowles and Jones, Kendall's 1953 work was published in the rather obscure *Journal of the Royal Statistical Society* and received little attention. So, while there was scattered evidence of doubt, prior to 1959 no one seriously questioned the doctrine of technical stock market analysis.

Summary

In this chapter we have done two things. First, we defined what the random-walk model is—and is *not*. Secondly, we examined the model's early history. It was this foundation, plus the discovery of the 1900 work of an intellectual "Einstein" and the reconsideration of Cowles' erroneous conclusion, that opened the floodgates of random-walk research during the 1960s. The next chapter highlights more recent research and begins to distill information that can be useful in developing profitable investment strategies.

chapter

7

The Renaissance of Investment Science

We have asserted that man's understanding of the stock market has doubled in the past ten years. This knowledge compression is due partly to modern, high-speed computers. It is astonishing to recall that the now-ubiquitous computer is a relative newcomer. The first electronic digital computer was completed in 1946 by Presper Eckert and John Mauchly at the University of Pennsylvania. Yet, it was not until 1954 that General Electric installed the first computer in a commercial firm. In that same year, Remington Rand (now Sperry Rand) made their now-classic marketing estimate that only 50 computing machines could be sold!

Today's 125,000 computers have proved differently, impacting on the stock market as a spectacular growth industry and as a much needed tool for both investment research and back-office processing. This growth of faster and more cost-effective computers, coupled with suddenly renewed interest in stock market research, set the stage for developments which have more than doubled our understanding of stock price behavior.

Most of the major research findings of the last decade, however, were reported in obscure academic journals. Little effort has been made to explain their meaning to investors. As a result, this important knowledge has not changed many popular investment practices which the new findings condemn as having no value. Sensible investing demands that you understand the significance of this research. An understanding of one facet of this research—that dealing with the random-walk model—is best gained by tracing the model's evolution through the progressively more rigorous studies of the 1960s.

60

The First Splash

Around 1960, Haloid (now Xerox) machines in universities across the United States were busy running off copies of Bachelier's 60-year-old dissertation, which had been discovered by Professor Paul Samuelson and others at M.I.T. At about the same time, widely read papers by Harry Roberts of the University of Chicago, and M. F. M. Osborne, an astronomer at the United States Naval Research Laboratory in Washington, D.C., kindled interest in using computers to study the random-walk model.

Professor Roberts' 1959 paper [143] was significant for several reasons. After placing the earlier work of Holbrook Working and Maurice Kendall in the context of the random-walk model, Roberts showed that a series of randomly generated price changes would look very much like actual stock data. By noting that this chance behavior produced patterns, Roberts was the first modern author to conclude that "probably all the classical patterns of technical analysis can be generated artificially by a suitable roulette wheel or random-number table." [143, p. 10] Osborne's paper [135] developed the hypothesis that the subjective sensation of profit is the same for a price change from $10 to $11 as from $100 to $110. This means that one should study the logarithm of price changes which Osborne showed conformed to the random-walk model.

With the publication of these widely read papers, *the seed of the random-walk controversy was planted in the United States!*

Possibly the most important research during this period was reported in 1960 and 1961 by Working [177] and Sidney Alexander [2], respectively. Each author discovered independently that research based on weekly or monthly stock price *averages* could show erroneous correlations that would not appear if unaveraged prices were used. This fact was extremely important because Cowles' early research that refuted the random-walk model had been based on price *averages.*

In an article published concurrently with Working's in 1960, Cowles [28] revised his 1937 conclusions. In 1937, Cowles and Jones had reported apparent predictability of monthly price changes, even though they found *no* predictability over three-week intervals. When Cowles realized that data composed of *averages* could produce his original results as a statistical artifact, he withdrew his earlier findings which were based on *average* monthly prices. The revised conclusion revealed no evidence that historical month-to-month price data could be used to predict the direction of next month's price change!

Working's 1960 demonstrations that studies of average prices could show fallacious period-to-period correlation, and Cowles' declaration that his 1937 conclusions suffered from this statistical bias, combined to open new avenues of research interest. Furthermore, the ever-increasing availability of electronic computers, and the introduction of high-level programming languages like FORTRAN, provided the long-needed tools for detailed statistical analysis. A careful research study was now needed to show whether or not the random-walk model was *indeed* a tenable representation of price movements in modern markets.

OK, Period-to-Period Price Changes Are Random, but. . . .

The random-walk model states that *any price change is independent of the sequence of previous price changes*. It is important to understand, however, that "price change" implies period-to-period data. For example, one can test the validity of the random-walk model for daily (day-to-day) price changes, monthly (month-to-month) price changes, or any other interval. This interval between price observations is called the "differencing interval." The daily price quotations in newspapers represent a one-market-day differencing interval. Similarly, the quotations in the financial weekly *Barron's* have a one-week differencing interval.

Since the random-walk model is concerned with how prices change from period to period, *one must specify the differencing interval when discussing the model*. Differencing intervals can vary from the shortest possible interval (consecutive transactions shown on the ticker tape) to extremely long intervals of a year or more. Also, instead of occurring between fixed times, differencing intervals can be defined by the occurrence of particular *events*, such as reaching a new price high, the formation of a pattern, and so on. Thus, the research question is *not only* whether the random-walk model is valid. Instead, research must ask, "Is the model valid for some particular differencing interval?" That is, is the relationship between day-to-day price changes random? Week-to-week? Month-to-month?

The early random-walk experiments by Kendall and Osborne were criticized for assuming "fixed differencing intervals." Their research had shown that a series of price changes, measured at *fixed* one-week or one-month intervals, could not be used to predict price movements. But suppose a prediction scheme relied on certain "events," such as large price changes or specific chart patterns, which occurred at variable-time intervals?

There are myriad adaptations of variable-time models, but they all monitor a continuous series of price changes in search of some extraordinary "event." One common variable-time model forms the basis for "point-and-figure" charting, a method of technical analysis of stock prices. This method observes and records the "event" of a stock's price moving by some predetermined amount. These chartists plot *x*'s and *o*'s for rising and falling stocks, but only at the variable times when they move by a specified amount, often one dollar per share.

Variable-time models seek to reveal complicated patterns of price behavior which elude fixed-time models. But, even though no study can undertake an exhaustive analysis of the infinite number of possible variable-time models, there is a single premise underlying all technical prediction methods. This premise is that the market repeats itself in patterns, and that historical information about price movements is useful for prediction. Consequently, the commonly used techniques of technical analysis—be they fixed- or variable-time models—can be classified and explicitly tested against the random-walk model.

Bolstering Random-Walk Research

In 1961, Sidney Alexander [2] of the Massachusetts Institute of Technology reported the first scientific investigation of a variable-time model of stock price behavior. Alexander tested a variable-time model which was based on the "filter technique."[1] He contended that, if his filter technique could show a profit, this profit would be indicative of nonrandom price movements. He evaluated his filter technique with Kendall's [85] data and reported that it was more successful than a buy-and-hold

---

[1] Filter techniques are based on the assumption that trends exist in stock prices but that these trends are obscured by insignificant fluctuations or market "noise." The filter precept is utilized to justify a procedure whereby all price changes smaller than a specified size are discarded or filtered out. The remaining data are then examined. A typical filter rule might be: If the stock price advances 5 percent (signalling a breakout), buy and hold the stock until it declines by 5 percent (signalling the start of a reversal). At that time, sell the stock held and sell short an equal amount until the stock again moves up 5 percent. Under such a rule all moves of less than 5 percent are ignored. Filter techniques seek to discover "significant moves" by studying price changes of a given magnitude, irrespective of the length of time between them. In short, the filter technique substitutes the dimension of the "move" for the dimension of "time." This precept is also the basis of the point-and-figure chart technique (cf. Cohen [18] and [19]).

strategy. His success lead him to conclude that ". . . price changes appear to follow a random-walk over *time,* but a move, once initiated, tends to persist." [**2**, p. 26] And, "it must be concluded that there *are* trends in stock market prices." [**2**, p. 23]

Alexander said, in effect, that the random-walk model describes the week-to-week, or the month-to-month price movements, but it does not invalidate technical prediction schemes based on filters. This conclusion was good news for Wall Street's technicians who search historical price data for variably-timed beginnings of "moves."

It should be emphasized that Alexander's findings were consistent with the previous reported findings that period-to-period price changes occur without trends. Alexander said that if one looks at *all* of the price changes, no patterns will be found. But, Alexander asserted, if you discard, or "filter out," all of the small moves and small sequences of moves, the trends, once initiated, tend to persist.

In another 1961 paper, the renowned Harvard economist and adviser to President Nixon, Hendrik Houthakker [**73**], also reported favorable experiences with a variable-time decision rule applied to commodity futures. In effect, Houthakker advanced the hypothesis (cf. Darvas [**35**] et al.) that changes in prices are characterized by long "runs" (that is, a series of price changes in the same direction). If such an hypothesis were correct, standing sell orders, called "stop orders," could be used by a speculator to sell when adverse runs were encountered. Conversely, a standing sell order would not be triggered when favorable runs were being experienced. Thus, if a trader wished to limit his losses to, say, 5 percent, he would place a stop order to sell when the stock's price dropped to 95 percent of his purchase price. If price fluctuations were not random, and if a price fall were likely to lead to a further fall, such a trading policy would reduce losses without affecting the upward runs of profits. Hence, average profit would increase. Houthakker's test of his trading rule on wheat and corn futures proved quite successful and led him to say, "I feel that . . . [the results] . . . indicate the existence of patterns of price behavior that would not be present if price changes were random." [**73**, p. 168]

Both Alexander's and Houthakker's results were quite surprising, since experiments with variable-time decision rules by other researchers met with failure. This author's own experiments in the early 1960s with numerous variable-time decision rules tested against a four-year file of daily data on 790 actively traded stocks proved most unsuccessful. Derivations of the "best" decision rule parameters, such as length of moving average, filters, thresholds, etc., made for numerous samples consistently showed no reliability. Similar discouraging results were reported in this area by Barney [8], Bauer [9], Johnson [79] and Levine [96]. Other investigators, less willing to report their failure to uncover successful trading strategies, doubtlessly exist. But how could the research reported by Alexander and Houthakker be explained?

As other scholars became intrigued by the reported findings of Alexander and Houthakker, they discovered several problems with their research. Professor Paul Cootner [24] at M.I.T. first noted a procedural error in Alexander's computations. And, while Alexander's results are impressive, he did not state his conclusions in terms of the statistical confidence one should place on the results. Thus, the likelihood of obtaining similar research results purely by chance, or "dart board" selection, was not known.

Similarly, Houthakker's work was based on tests of prices of commodity futures—not stock prices. Commodity futures have been shown to have seasonal patterns. Upon careful examination it is clear that Houthakker's "trends" could have been derived from seasonal movements, not behavior inherent in the price movements.

Overcriticism or Trends?

By 1962, the academic debate on the validity of the random walk began to accelerate—although it was still almost unknown on Wall Street. In 1962, Professor Cootner [25] published an extensive study of weekly data on 45 stocks. Essentially, he reported that prices appeared to move randomly when studied at one-week intervals. But he also found evidence of trends in the same data at 14-week intervals.

Cootner's research thus focused attention on a common area of confusion surrounding random-walk research—the differencing interval. *Remember that the random-walk model states that "future" price movements cannot be predicted from "past" price movements.* Cootner's research emphasized that there is not *one* random-walk model, *but one for every definition of "past" and "future."* In one case, Cootner defined "past" and "future" as "one week." This test of the random-walk model concluded randomness.

Yet, Cootner's research also showed that, when "past" was defined with a longer differencing interval, such as 14 weeks, the random-walk model was *not* valid! Thus, predictions based upon the more distant past might be useful. Investors, however, were faced with evidence that was counter to their intuition. In the race for "hot new information," this research still said *information on recent price changes is worthless!*

Further evidence that studying weekly price changes was futile came from Arnold Moore's 1962 doctoral dissertation at the University of Chicago. Moore's research [122] validated the random-walk model for *weekly* price changes with a sample of 33 representative stocks from the New York Stock Exchange.

Eugene Fama's 1965 doctoral dissertation [40] at the University of Chicago is one of the most definitive studies of the random walk ever conducted. He tested the validity of the model on data covering daily to two-week differencing intervals for the 30 stocks in the Dow Jones Industrial Average—spanning periods from five to seven years. After this exhaustive study, Fama reported no evidence of trends in stock prices for any differencing interval he tested. The conclusion: Information on stock price changes over any or all days during the past 16 days is useless!

"The Case against the Random Walk"

In 1966, *Fortune* ran an article entitled "The Case Against the Random Walk." This article reported on Robert Levy's doctoral dissertation at the American University in Washington, D.C. *Fortune* described Levy's research to be a "decisive refutation of the random walk." [187, p. 160] Before we look at this "case against the random walk," we should recall two things. First, the random-walk model requires an explicit definition of "past" over which price differences are analyzed for predictive potential. There are any number of random-walk models— each with its explicit definition of "past." Secondly, earlier research, dating back to Cowles in the 1930s, and more recently to Cootner, has correctly indicated that, when stock price changes are studied over *long* differencing intervals, there are discernible trends.

Levy's research [97] found that stocks which had higher-than-average price changes in the preceding six months tended to show higher-than-average price changes in the next six months. Random price behavior, on the other hand, should have resulted in only average results for the second six-month period. This phenomenon has been called "relative strength continuation." Thus, stocks with relatively above- (or below-) average price performance in the past six months tended to have above- (or below-) average performance in the next six months.

This phenomenon is not new, nor does it refute the random-walk model. Levy's findings were perfectly consistent with other research. Cowles reported in 1937 that, "taking one year as the unit of measurement . . . the tendency is very pronounced for stocks which have exceeded the median in one year to exceed it also in the year following." [**29**, p. 285][2]

One must exercise caution in interpreting Levy's statement that ". . . stock prices follow discernible trends and patterns which have predictive significance; and the theory of random walks has been refuted" [**97**, p. 354]. This should be read in conjunction with Levy's further findings that ". . . short-time [*sic*, with a one-month differencing interval] results did not reveal any discernible pattern" [**97**, p. 181]. More accurately, then, his statement should read "the random-walk model has again been refuted *when the differencing interval is six months.*"

Seeking further clarification of this important issue, Michael Jensen [**75**] showed that Levy's work contained an error by overstating the returns earned by his "relative strength" trading rules (see [**98**] and [**99**]). Still, some of Levy's decision rules showed more profit than could be attained from a buy-and-hold strategy. What perplexed Jensen was that Levy tested 68 different decision rules on the *same body of data* and that 20 of his decision rules actually produced returns higher than would a buy-and-hold investment policy. But Jensen has pointed out that, when the correct rate of return calculations are used, none of Levy's "profitable" trading rules showed returns *after transaction costs* that exceeded the correct buy-and-hold returns.

At best, Levy was reporting evidence of a subtle form of long-term, nonrandom behavior that apparently could not be used to beat average market returns. Furthermore, Levy tried a large number of trading rules on a single body of historical data until he found some that worked. This "shoot until you hit" methodology led Jensen and George Benington, of the University of Rochester, to remark

. . . given enough computer time, we are sure that we can find a mechanical trading rule which "works" on a table of *random* numbers—provided, of course, that we are allowed to test the rule on the *same* table of numbers which we used to discover the rule. We realize, of course, that the rule would prove useless for any other table of random numbers, and this is exactly the issue of Levy's results.

---

[2] Cowles' article manifests the error in statistical methodology that invalidated the apparent predictability of monthly prices. It should be noted, however, that the above quotation is not affected by this error.

. . . the only way to discover whether or not Levy's results are indicative of substantial dependencies in stock prices or are merely the result of the selection bias is to replicate the results on a different body of data. [77, p. 470]

Jensen and Benington did just this. They selected two of Levy's rules which were purported to earn substantially more than the buy-and-hold policy. These rules were tested on 29 independent samples of 200 securities each over successive five-year time intervals in the period from 1931 to 1965. Jensen and Benington concluded that, after allowance for transaction costs, Levy's trading rules did not, on the average, earn significantly more than the buy-and-hold policy. They concluded, "Levy's conclusion that '. . . the theory of random walks has been refuted,' is not substantiated." [77, p. 481]

Victor Niederhoffer, individually [128, 129, 130] and with Osborne [132], studied the other end of the differencing-interval time spectrum. They analyzed the most basic discernible stock market data—successive transactions on the ticker tape. Their research on this smallest-possible differencing interval provides striking evidence of dependence between successive stock transactions. They report:

The record of stock market ticker transactions displays four nonrandom properties: (1) There is a general tendency for price reversal between trades. (2) Reversals are relatively more concentrated at integers where stable, slow-moving participants offer to buy and sell. There is a concentration of particular types of reversals just above and below these barriers. (3) Quick-moving competitors cognizant of these barriers can take positions at nearby prices, thus "getting the trade" and hoping to make a profit. (4) After two changes in the same direction, the chances of continuation in that direction are greater than after changes in opposite directions. [132, p. 914]

Unfortunately, such short-term and small-percentage dependencies, although consistent, provide no successful trading strategies when transaction costs are included.

Summary

This chapter has examined the historical milestones of one facet of the new science of investing—the random-walk model. This research chronology demonstrates two things. First, it illustrates how the renaissance of investing knowledge has evolved from a sequence of progressively more rigorous, and more probing, computer-based investigations. Secondly, the conclusion that has been reaffirmed by each investigation is that *no research to date has refuted the random-walk model when the differencing interval is between one day and three months*. When the time period between observations is at least 14 weeks, Cowles, and later Cootner and Levy, as well as this author, have demonstrated that period-to-period price changes exhibit some statistical dependence, and thus can be used for prediction. Niederhoffer and Osborne demonstrated that successive ticker transactions similarly behave in a nonrandom, and predictable, fashion. But, unfortunately, any extra profitability attributable to trading schemes based on these findings is generally obliterated by the cost of commissions on transactions!

We warned you in Chapter 4 that intuition can be misleading—and even dangerous. Now, in light of the often counter-intuitive evidence summarized here, it appears that investors are mislead when they rely on the intuitively appealing approach of many technicians who study recent price data. In spite of this evidence, market technicians who plot elaborate charts of price data in an effort to predict the future still enjoy a disturbingly high following. The New Science of Investing indicates that it is time to lay these theories to rest. Do not be misled into believing that recent price movements can predict future price movements. The overwhelming evidence is that they cannot!

Technicians usually respond to this evidence by saying "OK, but how about. . . ?

chapter

8
OK, but How About . . . ?

By the mid-1960s, growing evidence supported the random-walk model of stock price behavior. Nonetheless, these findings were not readily accepted outside of academic circles. The reasons for this oversight all make it just a little bit easier for an investor to have faith in his "intuition."

The first reason for ignoring the emerging evidence against technical analysis was the noncomprehensive nature of the tests and data which had been used to verify the random-walk model. Fama's [40] test data, for example, consisted of daily prices for only the 30 stocks of the Dow-Jones Industrial Average. Also, in deference to technical analysts, one must admit that the statistical tools (serial correlation, run tests, and so on) used to study stock price behavior were inadequate to detect the complicated patterns (for example, head-and-shoulders) which are reputed by some chartists (cf. Jiler [78]) to serve as predictors. Furthermore, research on the random-walk model had generally neglected trading volume information. Yet, many technicians contend that volume is a necessary adjunct to historical price data.

Another, somewhat related, reason for limited acceptance of the random-walk model stemmed from the fact that "randomness" can only be defined negatively. There is no single test for randomness. A conclusion of randomness can be drawn only when one is unable to discover any systematic price movement. Thus, when research does not reveal predictive price patterns, one can only conclude that those *particular* price changes are random. As such, each test must carry the proviso that some other test on some other price data *might* be able to detect a meaningful pattern. Since each test covers only a particular class of

70

patterns on the particular data available, only an infinite number of experimental tests could *prove* randomness in all stock price behavior. These reasons, coupled with the fervent belief held by every technician that "his" system can predict price movement, produced, by the mid-60s, a flood of "OK, but how about . . . ?" challenges to the random-walk model.

As a result, practitioners and academicians did not agree on the relevance of the random-walk model of stock price behavior. It was then, *as it is now,* hard to find a practitioner who did not believe the mystique of technical analysis and who would not contend that historical price activity could be used "sometimes" to predict stock price change. On the other hand, by the mid-60s it was almost as difficult to find a scholarly researcher who believed that historical prices could be of any substantial value in predicting future stock price change. The academicians who contended that the random-walk model explained stock price behavior did so because thorough studies have been unable to verify the usefulness of price patterns in forecasting a stock's behavior. Conversely, most practitioners (if they were aware of the debate at all) did not believe the tests employed by the researchers would be able to detect *complex* patterns, as they claimed to do.

Round Two—Shoring Up the Weaknesses

Early studies of speculative price behavior searched almost exclusively for patterns present throughout the time period studied. It was quite possible, however, that a test which looks at *all* price data might indicate randomness, while a test that looked at only *some* of the price changes (for example, "large changes") would show predictable patterns. Furthermore, the tests were often made on less-than-comprehensive data.

Early investigations tested *fixed-time* versions of the random-walk model. Thus, most scholars based their findings on small samples of selected stocks which were analyzed using fixed differencing intervals such as day-to-day, week-to-week, etc. As a result, in the mid-60s it was not known whether the findings obtained from these limited tests on limited empirical data would be substantiated for a much larger sample of stocks, studied over various intervals. Further, it was not known whether industry or price-range differences might repudiate the random-walk description of stock price behavior.

In addition to the work needed on fixed-time models, the mid-60s raised many unanswered questions concerning *variable-time* or event-triggered models. For example, there had been no rigorous investigation of the assumptions underlying "chart" theories of investment selection. Under a chart theory, certain pattern formations, which may be detected visually from appropriate graphic displays of stock price data, are said to presage future price behavior. It was unknown whether or not a systematic investigation of visual patterns would reveal dependencies undetected by traditional statistical analysis.

The Reasons People Won't Listen

These early shortcomings of research on the random-walk model may be summarized by enumerating the most common reasons practitioners gave—and continue to give—for rejecting this description of stock price behavior. Technicians who were aware of the random-walk model often:

1. Contended that the random-walk model had not been tested on enough stocks over a long enough period of time.
2. Questioned some perceived assumption underlying the random-walk model—regardless of the criteria (stock exchange, industry, or price range) used in picking the stocks employed to test the model.
3. Felt that research on the random-walk model was incomplete because it did not include trading volume information, which was seen as a necessary adjunct to historical price data.
4. Believed that the random-walk research was too limited because it searched almost exclusively for patterns present throughout the entire time period.
5. Contended that the statistical techniques used to confirm the random-walk model were unable to detect the complicated relationships interpreted visually or graphically by chartists.
6. "Intuitively knew" that prediction schemes based on historical price and volume changes could forecast stock price movements.

This author sought to investigate these issues in his doctoral dissertation.

OK, but How About Low-Priced Stocks? Stocks on the American Exchange? Industry Differences?

The random-walk model, as of the mid-60s, had only been validated using data for a small number of stocks—typically for 30 or fewer large companies. To overcome such limitations, this author studied the daily prices and volume for 790 actively traded stocks on the New York and American Stock Exchanges over several three-year periods [**67**].

The first research question was: Does the random-walk model hold for all actively traded stocks? Using a large variety of computer programs and statistical tests, the findings were quite conclusive: There was no systematic behavior in stock prices that could be used for profitable prediction when the data were studied with differencing intervals between one and sixteen days. Further, there were no systematic differences that would allow profitable prediction when the findings were cross-tabulated by stock price range, stock exchange, or industry.

In summary, this author's findings from an exhaustive investigation of fixed-time stock price dependencies utilizing traditional statistical tools offered no evidence that profitable prediction schemes could be developed from recent historical price data. These findings are consistent with Fama's evidence [**40**] and indicate that *knowledge of a stock's price behavior during the preceding 16 days provides no useful information* for predicting the direction of future price change.

OK, but How About Prices and Volume?

Is it true, as many technicians contend, that it is the *combination* of price and trading volume data that provides useful predictive information? To answer this question this author used his computer-readable file of prices and volumes on 790 stocks. A comprehensive appraisal was undertaken of the possibility that price change can be predicted from the simultaneous interaction of preceding price and volume changes. While the details of this research are beyond this book's scope (they are available in this author's doctoral dissertation), the results are significant for anyone who invests. This research shows that knowledge of preceding volume changes,[1] even coupled with information on preceding price changes, does *not* improve one's ability to predict the direction of the next price change.

In sum, these results reaffirm previous findings that short-term (less than 16 days) stock price changes move in random, hence unpredictable, patterns. The introduction of the previous period's trading volume data

---

[1] It should be noted that "information" concerning various relative and absolute volume levels was also tested and that none of these schemes invalidated the above conclusions.

does not enable one to improve, even slightly, prediction of the direction of future period-to-period stock price change.

How About "Breakouts"?

There is conclusive evidence that knowledge of the direction of price and volume changes on any day cannot be used to predict the direction of the next price change. This conclusion was reached from analysis of fixed-time models. Most stock market technicians, however, do not purport to predict price changes solely from fixed-time models. They contend that situations arise *occasionally* which foreshadow certain kinds of predictable price behavior. Thus, technicians typically characterize the stock market by a variable-time or event-triggered model. This author has conducted exhaustive tests of the premises underlying such variable-time models. For example, do "large" daily price changes precede predictable events?

There are several conflicting viewpoints on how stock prices behave after large price changes. On the one hand, some investors contend that steep advances or declines are typically followed by reversals. They reason that reversals are brought about either by profit taking at the higher price or by bargain hunters attracted to the lower price. On the other hand, there are investors who contend that large price increases signal "breakouts" which are apt to continue. If the market contains both kinds of investors, however, their influences would offset each other. Then, large price changes might be followed by changes that behave just as if they were generated by a random process.

Mandelbrot [109] has suggested yet another model. He submitted that any large price change might tend to be followed by further large changes, either up or down. Fama has provided the following rationale for this model:

. . . this type of dependence hinges on the nature of the information process in a world of uncertainty . . . when important, new information comes into the market, it cannot always be evaluated precisely. Sometimes the immediate price change caused by the new information will be too large, which will set in motion forces to produce a reaction. In other cases the immediate price change will not fully discount the information, and impetus will be created to move the price again in the same direction. [40, p. 85]

Fama tested this hypothesis on ten stocks. He reported finding only slight evidence of large changes being followed by further large changes, and that such successive price changes were of unpredictable direction. These results have been substantiated by this author in a study of 790 stocks. That is, there is some evidence that "large" price changes occur in succession, *but the direction of the change is random.* This result interests economists but is of little value to investors, who are interested in the *direction* of the following price movement.

In addition, numerous other hypotheses have been tested by this author to establish the usefulness of coupling trading volume information, such as "volume shocks," with large price changes. In summary, there was no evidence that the occurrence of any special price or volume situation over the short run (less than 40 days) enables one to predict subsequent price behavior.

How About Chartists?

There are two kinds of chartists: bar chartists (cf. Edwards and Magee [38] and Jiler [78]) and point-and-figure chartists (cf. Cohen [18], [19], and Tabell [164]). In the context of the models that we have discussed, bar charting is a fixed-time model and point-and-figure charting is a variable-time model. Both kinds of charts plot price on the vertical scale. On bar charts, the horizontal scale is uniformly divided into fixed-time periods. On point-and-figure charts, the units on the horizontal scale are used to indicate reversals in the stock price's direction. These, of course, occur at variable-time intervals.

Once the stock's historical record has been charted, the technical analyst visually studies the configuration for predictive signals. While it is unlikely, it must be conceded that chartists might be able to detect visually extremely complex patterns that the traditional statistical tests used by researchers would be unable to perceive.

The validity of predicting stock price movement on the basis of chart patterns can, however, be tested rigorously by an unconventional use of computer capability. This is so because all charting theories rest on a single premise. They assume that visually detectable price patterns have repeating characteristics. This premise also has been rigorously tested by this author. It is again beyond the scope of this book to discuss such research on chart patterns in detail.[2] Here it suffices to summarize briefly the two methodological approaches and the general findings.

---

[2] Some of this author's early work on computerized detection and classification of chart patterns is reported in [67].

The first research approach sought to emulate the chartists' vision. Chartists look for specific kinds of patterns such as head-and-shoulders, saucer bottoms, triple tops, etc. The first phase of this research involved using a computer to search the price history of each of the 790 stocks for specified patterns that are purported by chartists to serve as predictors. The computer was instructed to "look for" the mathematical equivalent of what a chartist hopes to find visually. Next, the occurrence of any of these patterns was recorded, and the stock's succeeding price behavior was noted. Finally, a statistical analysis was conducted to determine if these patterns indeed preceded certain kinds of price performance. The investigation was unable to detect any evidence that the commonly used chart patterns actually forecast price changes.

The second research approach sought to have the computer derive original predictive patterns from the data. In this approach the computer was first instructed to group charts on the basis of the price behavior *following the chart*. For example, all chart patterns that appeared before dramatic price increases were grouped. Then these patterns, which all preceded similar kinds of price movements, were studied for similarities. Again, *this research offered · no evidence that predictable stock price movement follows visually detectable chart patterns.*

chapter
9
The Technician's
Coup de Grâce

Can a stock's future price behavior really be independent of its long-term price history? Here, intuition is substantiated, at least slightly, by the scientific evidence available thus far. Intuitively, a stock which performed well in the past six months or year might seem likely to continue good performance over the next six months or year. In a sense, a stock's behavior over this longer, past period indicates its fundamental quality. Even over the span of last year through next year, the company's management, products, markets, sales ability, etc. would seem unlikely to change drastically in quality. Thus, firms with better-than-average records in the past six months or year would seem likely to continue such better-than-average performance in the following six months or year.

As discussed, Alfred Cowles reported such year-to-year performance persistence for better-than-average stocks as long ago as 1937. In 1966, Robert Levy used the term "relative strength continuation" to describe a similar phenomenon, which he had observed for six-month periods. Levy's philosophy implied he was "better able to detect values by studying price and volume patterns and trends than by studying balance sheets and income statements." [184, p. 80] Levy's approach to technical analysis was based on comprehensive research, rather than intuition. Yet, as other researchers warned, any prediction system which is perfected on historical data makes the assumption that the future will behave like the past. For example, when Levy found that stocks which had performed well in the past six months tended to persist in their good performance, it was also natural to test the past four months, five months, seven months, eight months, etc. By doing this, one can "fine tune" a system that will perform very well in the future, as long as *the future behaves like the past.*

Don't Technical Schemes Work "Sometimes?"

For some readers the evidence presented here must seem contradictory to their personal experience. Such people "know" that technical prediction schemes based on historical price and volume changes work. But, do they? The evidence on this point is quite clear. There is *absolutely no evidence* that knowledge of the price and volume performance of a stock over the preceding 40 days is meaningful in predicting the future price behavior of that stock. Yet, many practitioners persist in using this kind of technical analysis.

Those who use technical information for investment decisions must occasionally feel successful. Otherwise, they would not continue the practice. Success in the stock market, however, must be gauged against a realistic bench mark. One would *expect* a certain level of investment outcome even if technical analysis is indeed useless. Stated another way, the bench mark for comparing investment performance should be the results one would expect from purely *random* investment in the stock market.

Suppose that, instead of basing investment decisions on the results of elaborate technical analysis, an investor selected his stocks by throwing darts at the financial page of a newspaper. Further, suppose he chose his transaction dates by throwing darts at a calendar. What would be the investment outcome of such random stock selection? Professors Lawrence Fisher and James Lorie of the Center for Research in Security Prices at the University of Chicago have answered this question.

Fisher and Lorie's work [49] revealed that the median rate of return from *random* investment in common stocks was 9.8 percent compounded annually. They arrived at this conclusion by repeatedly computing the return from individual stocks selected at random from a list of all NYSE stocks. This stock price data spanned from 1926 to 1960, and random buy-and-sell dates within that period were chosen for each hypothetical investment. They also found that *78 percent of the random transactions were profitable.* Furthermore, the holding of more than one stock, as in a diversified portfolio, would have led, on the average, to a positive return more often than 78 percent of the time.

Thus, research into the behavior of security prices indicates that:

1. There is no evidence that technical stock market prediction schemes based on price or volume information drawn from the preceding 40 days provide any useful information.

2. Purely random purchase and sale of common stocks during several past decades would have returned nearly 10 percent compounded annually and would have resulted in a profit on 78 percent of such transactions.

These findings become especially interesting when you consider that technicians generally claim to make accurate predictions no more than 70 percent of the time. For example, Edmund W. Tabell, considered the dean of chartists until he died in 1965, said that he was right only about 70 percent of the time. Admittedly, the longer a position is held, the more likely that it will become profitable, and Tabell made no statement as to how long or short a time it took for him to be "right." Also, the annual rate of return achieved on overall investment is usually more important than the percentage of individual buys with profitable outcomes. Nevertheless, it is this author's conclusion that people who give the credit to technical analysis for their success in the stock market have, in fact, *not been aided in any way by technical analysis.* They have merely obtained results consistent with the expected returns from comparable random investment.

How About Filter Rules?

The use of filter rules as a technical timing mechanism for stock trading deserves special attention. Despite a wealth of evidence that they are worthless, filter rules attract many devotees. There *is,* however, evidence obtained by this author and others that stock prices behave as if they fluctuate randomly but *within barriers.*

A security appears to have some real or "intrinsic" value, and its prices tend to fluctuate randomly around this value. There seems to be a point above the intrinsic value when people will say "the price is too high," and the price will then tend to return to its real value. Similarly, a price seems to exist below the intrinsic value at which investors will say "it's too low" and bid the price back up to the intrinsic value. Thus, it would be logical to have prices moving randomly within "reflection barriers" as shown below.

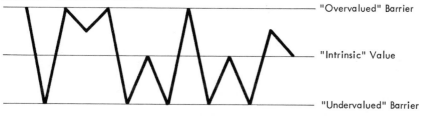

"Overvalued" Barrier

"Intrinsic" Value

"Undervalued" Barrier

If this is true, we would see evidence that prices tend to reverse themselves as they neared the barriers. Cootner [25], Fama [40], and this author [67] have all provided evidence that would support this theory. But the problem is "how can this evidence be used to devise a profitable stock market trading scheme?" This is the "game" the filter technicians play!

When devising a filter approach one must hypothesize what will happen when a barrier is exceeded. Most technicians who utilize filter approaches have hypothesized that any major price movement will cause a shift of the *entire* trading range. Thus they reason, as Alexander did in 1960, that the stock's price will behave randomly until there is a "breakout"—whereupon a new intrinsic value is established. Filter technicians contend that they can detect these shifts. Thus, the problem of the filter builder becomes one of deciding on a filter of proper size. If the market fluctuates randomly about the intrinsic value, the filter must not be too narrow, or it will signal too many false starts.

For example:

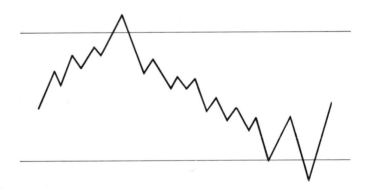

But similarly, if the filter is too wide, it will miss the "breakouts."

Fama and Blume [41] have conducted one of the most thorough analyses of the filter technique reported in academic literature. Their approach used a variety of filter sizes to see if they could determine the "best" size. *In no case did they report a strategy that would have been more profitable (after commissions) than a buy-and-hold strategy.*

Other techniques have tried to pinpoint breakouts from the elusive "intrinsic value." James Van Horne and George G. C. Parker [169] have reported the results of attempts to use moving averages for this purpose. *In no case did they report a strategy that would have been more profitable (after commissions) than a buy-and-hold strategy.*

Can Performance Be Explained?

What "performance" *really* means is discussed in a later chapter, but a preview is in order here. Consumer-investors are bombarded by much advertising literature which shows performance. But, of course, investment performance is the record of what you could have had, and not what you will get. A frustrating element of investing is that the outcomes of alternative decisions are available in the daily newspapers. In the business of life, major decisions preclude knowing the outcome of an alternative choice—both paths cannot be traveled. Yet, there in the morning paper the investment "could have been's" appear.

Before using past performance data, one must first ask, "is the future going to be like the past?" Richard Brealey, in his outstanding book *An Introduction To Risk And Return From Common Stocks,* has cautioned his readers that "the fact that a trading rule would have been profitable in the past does not necessarily indicate that it will offer a valuable investment tool. A formula that is capable of explaining past events may owe its success to coincidence." [12, p. 37]

Suppose you have the price record of every exchange-listed stock over the past three years. Imagine that, using this historical record, you have succeeded, after many tries, in perfecting complex decision rules which provide substantial profits in excess of what would have been obtained from a random buy-and-hold strategy. Should you use your newly discovered strategy in the future? Again, Brealey reminds us,

A decision rule will . . . only prove useful as a guide to the future if it is supported by a basic underlying rationale that gives some reason to believe that the relationships on which it relies will persist in the future. Not only do most technical systems lack this theoretical underpinning, but it is uncertain whether a sufficiently strong theory can ever really be developed to justify faith in a continuance of a major market imperfection. [**12,** p. 37]

What is Brealey really saying? If a system has worked, isn't that enough? One such classic decision system has been suggested and is not at all complex. The rule simply says buy stocks whose names end in *x*. In the 1962–69 market rise and technology-glamour boom, this rule gave good performance—Ampex, Magnavox, Memorex, Syntex, Tampax, Telex, and, of course, Xerox (maybe it's the two *x*'s that did it). But, the more recent fortunes of these "*x*-rated" stocks have, in some cases, dwindled. The good mechanical or "technical" rule of one era may not work well in the next. Academicians are merely reminding the public that, if 10,000 people using Ouija boards predict market swings, some will, by sheer weight of numbers, be correct in their predictions. But, there must be some underlying rationale providing reason to believe that the technique will work *again.* Applying filter rules that worked in the past makes the assumption that *the market will continue to move with swings of the same duration and magnitude!* Unfortunately for the filter devotee, even a casual stock market observer knows that prices do not move in such a systematic fashion.

So Where Do We Stand?

Academic research, which has no vested interest in holding out false hopes of prediction, is in overwhelming agreement—technical market prediction schemes based on price and volume movements over the preceding 40 days appear useless. Most market practitioners will react to this statement by asserting that they only use such technical analysis "sometimes." This is ridiculous! The evidence is overwhelming that such analysis should *never* be used. Why then does this kind of technical analysis persist? Why does the investing public support advisory services that rely on charts? Isn't it strange that a hospital patient who will literally trust his life to a computer's ability to read his electrocardiogram will not listen when told that the same pattern detection techniques fail to detect useful patterns in stock price data?

In spite of this research, "technical" jargon remains an integral part of Wall Street's vocabulary. Financial pages make frequent references to things like a "technical correction" even though few commentators agree on its definition or occurrence. Unfortunately, most of this gobbledygook appears to serve the purpose of the psychiatrist's ink blot—to project meaning into nothing.

Yet, in spite of its thoroughness, several provisos should be made regarding the research summarized here. First, it should be emphasized that technical analysis, as discussed here, means analysis based on recent (within 40 days) price and/or volume information. Secondly, direct comparisons against what technicians actually do is difficult because they usually interpret basic price data with "necessarily secret" formulas to calculate percentage strengths, moving and geometric averages (see James [74]), ratio lines, trend forecasts, and the like. Thirdly, prediction schemes within the commonly used rubric of "technical analysis" by no means limit themselves to the study of price and volume information. Hence, our analysis of the technical point of view will not be complete until we examine in a later chapter the usefulness of such nonprice technical indicators as splits and odd-lot sales.

In spite of these provisos, several comments can be made about technical analysis. It is doubtful that the tea leaves left behind by today's stock market can foretell tomorrow's. The more scientific approach of the next section, instead of analyzing market history for patterns, begins by studying the *causes* of price movements. For now, an important *don't* of successful investing is: *Do not use technical analysis based on recent historical price or volume information.*

The Epitaph

Given the wealth of evidence against such analysis, and nothing credible in its favor, it would appear that William Shakespeare wrote its fitting epitaph:

> It is a tale
> told by an idiot,
> full of sound and fury,
> signifying nothing.

part I
understanding the new science

B THE TENETS OF FUNDAMENTAL ANALYSIS

chapter

10
What Causes Price Movements?

The evidence supporting the random-walk model does not mean that price changes are uncaused. The random-walk research merely concludes that recent price changes cannot be used to predict either the direction or magnitude of subsequent price changes. Price changes result from the combined actions of buyers and sellers which shift the market's equilibrium between demand and supply. For example, when the demand for a stock increases, relative to its supply, this imbalance causes a price rise that is sufficient to attract enough sellers who create additional supply and restore the market to economic equilibrium.

Since price changes are caused by changes in either the net supply or demand for investments, above-average investing strategies can be developed if one can:

- Determine what causes people to change their minds, and
- Act on this information before it is fully reflected in the price of the investment.

This logical approach to achieving above-average rates of return introduces the issue of the "efficient capital market theory."

The Efficient Capital Market Theory[1]

The setting for an "efficient capital market" is a market in which many people, with similar investment objectives and access to the same

---

[1] Some authors, such as Lorie and Hamilton [107], distinguish between three levels of "efficient" markets. They define a "weak form" as a market in which historical price data is efficiently digested and, therefore, is useless for predicting subsequent price changes. This is distinguished from a "semistrong form" in which

87

information, actively compete. The stock market certainly provides this setting. Many people—both professionally and privately—continually search for undervalued securities. Also, in their quest for wealth, investors have similar basic objectives. Everyone prefers a high rate of return to a low one, certainty to uncertainty, and so forth. Furthermore, unless they are trading illegally, the law guarantees that both parties in a securities transaction have access to the same material facts.

Scholars have hypothesized that in such a market setting—with many people playing the same game, having similar objectives, and equal access to information—it would be impossible for any investor to have a consistent advantage over the market, which reflects the composite judgment of its millions of participants. This hypothesis is known either as the "efficient capital market theory" or the "fair-game theory." "Efficient" means that the market is capable of quickly digesting new information on the economy, an industry, or the value of an enterprise, and accurately impounding it into the price of the stock. A "fair game" means that participants in such markets cannot expect to earn more, or less, than a fair return for the risks involved.

The efficient capital market theory hypothesizes that all available information is continually analyzed and reanalyzed by literally millions of investors. It holds that in this kind of market, news of, say, an earnings increase, is quickly and accurately assessed by the combined actions of investors and immediately reflected in the price of the stock. The purported result of this efficiency is that, whether you buy the stock before, during, or after the earnings news, or whether you buy another stock, you can expect a fair market rate of return commensurate with the risk of owning whatever security you buy. (Risk is discussed in detail in later chapters.)

It is important to note that this theory might be true for one kind of information, say earnings, but might not be true for other types of information, say dividend changes. Similarly, it might hold true for information on particular instruments, say stocks, or in certain markets, such as the New York Stock Exchange, but not for other instruments or markets. We might reasonably expect, for example, that the efficiency of widely held common stocks is different from what we later term the "forgotten instruments"—speculative bonds, convertible bonds, puts,

---

all publicly available company-related data is assumed to be fully discounted in the current price of the stock. Finally, they discuss a "strong form" in which not even those with privileged information can secure superior investment results. Our discussion of the efficient capital market concept encompasses both the "semi-strong" and the "strong" versions by distinguishing between the two when necessary.

calls, and so forth. Alternatively, there may be opportunities to be gained by combining instruments from markets with differing efficiencies through hedging strategies. Thus, when you refer to the efficient capital market theory, you must specify: the "information," the "instrument," and the "market."

This theory does not deny the profitability of investing. It merely states that the rewards one earns from investing in well-organized, highly competitive markets will be fair, on average, for the risks involved. But this theory also holds that acting on publicly available information *cannot* improve one's performance beyond the market's assessment of a fair rate of return.

If the stock market is a fair game, much of the hope for extraordinary gains from investing is removed. The unlikelihood of making a big killing, however, would not lessen the importance of investing. It would merely change the underlying philosophy from one of trying to beat the other guy to one of asset management designed to attain a fair and stable rate of return consistent with one's personal financial plan. Also, this theory focuses our search for useful market predictors on that information which might cause people to change their minds about investment values.

Rather than the all-encompassing specter of gloom which some practitioners mistakenly assume it to be, the efficient capital market theory is a useful bench mark for the new science of investing. From its perspective, researchers can determine which information is "efficiently" and "inefficiently" processed by competing investors in various markets and for various investment instruments. They can hypothesize cause-and-effect relationships and study how efficiently a particular security and market digests a particular kind of information. In this way it is possible to analyze both the likelihood and magnitude of price changes caused by certain information, as well as the market's ability to efficiently impound this news into securities prices.

Investors tend to focus on one market (listed securities), one instrument (common stock), and one or two categories of news items (earnings and dividends). It is likely, therefore, that other fruitful (that is, where the information processing is inefficient) areas exist. Those who can discover and accurately assess these inefficiencies can profit from their differential knowledge. Unfortunately, however, as any heretofore unrecognized information is disseminated among competing investors, its value to users is destroyed by the equalizing forces of an efficient capital market. Even if research can pinpoint news items which are efficiently processed for particular instruments in particular markets, such knowledge enables investors to avoid analyzing this useless, fully discounted information—*an important decision in itself.*

If You Want Above-Average Performance . . .

To consistently attain above-average investment performance, an investor must *know:*

1. the *likelihood,*
2. that certain *information,*
3. will influence certain investment *instruments,*
4. in certain investment *markets,*
5. in known *directions,*
6. by approximate *magnitudes,* and
7. act on the information *before other investors.*

If this cannot be done, investment analysis becomes an expensive exercise in wishful thinking! The fact that well over 100,000 professional security analysts, brokers, and portfolio managers, not to mention 31 million investors, are all trying to do the same thing makes the game of investing *very competitive.* In this league, an above-average batting record comes down to having a game plan and knowing when to swing and when not to. To win consistently, you must know *what* to do, *how* to do it and *when* to do it.

Dissecting the Causes of Price Movements

Several kinds of information can precipitate price movements of various instruments in various markets. Three broad categories of such information are:

1. *Economy-related information.* General economic news typically affects the market as a whole. On days when several hundred stocks reach new lows, while only a few reach new highs, it is clear that even the stocks of well-managed companies in growing industries cannot withstand a bear market.

2. *Industry-related information.* Instead of affecting the general economy, news sometimes only has an impact on an industry. For example, the testimony of Robert B. Choate, Jr. before a Senate consumer

subcommittee in 1970, that dried breakfast cereals contained little or no nutritional value had an adverse industry-wide effect on all dried cereal manufacturers. Similarly, industry-wide strikes affect only firms in that or related industries.

3. *Company-related information.* News about a company's earnings, dividends, forthcoming stock splits, patents, merger offers, new discoveries, and so forth—with little or no bearing on its industry or the general economy—can prompt a change in the price of a company's stock.

If one is going to attempt to predict price movements, a logical first step is to determine the relative importance of each of these three basic kinds of information. For example, if the relative importance of information related to the company, the industry, and the economy is about equal, it might behoove analysts to allocate their research efforts to these three areas equally. Similarly, if 80 percent of a price movement is caused by movement of the market at large, any researcher who devoted most of his attention to company-related information might be grossly misallocating his efforts. In such a situation, the relative importance of information on individual companies would be swamped by the effect of market swings.

Benjamin King [88], in his doctoral dissertation at the University of Chicago, sought to determine the relative importance of these underlying causes of price movements: the market, the basic industry (such as, metals), the industry subgroup (such as, nonferrous metals), and the company. After studying 403 consecutive months of data (1927–1960) for 63 NYSE stocks, King reported:

1. a strong tendency for stocks to move with the market,
2. stock price comovements which corresponded almost exactly to industry classifications, and
3. only a minor proportion of overall price movement that could be attributed to company-related factors.

King's research is startling in its consistency. First, his findings parallel earlier but less comprehensive results reported by Granger and Morgenstern [61], and Godfrey, Granger, and Morgenstern [58]. Secondly, King's market and industry comovements were remarkably consistent, especially when you consider the industry changes that doubtless occurred over the more than 33 years spanned by his study. In the most recent period he examined (1952–1960), King showed that, on average, price changes were attributable to the investing public's reaction to four discernible components in the following proportions:

1. the market as a whole—31 percent
2. the basic industry—12 percent
3. the industry subgroup (or other common factors)—37 percent
4. the particular company—20 percent

On average, 31 percent of a stock's price movement was ascribable to general economic factors influencing the market as a whole. About half of the movement was traceable to the influence of a firm's basic industry and its industry subgroup—12 percent and 37 percent respectively. After these market and industry comovements were accounted for, only a scant 20 percent of the total price movement could be attributed to the individual company!

These aggregate figures do not present the entire picture which King developed. There were some interesting differences within the composite averages. These differences are summarized in Table 10–1 using King's most recent data.

TABLE 10–1
Classification of Price Comovements by Industry Membership

Industry Membership	Percentage Movement Explained by:			
	Overall Market	Basic Industry	Industry Subgroup	Individual Company
Railroads.	47	8	26	19
Metals.	46	8	31	15
Petroleum	37	20	28	15
Utilities.	23	14	41	22
Retail Stores.	23	8	42	27
Tobacco	9	17	49	25
Average.	31	12	37	20

Source: Derived from data in King [88] (also see Brealey [12, p. 61]).

These data show that the shares of railroads, metal companies, and petroleum firms rank highest in overall market dependence, with the stocks of tobacco firms being relatively insensitive to overall market swings. The industry columns confirm King's statement that the "general adherence to the pattern of industry comovement is ineluctable . . . the strongest industry effects are those for petroleums, utilities, and tobaccos—the weakest for metals, [retail] stores, and rails." [88, pp. 203–4]

The significance of King's research can be summarized as three major contributions. First, he showed that, on the average, roughly one third of a stock's movement can be traced to general market swings. Secondly, and very important, there are clear industry differences. In the tobacco industry, for example, King could trace only 9 percent of the price variations to general market swings. By contrast, he could attribute 46 percent of the price movement in the metal industry stocks to general market swings. Thirdly, this relationship between stock swings and market swings appears to be consistent over time. Thus, even today, there is reason to believe that tobacco stocks are still not as sensitive to general market swings as metal stocks, and so forth.

King's research was expanded and updated in 1968 by Marshall Blume [10] in his doctoral dissertation at the University of Chicago. Blume, who studied 251 securities, demonstrated quite conclusively that there is an overwhelming tendency for certain stocks to move with the market, and that this relationship is persistent over time. That is, stocks which are very sensitive—say, those which tend to move 1.5 percent for every 1 percent change in the market—tend to maintain this level of sensitivity over time. Similarly, stocks which are insensitive to market swings—say, those which tend to move only 0.5 percent when the market as a whole moves 1 percent—continue to behave in this fashion. Thus, Blume's dissertation undeniably confirmed the hypothesis that individual stock movements establish and tend to maintain a consistent relationship to overall swings in the market.

How Wall Street Organizes Its Research

These findings are significant in view of the way many Wall Street professionals "pick stocks." Traditionally, brokerage firms, bank trust departments, and investment advisory services organize their research departments around industries. The rationale for this approach is that, by concentrating his efforts, each analyst can become an expert on both the industry and the companies within that industry.

A potential problem with this approach is that it is often difficult for security analysts to balance their in-depth company analyses with both general economic and inter-industry assessments of their industry's competitive position. One reason for this difficulty is that their performance is generally measured by their ability to *pick stocks*. Thus, instead of considering the general economy, or the relationship of their industry to the economy and other industries, or how their research will serve the overall needs of investors, many analysts spend the majority of their time trying to select the best stocks *within their industry* specialty.

From the evidence summarized here, *even if they could predict with complete accuracy,* they could then only explain 20 percent of the typical stock's price variations. The dominance of this company-level research often blinds investors to *more important* general economic and inter-industry forecasting, or even to the personal issues of risk and investment objectives.

Security analysts should discipline themselves to balance in-depth company studies with both general economic and inter-industry analysis. It is important to remember that, on average, almost one third of a stock's price movement can be attributed to overall market forces. Furthermore, the consistent differences among industries lend themselves to different approaches for each industry. Metals and rails, for example, tend to move with the overall market, while tobacco firms do not. Also, basic-industry associations are important in petroleum and tobacco, but not to so great a degree in rails, metals, or retail stores, and so forth. Practically speaking, if 85 percent of the movement of petroleum stocks is tied to the economy and the industry, little effort need be expended on choosing *between* the stocks of oil companies.

For most investors, however, the importance of economic and industry comovements lies in the concept of, rather than in the specific nature of, comovement patterns. This concept is important to the new science of investing because it allows us to evaluate our forecasting ability separately for each of the four levels of the information hierarchy—the overall economy, the basic industry, the industry subgroup and the individual company.

How To Distill Useful Information

When placed in the context of the efficient capital market theory, the foregoing research should prompt us to look for useful information by:

1. specifying the investment "instrument" that interests us (for example, common stock),
2. defining the "market" to be studied (for example, the NYSE), and
3. tabulating the kinds of "information" that *might* affect the value of this instrument at the four levels of the information hierarchy.

This procedure is illustrated in Figure 10–1.

When *possibly* useful information is placed in the perspective of Figure

FIGURE 10–1
The Investment Analysis Function

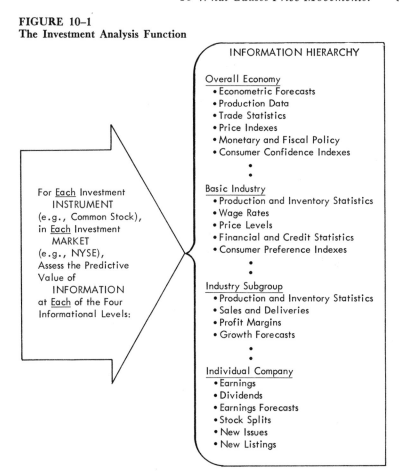

INFORMATION HIERARCHY

Overall Economy
• Econometric Forecasts
• Production Data
• Trade Statistics
• Price Indexes
• Monetary and Fiscal Policy
• Consumer Confidence Indexes

Basic Industry
• Production and Inventory Statistics
• Wage Rates
• Price Levels
• Financial and Credit Statistics
• Consumer Preference Indexes

Industry Subgroup
• Production and Inventory Statistics
• Sales and Deliveries
• Profit Margins
• Growth Forecasts

Individual Company
• Earnings
• Dividends
• Earnings Forecasts
• Stock Splits
• New Issues
• New Listings

For Each Investment
INSTRUMENT
(e.g., Common Stock),
in Each Investment
MARKET
(e.g., NYSE),
Assess the Predictive
Value of
INFORMATION
at Each of the Four
Informational Levels:

10–1 for specific investment instruments in specific markets, one can assess how efficiently information is processed at each hierarchical level. If the information is quickly and accurately impounded into the instrument's price, the market would be deemed economically "efficient" in terms of the impact of that information on that instrument. But, if for some reason the market does not fully react to a certain kind of news, or reacts slowly, the discovery of this economic "inefficiency" will permit one to profit in excess of a "fair game."

It should be reiterated, however, that one does not have to discover market inefficiencies to profit from investments. An efficient market is one in which everyone can expect a "fair return" for his risks. If such a market is efficient at digesting earnings information, for instance, it would mean that acting on such information could not increase your expected return above a fair-game return. Importantly, and unlike the situation in Las Vegas, this expected return is a positive and profitable economic reward for investing.

We will use the framework shown in Figure 10–1 to explain the research bearing on the usefulness of various types of information for predicting market- , industry- , and company-caused price changes. We will begin where much modern research has been focused—the worth of common stocks.

chapter
11
But Some Stocks Are
Worth More than Others

A wealth of evidence shows that stock prices on the NYSE tend to move together, reflecting the public's reaction to the overall economy or an industry. In spite of this, most security analysis is directed toward individual companies. It is important, therefore, to understand how security analysts determine that some stocks are worth more than others—by what is known as fundamental security analysis.

What Constitutes Worth?

When you buy a share of stock you forgo present spending in exchange for expected future benefits. Since you know today's stock price, investing involves a certain sacrifice for an uncertain benefit. These uncertain future returns come from the firm's earning power, which will determine the extent of its dividend distributions and affect, in varying degrees, the future selling price of the company's stock. A cornerstone of fundamental security analysis is that a share of common stock is worth the present value of the future income its owner will receive. Since the income from dividends and the eventual selling price are to be received in the future, their worth must be discounted to reflect interest rates and risk. The price the next buyer is willing to pay, in turn, hinges on his own perception of his returns and his eventual selling price.

Thus, when an investor buys stock he acquires the legal right to share in the company's future earnings through any income distributions or growth. The amount that investors will pay to share in the company's future is generally many times the company's current annual earnings. For example, a stock or a bank savings account that earns 5 percent annually requires an investment of 20 times earnings. A critical valuation bench mark used by security analysts, therefore, is a stock's price-earnings ratio. This is simply the ratio of the stock's current price to its rate of annual earnings, usually as projected for the current or subsequent year, or as calculated for the preceding 12 months. The historical price-earnings ratio, or P/E, as it is generally called, for the Dow Jones 30 Industrials over the 1961–1973 span is shown in Figure 11–1.

Since 1961, the P/E for the Dow Jones 30 Industrials has averaged about 17 and has ranged from 12.8 to 24.2. The market's P/E, measured by this index or others, provides a bench mark for comparison with the P/Es of individual stocks. Table 11–1 shows a representative list of P/Es

TABLE 11–1
P/E Ratios for 35 Large Compaies as Reported on Tuesday, February 6, 1973

Company	P/E Ratios	Company	P/E Ratios
Aetna Life & Casualty	11	Kennecott Copper	9
American Smelting	10	Litton Industries	–
AT&T.	11	McDonnell Douglas	10
Avon Products.	60	Mobil Oil.	12
Chase Manhattan	12	Penn Central.	–
Coca-Cola	45	Philip Morris.	27
Continental Can.	10	Polaroid	78
Delta Airlines	22	Procter & Gamble.	31
duPont	20	Safeway.	11
Eastman Kodak	46	Sears, Roebuck	29
Exxon	13	Tenneco	11
Ford	8	Texaco	12
General Electric.	24	Texas Utilities.	16
General Foods	12	Union Carbide.	13
General Motors	10	U.S. Steel.	10
Gulf Oil	11	Weyerhaeuser	21
IBM.	39	Xerox.	48
IT&T	13		

Source: *The Wall Street Journal*, February 6, 1973.

as of February 6, 1973 for selected large companies. Notice that a P/E could not be calculated for Litton Industries or Penn Central because neither had positive earnings. Also note that the P/Es listed range from a high of 78 for Polaroid to a low of 8 for the Ford Motor Company. This means that investors evaluate some companies' earnings at almost *ten times* those of other companies.

The variations in P/Es stem from the fact that investors anticipate more growth and/or certainty in the earnings of particular stocks, and are willing to pay a higher price for a share of the future growth and

FIGURE 11-1
Price Earnings Ratios for the Dow Jones 30 Industrials 1961–1973

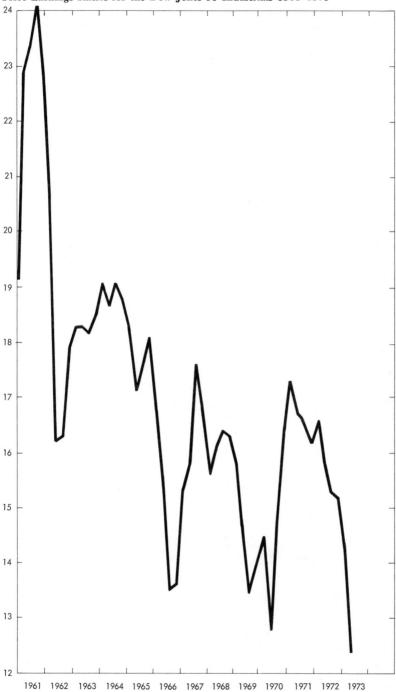

earnings of these companies. Thus, high P/Es reflect investor optimism about a company's future growth. For example, the P/Es in Table 11–1 show that on February 6, 1973 investors were four times more optimistic about the future of Xerox, with a P/E of 48, than they were about the future of Mobil Oil, with a P/E of 12. Similarly, the P/E ratios in Table 11–1 indicate that optimism about the future of oil companies, as represented by Exxon (P/E = 13), Gulf (P/E = 11), Mobil (P/E = 12) and Texaco (P/E = 12), was roughly the same for all members of the industry.

A daily measure of the market's relative optimism about the future of any listed company can be found by examining the P/E ratios that are published by *The Wall Street Journal* and other major newspapers. These ratios are calculated daily from the previous day's closing price and the most recent 12-month earnings.

To accentuate current earnings as a percentage of current price, some analysts like to turn P/E ratios upside down. The British call this inversion of the P/E ratio the "earnings yield." Thus, a P/E of 20, which is $^{20}\!/_1$, can be converted to an earnings yield of $\frac{1}{20}$, or 5 percent. This means that the stock's current earnings yield a 5 percent return on the current purchase price. Similarly, a stock selling at 40 times earnings currently earns only $\frac{1}{40}$, or 2.5 percent, of the current purchase price each year. Why do people buy stock whose current earnings are only 2.5 percent of the purchase price, when they could buy another stock at the same price that would yield 5 percent? The reason is that they expect the future earnings of the current low-yield stock to grow faster, and/or to be more stable, than those of the stock with the current high yield. Whichever form of the ratio one prefers, the key to using this measure is to realize that *it reflects the market's anticipation of growth and/or certainty of future profits.*

Are Stock Prices Related to Earnings?

High P/Es result from a high anticipated growth rate and/or certainty of earnings. Probably the most widely read study of differences in P/E ratios was conducted by Volkert Whitbeck and Manown Kisor [174] at the Bank of New York. They sought a definitive answer to why IBM was then selling at 35 times earnings, while General Motors was selling at less than 18 times earnings. (As of this writing, the gap has widened somewhat to 39 and 10 respectively.) In their analysis Whitbeck and Kisor showed that IBM had experienced an annual earnings per share growth rate of 16.1 percent. During the same period, GM had experienced an average growth rate of only 5.3 percent per annum. In addition, Whitbeck and Kisor demonstrated that IBM's expansion was not only more rapid but also more stable. They reported that ". . . IBM commands a higher price/earnings (P/E) ratio, not because of its past performance, but, rather, because the market, on balance, expects more *in the future* from IBM than it does from GM. As investors, we buy common stocks not simply for records prior to purchase, but, more fundamentally, for what we anticipate from them after our commitment." [174, p. 337]

Here, then, is the issue. Theoretically, a stock's price is governed by its future stream of earnings. In reality, investors have different expectations about the future earnings ability of different companies. A share of stock is worth what someone will pay for it, and investors value earnings differently depending on the company. So, to predict which stocks are the best buys, three important questions must be answered.

1. Do anticipated growth and certainty in a company's earnings account for its relative market price (that is, its P/E relative to the market's P/E)?
2. If you could forecast earnings, could you then forecast stock price changes?
3. Can we accurately predict future earnings?

Does Anticipated Earnings Growth Explain Relative Differences?

The researchers at the Bank of New York concluded that differences among anticipated growth rates explain about 60 percent of the differences in normal P/E ratios. Similarly, John Cragg of the University of British Columbia reported that anticipated growth in earnings explained, on the average, 67 percent of differences in P/E ratios. (See [12, p. 79])

Richard Crowell [31], in his doctoral dissertation at M.I.T., studied the relationship between anticipated earnings and P/E ratios in different industries. Of the 12 industries analyzed, Crowell demonstrated that, at one extreme, 69 percent of the differences in P/E ratios for bank stocks could be explained by differences in anticipated growth rates; at the other extreme, only 5 percent of the differences in the P/E ratios accorded steel stocks could be traced to differences in anticipated growth in earnings. This research confirms that *differences among the relative P/E ratios of various stocks can be explained only partially by differences in each company's anticipated earnings growth rate.*

Where Do We Go from Here?

Further research relating earnings to stock prices was reported by Professors Philip Brown and Ray Ball. [14]. For selected companies, they adjusted stock price changes to eliminate the movements attributable to swings of the general market. Then they studied these "nonmarket" stock price changes for 12 months before, and 6 months after, the date of each company's reported earnings. They found that, when actual earnings were above the forecast earnings, the price of the stock would typically rise during the preceding 12-month period, and that the rise faltered in the 6-month period after the actual earnings announcement. This is depicted in Figure 11–2, where "0" on the horizontal scale denotes

FIGURE 11–2
Average Price Movement During Months Preceding and Succeeding the Earnings Announcement of Stocks of Companies Producing Unexpectedly Good Earnings*
Price Change Not Attributable to Market Change

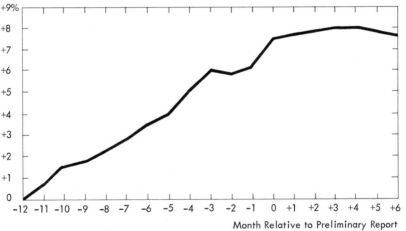

Month Relative to Preliminary Report

* After Brown and Ball [14] and Brealey [12].

the official earnings announcement. They also reported that price movements during the months preceding and following unexpectedly bad earnings announcements showed declines. Figure 11–3 traces the average price movement when actual earnings were below the forecast level.

The information portrayed in Figures 11–2 and 11–3 is very revealing.

FIGURE 11–3

Average Price Movement During Months Preceding and Succeeding the Earnings Announcement of Stocks of Companies Producing Unexpectedly Bad Earnings*

Price Change Not Attributable to Market Change

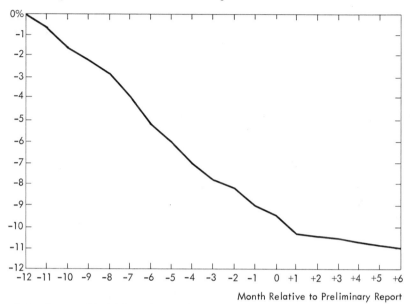

Month Relative to Preliminary Report

* After Brown and Ball [14] and Brealey [12].

It shows what typically happens to a stock's price in the months that precede and follow an unexpected earnings performance. Note that *by the time the earnings report was issued, the market had almost fully anticipated the report.* Also note that, *the stock price made little adjustment after the announcement of either favorable or unfavorable earnings.*

This research indicates that, on the average, stock prices react well in advance and over time to the reported annual earnings of companies. As noted, the theoretical worth of a share of common stock is linked to its future stream of earnings. Research indicates that the process by which the market anticipates this future earnings stream is both steady and accurate. The market action, derived from the aggregate actions of millions of investors, does a remarkably good job of accurately anticipating published earnings announcements.

If You Could Forecast Earnings . . .

Modern research has shown that there is a strong, but not perfect, relationship between stock prices and earnings. The research of Whitbeck and Kisor, Cragg, and Crowell has shown that differences in P/E ratios are only partially explained by differences in anticipated earnings growth. Brown and Ball have shown that, on the average, the price change in response to earnings changes is gradual and extends over many months while the actual earnings are being achieved. These studies can be capsulized by saying that *there is a partial relationship between stock prices and earnings*. This relationship is not simple or completely forecastable. The question remains: If you could forecast earnings, could you then forecast stock price changes?

Henry Latané and Donald Tuttle, at the University of North Carolina, studied the relationship between earnings changes and price changes. [93] Suppose, for a moment, that someone had the ability to forecast earnings with complete accuracy. Could such information be used to predict stock price changes? Latané and Tuttle sought an answer to this question by comparing changes in earnings with changes in the corresponding stock's price for 48 stocks over a 14-year period. They found large year-to-year differences among the proportion of price changes that could be explained by changes in earnings. However, while this proportion of price variations that could be explained by earnings changes ranged from 64.5 percent to 0.8 percent, *the correlations were all positive*. That is, increases in stock prices were generally associated with gains in company earnings. Likewise, declines in prices were, on the whole, associated with decreases in company earnings.

In some years, this tendency was almost eliminated by other factors, while in still other years the influence of earnings on prices was quite strong. Over the entire 14-year period studied, Latané and Tuttle reported that only 17.4 percent of all price variations could be explained by earnings changes. While 17.4 percent is a surprisingly small proportion of stock price movement that can be traced to changes in company earnings, Latané and Tuttle nonetheless observed that "perfect knowledge of future earnings would be of great value in selecting stocks." [93, p. 347]

Brealey has expanded the work of Latané and Tuttle to determine just how much benefit could be realized by such "perfect knowledge of future earnings." Commenting on their research Brealey stated that

The average annual price appreciation of the 48 stocks was 12.2 percent. If, however, at the beginning of each year, an investor had been able to select from this group, stocks of those eight companies [out of the 48 studied] that were to show the greatest proportion of earnings increase, his average annual profit would have been 30.4 percent. [12, p. 85]

Thus, two conclusions are well supported in the research literature. First, P/E ratios reflect, to a major degree, the anticipated growth in company earnings. Secondly, if *one* could accurately forecast future earnings, an above-average investment strategy could most certainly be devised. Use of the term "one," however, is more than literary impartiality. Indeed, if *many* could predict future earnings accurately, the profitable strategy of *one* would succumb to an efficient capital market.

So, if accurate earnings forecasts can provide investors with above-average performance, the important question becomes, "Can changes in earnings be predicted?"

Can Changes in Earnings Be Predicted?

There are many reasons to expect that companies with consistently strong earnings records should continue to be capable of producing good earnings in the future. Similarly, companies with low profitability in the past *intuitively* seem likely to have such difficulties in the future. Some of the super-growth stocks of the past, such as Avon Products, IBM, Polaroid, and Xerox, enjoyed a certain monopolistic advantage in rapidly expanding markets, enabling them to post consistently good earnings performance. It therefore seems reasonable that companies with satisfied customers and large, successful investments in product development, personnel, plant, and equipment should have a competitive advantage that is likely to persist.

Do good earnings records persist? Richard Brealey sought to answer this question in his seminar papers at the University of Chicago. He has since reported this research in his outstanding book *An Introduction to Risk and Return from Common Stocks*. By studying the earnings changes of approximately 700 industrial companies over a 14-year period, Brealey found that, contrary to intuition, year-to-year earnings changes do *not* tend to persist! In fact, they even show a slight tendency to reverse. Thus, news that a company has had a consistent pattern of earnings growth does not increase the odds that such growth will continue in the future.

We have seen that stock price changes, when studied over relatively short differencing intervals, behave in accordance with the random-walk model. This means that recent historical stock price data is useless for predicting either the direction or magnitude of succeeding price changes. *Now, Brealey has offered scientific evidence that period-to-period "earnings" changes also behave in accordance with a random-walk model.*

If this is true, the study of the recent pattern of earnings changes is also worthless! These findings are indeed counter to the intuition of most investors and merit careful examination.

Since it is probable that any given investor would be interested in the earnings of companies in a few specific industries, Brealey classified his findings separately for 62 different industries, and still found no evidence that period-to-period earnings changes occur with discernible patterns or trends. In fact, after rigorous tests, he reported that ". . . a good year or succession of good years was more frequently followed by a poor year and vice versa." [12, pp. 94–95] Contrary to our intuition, a sequence of favorable earnings changes does *not* tend to persist. If anything, there is a slight tendency for good earnings records to reverse!

Similar findings have been reported by Joseph Murphy, Jr., who studied the earnings of 344 companies in 12 industries during 38 different time periods. Murphy's research, conducted at the University of Minnesota, reported that

. . . there appears to be little significant correlation between relative rates of growth of earnings per share in one period and relative growth in earnings per share in the next period. Only rarely did companies which recorded superior growth in earnings per share in one period show more than an even chance of recording above average growth in the next period. [124, p. 73]

Thus, if we *could* accurately forecast future earnings changes, such forecasts would undoubtedly provide above-average investment returns. Caution needs to be exercised, however, so that we do not attempt to predict future earnings changes solely on the basis of past earnings.

Logically, the most successful investing strategies will focus on the most important and/or the most predictable forces governing the movement of stock prices. In practice, earnings receive the most attention. In the next chapter we will look at both the *importance* and the *predictability* of earnings changes.

12
Predicting Earnings Changes

Intelligent discussion of the random-walk model, when applied to either price or earnings changes, must include the time span from which one attempts to predict. Random-walk research on price movements has shown, for example, that *recent* price and volume changes do not provide predictive information. Conversely, however, we have seen that long-term price movements, as well as short-term intraday price movements, are not random. The preceding chapter concluded that quarterly earnings changes also take place in accordance with the random-walk model. Two unanswered questions remain: first, whether long-term earnings changes—like long-term price changes—are predictable from past performances; secondly, whether earnings can be forecast from information other than past performance.

Long-Term Trends in Earnings?

John Lintner and Robert Glauber [101] of Harvard have studied the earnings of 323 companies over varying periods of up to five years in an attempt to discern predictive patterns. Somewhat surprisingly, while there is evidence of long-term patterns in price movements, Lintner and Glauber were unable to detect consistent patterns in long-run earnings that could be used to produce above-average investment results.

Manown Kisor and Van Messner [89] studied earnings changes over six-month intervals. They first showed that, *if* they could calculate the *direction* of earnings changes six-months hence, *irrespective of the amount of the change,* they could outperform the market. But using a sample of 813 industrial companies, they found only *one* pattern that

FIGURE 12-1
Pattern of Earnings Changes with Useful Information Content
Relative Earnings*

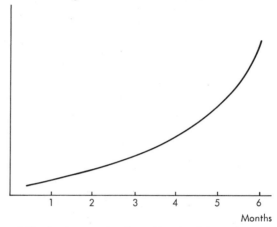

Months

* That is, after removing the performance of the market.

could be used to predict the direction of subsequent earnings changes. The pattern, which they called "increased momentum in relative earnings," shows *acceleration* in the rate of change in a company's earnings relative to the earnings performance of the general market. Thus, Kisor and Messner showed that, when the path of a company's relative earnings assumes the shape depicted in Figure 12-1, the likelihood of some increase in earnings for that company over the subsequent six months is significantly better than it is for the totality of companies whose shares make up the market as a whole. Thus, there is evidence that a company whose earnings advance *substantially* ahead of the market in one six-month period will continue to sustain positive earnings growth in the succeeding six months.

The Kisor-Messner findings tend to parallel Levy's [97] and this author's [67] evidence that stocks which advance in *price* substantially ahead of the market in one six-month period tend to have above-average price appreciation in the following six-month period. With the exception of a six-month pattern of *accelerated* earnings growth as depicted in Figure 12-1, however, there is overwhelming evidence that future earnings changes cannot be forecast solely on the basis of past earnings changes.

If Changes in Earnings Are Random, What Does It Mean?

When researchers report that earnings changes behave in accordance with the random-walk model, they are saying that historical earnings changes cannot be used to predict future earnings. This in no way negates the possibility that other information might be used for extremely accurate predictions. The research summarized here concludes only that, besides the exception that was noted, neither the direction nor magnitude of earnings changes can be predicted from the historical patterns of earnings changes.

Does anyone really *try* to predict earnings from historical patterns? Yes!!! Because it seems intuitively correct, there is much evidence that investors, as well as Wall Street professionals, rely heavily on historical earnings to predict future earnings. John Cragg and Burton Malkiel [30] have studied earnings estimates made by professionals who specialize in bank trust management, investment banking, mutual fund management, general brokerage, and the investment advisory business. The remarkable conclusion of the Cragg-Malkiel study was that, when these experts were asked to forecast earnings, the overwhelming tendency was to base their predictions on recent changes in historical earnings. Even more startling was the fact that the predictions of the top analysts were ". . . no better than the simplest strategy of the naive investor—who simply believes the company growth will parallel changes in gross national product." [152, p. 43]

Despite scientific research to the contrary, it appears that many people base earnings projections on intuitively safe, but in fact apparently useless, historical earnings data! Thus, while careful research confirms that you could reap handsome profits from accurate earnings forecasts, the common practice of extrapolating future earnings from past earnings does not provide satisfactory results. If you accept the validity of this research, the conclusion is clear. With one exception, *the study of changing patterns of earnings is worthless!*

It should be emphasized that this research does not mean that earnings cannot be forecast from information other than historical earnings. Thus, a vital question is whether or not earnings can be forecast from such things as balance sheet items, sales estimates, computerized cash-flow simulations, and so forth. To answer this question, we must first define what is meant by "earnings."

What Are Earnings, Anyway?

The concept of corporate earnings would seem to be simple enough. Since the securities legislation of 1933, the Certified Public Accounting (CPA) profession has had to certify the authenticity of earnings reported by publicly owned companies. This requirement of CPA-certified financial statements was intended to imbue stockholders' information with a kind of "Good Housekeeping 'Fiscal' Seal of Approval." Unfortunately, CPA-certification of earnings has not meant that the earnings were calculated in a manner easily comparable to previous years' earnings or to the earnings of competitors.

Most people assume that accounting is a profession dedicated to exactness. This image is propagated by the accounting profession's proclivity to report a firm's financial condition to the nearest dollar—even when dealing with millions. The fact is, however, that accounting statements have traditionally been prepared within the broad guidelines of so-called "generally accepted accounting principles," and the resultant statements have been far from precise or comparable. Due to the wide latitudes allowed within "accepted" principles, even CPA-audited earnings statements have sometimes been downright misleading when people assumed that the earnings of different firms were calculated in a comparable fashion.

These practices grew from the accounting profession's belief that its rules should not constrain management's flexibility. By the accounting profession's leave, corporate managers have exercised varying degrees of discretion in deciding on methods of "accepted accounting" for their operating decisions. As a result, companies that appear to be similar because of common products, size, and so forth, can, from an operating point of view, elect to manage their assets quite differently. One manufacturing company might, for example, purchase the newest production equipment, while a competitor might elect to sustain old equipment through heavy maintenance outlays. The accounting for these different operations can vary the reported earnings of different companies substantially. More important, however, is the fact that under the "generally accepted" guidelines even identical operating decisions can be accounted for differently.

This flexibility, plus the reality that businesses hire their accountants, troubles the client-accountant relationship. Accountants, by and large, are ethical men with high professional standards of honesty and integrity.

Within the relationship between the client and the CPA firm employed as its financial watchdog, the issue has often become "what the accountants will accept and certify." In this decision, the professional ethics of the accounting firm have rarely been compromised. Yet, *within* "generally accepted" accounting practices, there are a myriad of "accepted" precedents that can confuse the reported earnings. This problem was articulated in a *Forbes* Special Report:

> . . . accounting rules which, under the guise of affording management legitimate choices, result in distorted earnings figures. In all too many cases the question is not whether a given accounting treatment fits, but whether the companies' accountants can be convinced to accept it.
> Toward this end companies and their auditors, too, will go to great lengths to seek out precedents. . . . A single precedent, perhaps backed by the threat of the company "to take our auditing business elsewhere," can be enough to make a questionable accounting treatment "generally accepted." [**183**, p. 5]

"Smoothing" Reported Earnings

The cases of abuse, irregularities, and just plain confusion from mixing "apples and oranges" on certified financial statements have resulted in lawsuits against each of the Big Eight CPA firms. Numerous artificial increases in reported earnings through changes in depreciation schedules, flow-through of investment credits and the pooling treatment of mergers have been documented in the accounting journals (see [**82**]). Further, evidence from Barry Cushing's [**32**] doctoral dissertation at Michigan State University supports the widely held belief that companies resort to such accounting changes to smooth fluctuations in their reported earnings. But, for all of the confusion such accounting variations generate among the public, and for all of the grief they cause corporate officers and their CPAs, the "market" is remarkably "efficient" at properly reflecting the *true worth* of a company.

Corporate exececutives who contemplate changes in their investment credit or depreciation accounting should first consult Robert Kaplan's and Richard Roll's [**82**] study of the impact such changes have on securities prices. They concluded

> Earnings manipulation may be fun, but its profitability is doubtful. We have had difficulty discerning any statistically significant effect that it has had on security prices . . . firms that manipulated earnings seem to have been performing poorly. If this is generally true, one would predict that

earnings manipulation, once discovered, is likely to have a depressing effect on market price because it conveys an unfavorable management view of a firm's economic condition. [**82,** p. 245]

Yet, in spite of the market's apparent economic efficiency, the problems arising from subtle differences embedded in the reported earnings of similar companies has long complicated the job of both money managers and security analysts. The *Forbes* Special Study noted, for example, that

Sun Oil elects to charge off its drilling costs for new wells right away, while competitor Continental Oil capitalizes the costs of successful wells and writes them off gradually. . . . Delta Air Lines depreciates its planes over ten years, while United Air Lines, at the other end of the spectrum, writes off its 727 jets over as long as sixteen years. Douglas Aircraft elects to record some of its aircraft development costs as assets, while competitors may charge similar expenditures against current income. [**183,** p. 4]

Accounting Standards

Recognizing the problems that arise from accounting differences, and facing the threat of a more active role by the Securities and Exchange Commission in setting accounting standards, the nation's CPAs adopted new rules on March 1, 1973. This first retooling in more than 50 years of the standards under which accountants operate, now requires that *CPAs follow the opinions of the Financial Accounting Standards Board, when certifying financial statements!* The exceptions to this standard are carefully limited to unusual situations where it can be shown that preparation of reports according to the official standards would produce misleading results. Another important rule change put into effect in 1973 makes it difficult for firms to "shop around" for favorable accounting opinions. This new rule requires that newly selected auditors must consult with their predecessors about possible procedural disputes underlying the auditor change.

Doubtless the 1973 rules governing CPAs will improve the meaning and comparability of earnings. These rule changes will not (and should not), however, suddenly make all companies the same. To the degree by which management prerogative causes one company to differ from another, earnings can never be strictly comparable. Reported earnings, in reality, are the composite of hundreds of assumptions that have been distilled into one number—net earnings. This single, certified figure provides irreducible simplicity. This, coupled with the fact that earnings theoretically give a stock its value, has caused the investment community to adopt the consolidated assumptions underlying net earnings as the common denominator for stock valuation.

Unfortunately, due to both the different structure of each firm's assets and accounting flexibility, this bench mark for much fundamental security analysis has historically had the measurement accuracy of a rubber band! The tighter accounting standards adopted in 1973 promise to eliminate much of the confusion surrounding the calculation of earnings. It should always be remembered, however, that no two companies are the same.

The next time you contrast the earnings and P/Es of two companies, remember to ask *if the earnings of both companies were determined in exactly the same way.* The odds are that they are not really comparable. But, unless they are, it is dangerous to generalize from such comparisons. (For those who would like to confirm how dangerous a casual look at earnings can be, go back and look at the prior "good" earnings for the now-bankrupt Penn Central railroad—but this time read the footnotes!)

A monumental problem for people who try to forecast earnings is that "earnings" are not easily defined. Partially for this reason, it is often difficult for people who are not corporate insiders to forecast earnings changes accurately. Because corporate insiders have detailed knowledge of their own business, some people reason that they are in the best position to make accurate earnings forecasts. This consideration, plus the concern that the public often does not know about earnings changes until they occur, prompted the suggestion by former SEC chairman William Casey that companies should make their internal earnings forecasts public, thereby giving everyone equal access to the best available information.

chapter
13
Official Earnings Forecasts

Nuances of the debate over "official" earnings forecasts involve the pros and cons of making such forecasts voluntary or required, CPA versus SEC certification, plus whether or not to require them in new-issue prospectuses. (The latter point has been suggested as a means of tempering some of the unrealistic surges in "hot" new issues.)

Those who favor the idea of official earnings forecasts note that Great Britain requires such forecasts in new-issue prospectuses and emphasize that British investors consider such forecasts an essential part of the publicly available information. Companies that favor official forecasts do so because they resent watching the price of their stock fluctuate around outsiders' projections. For many companies, seeing the price of their shares inflated by heady outside projections, and then watching, at the first sign of bad news, the exodus of institutions and subsequent dramatic price drops has become an all-too-familiar pattern. To prevent such violent swings, some companies now routinely prepare public disclaimers for outside projections that they feel are unduly high.

Other proponents of required earnings forecasts contend that they will be based on the best available information and, because of the liability associated with misleading forecasts, they will meet the highest standards of excellence. Hence, they contend that requiring official earnings forecasts will guarantee that the best available information, prepared by the most qualified people, will be available to all investors.

Those who oppose published earnings forecasts argue that a certified earnings *forecast* can easily be construed as a guarantee that the forecast will be attained. Conversely, if the forecasts are not attained, managers fear they will appear inept. Critics of the idea contend that, in addition to inviting shareholder lawsuits, the idea is counter to the theory of investing whereby one forgoes current consumption in exchange for uncertain future rewards or losses. Harvey Kapnick, chairman and chief executive of Arthur Andersen & Co., sees two great dangers in earnings forecasts.

One is that management will be overly conservative in estimating sales and earnings in order not to get egg on its face when the results come in. This might dissuade investors from putting money into a company with a much brighter future than its management is willing to attest to publicly. The other is that some managements will overestimate future sales and earnings in order to boost the stock. [**186**, p. 37]

If We Had the "Best" Available Forecasts . . .

Several observations can be made concerning the notion of "official" earnings forecasts. First, there is little doubt that such forecasts, especially if sanctified by CPA or SEC guidelines or approval, will have an enormous influence on stock prices. For this reason, the linchpin of the debate becomes the *accuracy* of such forecasts. If insider forecasts are not accurate they will confuse, rather than serve, the public.

Secondly, even the most expertly derived forecasts will *sometimes* be wrong. To insure against lawsuits in such a situation, it is certain (from the October 8, 1971 opinion of U.S. District Judge Jacob Weinstein in a shareholder suit against Monsanto Co.) that earnings forecasts will have to be "appropriately prepared," "extensively reviewed," "honest," "reasonable," and made by the people "most qualified" to make them. [**194**, p. 14] This guaranteed "best effort" will undoubtedly necessitate a *sizeable* commitment of the average firm's managerial resources. (A sidelight example of how efficiently our capitalistic system responds to new opportunity is illustrated by the rash of profit forecasters that appeared after SEC chairman Casey said he felt such forecasts should be required by the SEC.)

Thirdly, when an earnings forecast is wrong, the price of a stock can literally collapse in the wake of its publication. Many investors remember what happened in 1971 when a respected analyst forecast a giant jump in Wrigley's profits, because of the 20 percent rise in chewing gum prices. When Wrigley announced only a 20 percent third-quarter increase in net, some institutions that had been courting the stock stampeded for the exits. Holders of the shares were caught in the classic liquidity trap, with lots of sellers and no buyers, and trading was temporarily suspended until late in the following session when the issue closed at 131¾—30 points lower than it was the previous day.

Another illustration of how sensitive institutions can be to deviations from earnings forecasts, especially on the part of companies whose stocks sport a high P/E, is the 1973 experience of Automatic Data Processing. Buoyed by the company's own earnings forecast for fiscal 1973 of $1.40 per share, against $1.00 in fiscal 1972, the stock closed on January 23, 1973 at 92½—with a P/E on fiscal 1972 net of 92.5. The following day, Automatic Data Processing announced that six-month earnings were up from $0.41 to $0.57 per share. Interpreting $0.57 as signifying that fiscal 1973's profits would be well below the company's forecast, some institutions rushed to unload their holdings and triggered a 28.4 percent price drop from 92½ to 66 in three days. Conversely, of course, it can be argued that the prices of both Wrigley and Automatic Data Processing were inflated by the overly optimistic forecasts, and the collapses merely returned the prices to where they belonged.

Fourthly, the suggestion that CPA firms might be called upon to validate earnings forecasts, and thereby prevent the overoptimism that characterized the Wrigley and Automatic Data Processing forecasts, has stirred up much furor. Those who oppose CPA involvement feel that CPAs are skilled in documenting the current financial condition of a firm and lack training in modern forecasting techniques. Others argue that, if a CPA certifies a forecast, he might be biased by this certification when the time comes to certify actual performance.

Fifthly, the myopia of focusing on one number—earnings per share—can be bad for both the company and the investor. Joel Stern [161] of the Chase Manhattan Bank has, for example, documented how the earnings per share criterion often leads to *bad,* long-run financial decisions. Forecasting is not an exact science. It attempts to answer "if" questions. "*If* sales increase, and *if* terms of retail notes are extended, and *if* . . . ." The results of such forecasts, however, are seldom *one number!* Instead, companies usually make "optimistic," "best guess," and "pessimistic" forecast boundaries. Forcing managers to make more precise projections, some contend, erroneously represents forecasting as an exact science.

The forgoing criticisms of official earnings forecasts would be purely academic if managers could not forecast accurately. The evidence is, however, that they can. Information compiled by Douglas Carmichael, director of technical research for the American Institute of Certified Public Accountants, and by Donald Chapin indicates that required earnings forecasts in Britain are consistently on the conservative side. The indications are, in fact, that the "name of the game" in Britain is to please the public by exceeding your forecast each year by 10 percent [**194**, p. 14].

Several recent and rigorous studies have sparked a heated debate over the accuracy of executives' earnings forecasts and the usefulness of interim earnings data in predicting annual earnings. David Green and Joel Segall [**62**] ignited the powder keg by showing that there was little difference between executive forecasts and naïve extrapolations. These findings were openly challenged by Philip Brown and Victor Niederhoffer [**15**] and an exchange of articles between the protagonists ensued. When the smoke settled around an exchange of articles, such as "Brickbats and Straw Men" [**63**] and "Return of Strawman" [**64**], the conclusion, now generally accepted, was that "managers' forecasts are substantially 'better' than those produced from naïve models." [**26**, p. 498]

The SEC policy

It is both logical, and experimentally verified, that corporations, which have more relevant information than outsiders and to some degree can control their performance, can do a superior job of forecasting earnings. To the degree that these forecasts represent reality, their widespread dissemination will move the market closer to reality, and to that degree stabilize prices. It was this needed stabilization around "reality" that prompted SEC chairman William Casey to advocate dissemination of official earnings forecasts.

Chairman Casey was unable to sway the SEC into requiring authenticated earnings forecasts. The current SEC compromise policy on forecasts holds that:

- Earnings forecasts are not required in SEC-related documents.
- Companies can, at their own discretion, include earnings forecasts in publicly circulated documents.
- Companies that prepare such projections must adhere to SEC guidelines and disclose all assumptions underlying their forecast.
- Any publicly circulated forecasts must be filed with the SEC.
- If forecasts are made available to some investors, the information must be simultaneously disseminated to the public at large.

Predicting Stock Prices from Earnings Forecasts

The major points should be reiterated:

1. The goal of security analysis is to select stocks likely to have above-average total returns—yield plus price appreciation.
2. Price is theoretically related to future earnings.
3. It can be shown that an accurate knowledge of future earnings changes would allow one to select stocks with above-average returns (see [133]).
4. The common practice of predicting future earnings from historical earnings trends is apparently worthless.
5. In an accounting sense, earnings are hard to define, difficult to forecast, and are subject to various accounting interpretations which complicate intra- and inter-industry comparisons.
6. Corporate insiders can do the best job of making earnings forecasts because they have the best available information and, to some degree, they can make their forecasts come true.
7. If the information that reflects "reality" is widely disseminated, stock prices will also reflect reality.
8. While the SEC does not yet require earnings forecasts, it does impose guidelines and sanctions over the quality and dissemination of forecasts that companies elect to publicize.
9. If accurate earnings forecasts are disseminated to all investors, their differential value to any single investor is nil.
10. Investment analysis directed solely at predicting a company's earnings in effect focuses attention on an area overshadowed by the larger force of public reaction to the industry subgroup, the basic industry, and the market as a whole.

Earnings and the Economy

Richard Brealey has said "when the wind of recession blows, there are few companies that do not lean with it. In consequence, aggregate corporate profits tend to rise and fall in line with economic activity." [12, p. 104] Jack Francis [50], at the Wharton School, has similarly reported that usually less than 1 percent of NYSE stocks move against major bull or bear markets. Francis also noted that those whose prices do move against the prevailing market do not do so in any consistent or recurrent fashion.

FIGURE 13–1
Aggregate After-Tax Profits

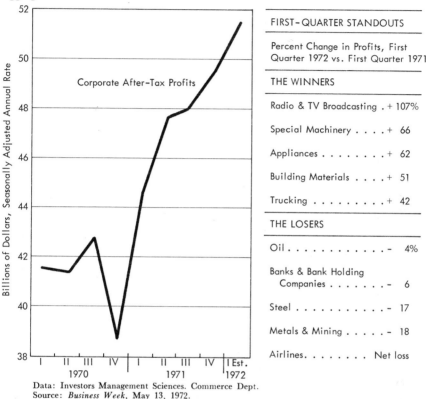

Data: Investors Management Sciences. Commerce Dept.
Source: *Business Week*, May 13, 1972.

The tendency for the economy and its component industries to sweep individual companies along can be illustrated by a glance at almost any quarterly summary of business activity. A chart from one such summary prepared by Investors Management Sciences, Inc. that appeared in *Business Week* is shown in Figure 13–1. The excerpts from the accompanying text note, in part,

. . . Of the 35 industries, only 6 reported earnings down for the quarter, and only 1, the airlines, lost money.

The big winner in the first quarter was the radio-TV broadcasting industry, with profits up by 107 percent. But, the year-ago quarter was a bleak period for broadcasters—the first three months after cigarette commercials were kicked off television.

Consumer spending was at a handsome clip . . . and . . . benefited a number of industries: applicances, with earnings up 62 percent; photo and optical, with earnings up 26 percent; automotive, with earnings up 21 percent; retailing, with earnings up 20 percent. . . .

There was tremendous strength in homebuilding. . . .

Plant and equipment spending was up . . . and that meant higher profits for most makers of capital goods.

Oil companies, on the other hand, were hit with both softer prices and the high cost of dealing with pollution.

Steel took its lumps. . . .[1]

And so it goes. Diversified portfolios in the "right" industries at the "right" economic time are sufficient, *without predictions about companies,* to yield above-average market returns. The significance of this statement is that, if a company will prosper little in "bad times," why even *try* to predict its earnings without first predicting economic and industry factors. Further, we would not expect the earnings of all companies to be equally sensitive to the economy's general health. We would expect companies that produce nondurable consumer products, such as food, cigarettes, beverages, cosmetics, and utility services, to be somewhat less influenced by recessions than the average concern. Shares of companies in such "defensive" industries vary with economic cycles less than other stocks. Likewise, we would expect "big-ticket" durable goods items to be more sensitive to the business climate than frequently purchased goods. Buying a car, building a new home, purchasing industrial machinery, or even enlarging one's wardrobe or traveling are somewhat postponable, and the level of such spending reflects the status of consumers' sentiments and the nation's economic prosperity.

The sensitivity of corporate earnings to the economic climate of particular industries has been studied by Richard Brealey. He studied 217 companies in 20 different industry groups to determine "the proportion of each company's earnings movement that could be explained in terms of the fortune of the industrial sector as a whole." [13, p. 105] A similar study has been conducted by Brown and Ball [14]. Both studies showed that the degree to which a company's earnings are tied to those of its industry varies from industry to industry. Brealey concluded:

. . . the impact of the economy on the earnings of a firm is not only important but also fairly consistent, so that an understanding of the implications of major economic events should be of considerable value in attempting to forecast earnings changes. There is some evidence that analysts are

---

[1] *Business Week,* May 13, 1972.

relatively deficient in such an understanding and that their forecasts tend to reflect that portion of earnings that is peculiar to the firm. This may again raise questions about the merits of the traditional division of responsibilities in institutions. [12, p. 111]

These research findings are perhaps startling, yet their implications are quite clear. Large portions of corporate earnings merely reflect the state of the economy and the health of the company's industry. Further, such relationships are quite consistent over time. The differential expertise of the individual company accounts for a *minor* portion of that company's earnings and the price performance of its stock. Furthermore, in some industries less than half of a particular firm's earnings changes are attributable to differences between it and competitor companies. [12, p. 105] Industries which have exhibited a strong tendency to reflect the economy include the auto, department store, nonferrous metal, paper, rubber, and clothing industries. Thus, earnings are largely dictated by exogenous (economic and industry-related) variables and hence are difficult to forecast from even perfect endogenous, company-related information. One can conclude:

1. The widespread practice of forecasting stock prices by first forecasting earnings could be justified if the resultant information were both *important* enough and possessed enough *predictive power* to justify the cost of developing it.
2. Accurate earnings forecasts (and certain other information, discussed next) are important and valuable, but the typical methods for making such forecasts are questionable.

part I
understanding the new science

C USEFUL INFORMATION
VERSUS MARKET "NOISE"

chapter
14
Company-Related Information

Reasoned investment selection comes from knowing what information is, and is not, completely reflected in the price of various investment instruments in different markets. The most popular instruments are stocks listed on the NYSE or the AMEX. Of the four kinds of information—the overall economy, the basic industry, the industry subgroup, and the company—most investors concentrate on company-related information. Yet, company-level information explains only a small portion of a stock's price movement. This fact alone, however, does not mean that such information is unimportant. If company-related information could predict the company-related portion of stock price movements, it might be the *most* useful kind of information.

Some investors argue that the specificity of company-related information makes it the most predictable level of the information hierarchy. On the other hand, skeptics argue that constant scrutiny of company-related information by millions of investors destroys its value to any individual. This chapter summarizes the scientific evidence on the following company-related information: earnings, dividends, stock splits, and professional opinions. Taken together, this research allows us to classify such information as being either useful (as generally interpreted), misleading (and requiring special interpretation), or useless.

Under the fair-game theory, when astute investors have equal access to all information, none can reliably expect to outperform the market. In looking for clues from company-related information, one can only expect above-average performance by illegal access to information not available to other investors, or by superior analysis of available information. It is the latter area—producing private knowledge from public information—that concerns the new science of investing.

Earnings

The preceding chapter examined the construction and usefulness of earnings forecasts. We concluded that, while accurate earnings forecasts could be used to select undervalued stocks, such forecasts should not be based on the pattern of historical earnings changes. Careful research has been unable to verify predictable relationships between successive changes in earnings. Yet, other information might be useful in predicting earnings, and hence, price changes.

The concept of "information," or "news," is synonymous with *surprise* or *change*. If a company's earnings have grown at 5 percent per year for the past four years, and all forecasts predict continued 5 percent growth, there is little information in an announcement that merely confirms this expectation. Surprises provide information! Hence, the real "information" in an earnings announcement is the degree to which it deviates from expectation. In the previously illustrated case of Wrigley and Automatic Data Processing, the market's expectation had been swayed by optimistic earnings forecasts. The surprise that earnings were below this expectation triggered landslide sales. Thus, to study the usefulness of earnings information one needs two things: the consensus of what investors expect earnings to be, and the subsequently announced earnings. The difference between these two figures is the surprise, or information, in the earnings announcement.

Philip Ball and John Kennelly [5] have contrasted the performance of stocks selected after "good," "bad," and "expected" earnings announcements. Contrary to the efficient capital market theory, they showed that stocks purchased after surprisingly good annual and quarterly earnings "surprises" would have provided abnormally high rates of return. Similarly, they showed that stocks purchased after surprisingly bad earnings announcements had worse-than-average subsequent performance. We can conclude from this research that the market adjustment in the weeks following surprisingly good (or bad) earnings announcements is sufficient to produce abnormally high rates of return for those who buy (or sell out) on the day of the official announcement!

Dividends

Research on dividend information has been directed toward two important decisions:

* Should you buy a high- or a low-dividend stock?
* Can dividend information be used to select stocks with above-average returns?

High- versus Low-Payout Stocks.   The rate of return from an investment depends on two factors—capital appreciation and income, as from dividends. Many investors are blinded by visions of grandeur about the expected capital appreciation of their investments. To such investors dividend income is something for widows or orphans. If you have a tendency to disregard dividends, you should consider the following quotation from Richard Brealey's outstanding book *Security Prices in a Competitive Market.*

If in 1926 a tax-exempt investor had purchased an equal amount of all New York Stock Exchange equities, and if he had reinvested all subsequent dividends he would have found that by the end of 40 years his capital had multiplied 35 times [after Fisher and Lorie [49]]. If he had been improvident and squandered all his dividends on bacchanalian pleasures, the value of his portfolio would have increased by a factor of only six. This example is presented not as a warning against prodigality but to demonstrate that the cumulative effect of dividend receipts can be very large [**13,** p. 4]

A company can do two things with its earnings. They can be distributed to stockholders as dividends, or they can be retained and reinvested, or plowed back, into the company. Retained earnings have an advantage, since they represent an automatic reinvestment of money that, if distributed to stockholders, would be taxed *before* it could be reinvested. Further, once earnings are distributed to stockholders, they cannot be reinvested without an underwriting or brokerage commission.

The portion of a company's total earnings which is distributed as dividends is called the "dividend payout ratio." Typically, a rapidly growing company, such as McDonald's, will retain all or most of its earnings to finance expansion. Similarly, companies with sufficient plant and equipment to meet the demand of their customers need little to finance expansion and can distribute a large portion of their income as dividends.

The importance of the dividend payout ratio lies in the differential between the timing and rate of taxes on dividends versus capital gains. Dividends are taxed currently as part of income, while long-term capital gains (assets held more than six months) are subject to taxation only upon sale of the appreciated asset and at rates which are generally half those on income. As a result, for the average investor, *a dollar of dividends is equivalent, after taxes, to about 75 cents of capital gains* (see [13, p. 19]) We could, therefore, reasonably assume that low-dividend-payout stocks are relatively more attractive for any investor subject to taxes. It follows, then, that the price of low-dividend stocks includes a premium for this advantage. This conclusion—that low-dividend stocks are worth more—is counter to one of the age-old tenets of fundamental security analysis. Authors such as Graham and Dodd have held that the market's pricing mechanisms are overwhelmingly in favor of liberal dividends [59]

Surprisingly, though, the factual evidence concludes that there is no substantial difference in the value that the market places on dividends versus capital gains. The market seems to have struck a balance between the traditional belief that liberal dividends are overpriced and the logic that, because of differential taxation, they should receive a lower price. This means you pay roughly the same price for $1 of future dividends that you pay for $1 of future capital gains. But, since your dividends are taxed at a higher rate, they are worth proportionately less. Hence, in the market's apparent confusion over the relative valuation of capital gains and dividends, and the resultant parity, there appears to be a slight unadjusted *penalty for owning high-dividend stocks.* We can conclude that, in the words of Brealey, ". . . almost any taxed investor will derive a somewhat lower net rate of return from high-payout stocks." [13, p. 20]

Dividend Announcements. We have shown that changes in stock prices are explained largely by reference to expectations about the company's future earnings. It is likely, therefore, that dividend announcements will also affect stock prices to the extent that they portend a firm's future prosperity or ill health.

Several researchers have examined the rationale underlying dividend decisions. These studies reveal how firms decide on the amount of earnings to distribute as dividends versus the amount to be retained by the company. For a variety of reasons, the paramount factor in this decision is the amount of earnings that management feels "should" be distributed. To the astonishment of many people, it appears that notions of the "appropriate," or "target," dividend so dominate this decision that retained funds are viewed as a leftover. If these leftover funds are not sufficient to finance expansion, most firms will either borrow the funds or defer the expenditure rather than tamper with the dividend level they feel their stockholders expect.

As one analyzes dividend decisions further, it appears that the target dividend is guided by management's desire to establish a pattern of stable dividend growth. This reluctance to change prevails in regard to both dividend increases and decreases, with dividend reduction typically viewed as a last resort. On the other hand, the hesitancy to increase a dividend is attributed to the fear that a higher-level dividend implies a commitment to *continue* at that level. Paul Darling [34] has supported this conclusion by showing that the level of dividends paid between 1930 and 1955 could not be explained by variations in earnings, but instead corresponded to management's optimism about the future.

Here, then, is an important focal point in considering the usefulness of dividend announcements. Studies that have relied on interviews with corporate management [100], and others that have studied dividend histories [42], conclude that firms do not make dividend changes without considerable assessment of the future. Decreases take place largely because firms have little choice other than to cut the payout. Increases, in addition to reflecting high current earnings, reflect management's optimism that the new dividend level can be sustained. It follows, then, that if dividend changes reflect management's opinion about the future, and if managers can correctly assess the future, dividend *changes* should serve as barometers of a firm's future prosperity.

This possibility raises two questions. The first, and most obvious, is whether or not dividend changes portend the future. If they do, the next question is whether or not the market *already knows* that prosperity or difficulty lies ahead, and has fully adjusted the stock's price by the time the dividend news is available.

Joseph Murphy [125] sought a definitive answer to these questions by studying the relationship between dividend changes and the subsequent earnings of 244 companies between 1950 and 1965. While the association between dividend changes and subsequent earnings was not as strong as one would like, Murphy did find a positive relationship. So, while dividend changes do not portend the future exactly, they do tend to reflect management's correct assessment of future earnings.

A more direct study of the relationship between dividend announcements and both subsequent earnings and price changes was made by Richardson Pettit [137] at the Wharton School of Finance. Pettit studied the impact of dividend announcements on the subsequent earnings and price performance of 625 companies over four and one-half years. He found that dividend announcements were closely associated with subsequent price performance, and concluded that "dividend announcements convey substantial information to market participants that causes them to revalue their shares." He also noted that the effect was generally proportionate to the amount of the dividend change. In terms of the market's efficiency, Pettit concluded that the "market's judgment concerning the information implicit in the [dividend] announcement is reflected almost completely as of the end of the announcement month." [137, p. 38] We conclude, therefore, that news of dividend changes contains useful information that is not immediately reflected in the price of the stock.

Stock Splits

A stock split is a management decision to increase (often double) the number of shares of stock outstanding. Many people fail to understand that, even though the company decides to give you more shares, everything else about the company remains unchanged. For instance, in a two-for-one stock split the price of each new share should be worth exactly half the price of each old share. After a split, each shareholder has exactly enough additional shares to compensate for the lower price. The total worth of his holdings, and of the firm's securities, remains the same. The investor's pieces of paper represent precisely the same proportion of ownership as before. In the words of A. Wilfred May, one of Wall Street's elder statesmen, "a pie does not grow through its slicing!" [115, p. 5]

Some people contend that the lower price per share brought about by a stock split will "broaden the market" for the company's shares and that the lower price will, in turn, stimulate investment demand. There is, however, no merit to this contention unless one speaks of those investors who could not afford to buy a *single* share at the former price. But, the argument runs, investors like to buy stock in round lots, and a split lowers the price of a hundred-share purchase. Some people favor splits because they expect lower commission rates from round-lot purchases. The problem with this argument is, that while commissions on some trades are less after a split, on other trades they are more. On the average, in fact, the lower share prices resulting from stock splits cause slightly higher commissions for the same dollar amount of trading.

Even though there is no theoretical reason to expect the value of one's holdings to increase owing to a stock split, as expressions of progress or optimism, splits might be self-fulfilling predictions. In the stock market, if enough people believe something will happen, their actions will make it happen—despite the fact that the logic underlying their belief is defective. This blindly fatalistic reasoning has been openly criticized by A. Wilfred May in a 1956 article entitled "Current Popular Delusions About the Stock Split and Stock Dividend." In this article, May characterized stock splits as a "speculative Frankenstein ending in stockholder disillusionment." [**115**, p. 5]

In both 1956 and 1957, C. Austin Barker published articles on stock splits in the *Harvard Business Review*. In his 1956 article, Barker concluded that "contrary to the general belief, stock splits do not automatically produce a lasting price gain." [**6**, p. 101] His 1957 study sought to determine whether or not stocks, after splits in a bull market, behaved differently than they did after splits in less buoyant markets. His conclusion was ". . . split-ups alone produced no lasting real gains in market price for widely held, nationally listed stocks, whether the split-up is effected in a normal market or in an outstanding bull market." [**7**, p. 551]

Other studies of splits have shown essentially the same thing. Research by R. C. Rieke [**141**] has shown that companies announcing stock splits have generally experienced a price improvement in the months preceding the announcement of the split. It appears, however, that, by the time the news of a pending split has been announced to the public, no significant price movement remains. The brokerage firm of Hardy and Co. analyzed the impact of the additional number of shares resulting from the stock split on subsequent stock price performance. As we would expect, this study also concluded that splits provided no useful information (see [**141**]).

An extensive study of stock splits by Eugene Fama *et al.* [**43**] monitored the behavior of 940 stocks for the 30 months that preceded and followed stock splits. The relative performance (that is, with market comovement removed) of a portfolio consisting of these stocks is shown in Figure 14–1.

In examining Figure 14–1, it is important to note that split information was not available until immediately before the split occurred (designated by "0" on the horizontal scale)—the point where the relative

FIGURE 14–1
Relative Pre- and Post-Split Performance of 940 Stocks

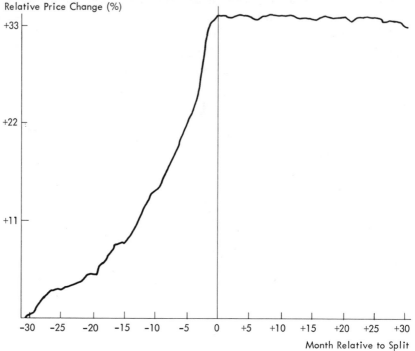

Source: Fama, Fisher, Jensen, and Roll [43] and Brealey [13].

price growth *stops*. This information, plus other data on the relationship of splits to the level of the market, indicates that splits are a *consequence* of rising stock prices, and not a *cause* of rising stock prices. Those who rely on news of impending splits should note that, for two and one-half years after the split, *the relative price remained within one percentage point of the split price*. Not surprisingly, Fama *et al.* reported that ". . . there seems to be no way to use a split to increase one's expected return. . . ." [**43**, pp. 20–21]

Another study of stock splits was reported by Hausman, West, and Largay in 1971 [**71**]. In this study Hausman *et al.* carefully synthesized the most recent research on stock splits and then, through their own research, reconciled some of the differences that have appeared between researchers. They reported that

. . . for stock splits, there is no evidence that after the announcement date the price appreciation is significantly higher than that expected from the underlying earnings and industry factors.

Our results clearly indicate that buying stocks on (or after) the date on which a split has been publicly announced does not lead to systematic price appreciation greater than the appreciation that might be expected from underlying factors such as corporate earnings and the industry-by-industry outlook for stock price movements. [**71**, p. 76]

People who believe that news of an impending stock split is useful could reason that, while the underlying value of the company is unchanged, the decision to split reflects management optimism about the future prosperity of the company. The research summarized here indicates, however, that the market efficiently discounts the news of impending stock splits. It is our conclusion that no convincing evidence supports buying stocks on news of impending splits. Such information is apparently useless.

Professional Opinions

Stock prices change because people change their opinions. One of this author's acquaintances, who has asked to remain anonymous, once confided that he had developed a technique for selecting undervalued securities. His problem was, however, that the market did not have the benefit of his careful analysis. Because "the market did not know any better," his favored securities remained undervalued.

At the other extreme, it is reasonable to expect that the publicized opinion of a respected professional could precipitate dramatic price changes, regardless of the underlying rationale. Walter Winchell's "Mr. and Mrs. America and all the ships at sea" radio tips caused such landslide reactions that he was restrained from giving further on-the-air recommendations. It is plausible that such stock market opinions could become self-fulfilling predictions. When people believe "IBM is going to go up," their actions will drive it up, and vice versa. If so, it might be a useful investment strategy to respond quickly to the opinions of widely circulated advisory services. Also, of course, one should not dismiss the possibility that advisory services are correct in their analyses, so that the market will subsequently adjust to the advisory services' correct assessment of a stock's value.

Researchers have long been intrigued by the possibility that advisory services can forecast. As long ago as 1933, Alfred Cowles studied the forecasting ability of 16 financial services, 20 insurance companies, and 25 financial publications. Cowles concluded that the 16 financial services were 1.43 percent worse than average, the 20 insurance companies 1.20

percent worse, while the 25 financial publications failed by 4 percent per annum. [27]

Several modern studies have measured the market's response to published investment advice. In 1958, Robert Ferber, at the University of Illinois, studied the price movements related to recommendations of four major advisory services. After removing market and industry comovements, Ferber found that "in the very short run, stock market service recommendations tend to influence the prices of approximately two thirds of the stocks in the direction indicated . . ." [46, p. 94] By the end of the first week after publication, the average profit attainable from this information was 1.1 percent. However, after this very short-run adjustment, Ferber found no evidence of a longer-run impact. Ferber also concluded that the short-run price adjustments were *caused* by the recommendation, and not *predicted* by them. He based this conclusion on ". . . the failure of the recommended stocks . . . to outpace the market . . . in the week or two immediately preceding the recommendation" [46, p. 94].

Other studies by Ruff [145] and Stoffels [163] confirm the general conclusion that professional recommendations accurately foretell future price changes and that there is a measurable short-term price adjustment to reflect the "news." Other evidence by Cheney [16] and Colker [23] indicates that stocks recommended by advisory services and brokerage houses tend to outperform representative market averages over the following year. We conclude, therefore, that widely distributed professional opinions can somewhat presage short-term and (to a lesser degree) long-term relative price changes.

Conclusions

Our examination of company-related information has led to several surprising conclusions. First, the market is often caught off guard by announcements of unexpectedly high or low earnings. After such news, it takes several weeks for the price of the stock to "catch up" to the new information. Hence, inordinately profitable investment decisions can be made in the week following announcements of unanticipated high or low earnings. Secondly, contrary to the thinking of many seasoned market professionals, as well as noted authors such as Benjamin Graham, high-dividend-payout stocks provide the tax-paying investor with a somewhat lower rate of return than low-payout stocks of comparable risk. Thirdly, presumably because corporations do not alter their dividends casually, dividend changes do mirror management's largely correct assessment of the firm's future prosperity. Fourthly, to the chagrin of many advocates, stock splits typically signal the *end* of price growth and not its continuation! Finally, professional opinions *cause* price movements. Thus, we conclude that an investor who stays on top of earnings and dividend announcements and who invests according to professional advice can attain above-average returns.

chapter
15
Market-Related Information

Following the examination of company-related information in the preceding chapter, this chapter reviews market-related information. Specifically, we will examine the usefulness of information about: new issues, new listings, secondary distributions, odd-lot transactions, short-interest positions, and odd-lot short sales.

New Issues

The function of the new issues market is to channel investment capital into promising new companies. The creation of a new issue involves three steps: origination, underwriting, and distribution. Origination involves the negotiations between investment banking firms and the issuing corporation to determine price, assure legalities, and so forth. Underwriting refers to the purchase or guaranteed sale of the issue by participating investment banking firms. Finally, distribution involves the sale of the shares to the public.

In these transactions the underwriter has a "two-hat" role of trying to obtain the *highest* offering price for the issuing company while, at the same time, insuring that the offering price will be *low* enough to be fully subscribed. If the offering is priced above what the market is willing to pay, the underwriter guaranteeing sale at the offering price can sustain large losses. Thus, one could reason that, to play it safe, underwriters will tend to underprice new issues.

Such underpricing was alleged in a 1963 SEC study and later refuted by Professor George Stigler at the University of Chicago. In a pointed article criticizing the SEC, Stigler contrasted the performance of new

TABLE 15–1
Price Changes of 135 Newly Issued Stocks Relative to Market

Year of Issue	Number of Years after Issue (by percent)				
	1	2	3	4	5
1923	– 7	–15	–22	–38	–33
1924	– 2	–24	–31	–34	–49
1925	–15	–33	–45	–58	–67
1926	–10	–18	–23	–37	–33
1927	–15	–31	–40	–27	+ 3
1928	–28	–50	–59	–55	–43
1949	– 7	–12	–13	–13	–35
1950	–16	–24	–47	–42	–53
1951	–16	–21	–24	–20	–25
1952	–12	–26	–29	–30	–30
1953	–12	–21	–25	–30	– 6
1954	–47	–51	–44	–52	–58
1955	–28	–35	–18	–22	–17
Average.	–18	–32	–38	–40	–38

Source: After Stigler [162] and Brealey [13].

issues for periods both before and after such issues were required to meet SEC registration requirements. His investigation found no evidence of under-pricing before or after SEC registration requirements were imposed. In fact, Stigler showed that the relative long-term performance of new issues was consistently below that of the market. Brealey has presented Stigler's findings in a quickly readable format that has been reproduced in Table 15–1. Note the remarkable consistency with which the subsequent prices of new issues tend to decline.

In an apparently contradictory study of the postoffering behavior of seasoned new issues between 1953 and 1963, Irwin Friend and James Longstreet reported ". . . no evidence of any penalty or premium associated with new issues. . ." [54, p. 492] Still another contradictory study by Frank Reilly and Kenneth Hatfield, at the University of Kansas, traced the relative appreciation of 53 new issues between 1963 and 1965 and came up with impressive results. Whether referring to a span ending a week, a month, or a year after the new issue, "all tests showed superior short-run and long-run results for the investor in new stock issues." [**140,** p. 80]

Results paralleling those of Reilly and Hatfield were reported by Dennis Logue in his doctoral dissertation at Cornell in 1971. Logue studied 250 new issues marketed between 1965 and 1969 and reported that "on average, the risk-adjusted rates of return of new issues bought at the offerings were significantly greater than they should be in an efficient market no matter if the holding period is two weeks, three months, or one year." [**104**]

Still different results were reported in a recent study by J. McDonald and A. Fisher [**118**], at Stanford University. They reported on the post-offering performance of 142 unseasoned new issues during 1969 and 1970. Their findings showed extremely large (plus 28.5 percent) returns, adjusted for market effects, for initial subscribers one week after the offering. From the end of the first week to the end of the first year, 51 weeks later, the mean adjusted return was minus 18.1 percent. McDonald and Fisher also showed that the size of the price change in the first week was unrelated to future performance.

Hence, research on the performance of new issues is contradictory. On the one hand, Logue concludes that the significantly better post offering rates of return indicate that "underwriters, in general, underprice new issues." On the other hand, Brealey concludes ". . . the inferior long-run rate of return from new issues implies too much capital rather than too little has been committed to these businesses." [**13**, p. 107]

This author's as yet untested explanation for these apparently contradictory results is that unseasoned new-issue performance is itself an indicator of investor optimism or pessimism. If investor optimism is running high, new issues would be likely to significantly outperform those high-risk stocks that they are usually measured against. This would explain the better-than-average performance of unseasoned new issues observed in certain bull markets. Conversely, if investor optimism is beginning to ebb, the unseasoned new-issue market would be expected to be overly vulnerable and to overreact. This generalization is confirmed by the studies of new-issue performance in bear market years. Unseasoned new issues probably constitute a risk category that tends to amplify market moods more than other over-the-counter stocks.

In summary, all studies agree that, if an investor has an opportunity to participate in a popular new issue, he is likely to enjoy above-average short-term gains. Whether this short-term price appreciation is attributable to market adjustments in the wake of the underwriter's conservative pricing, or results from the aggressive selling that accompanies a new issue, is immaterial. In the long run, new issues, like any investment, demand careful scrutiny. The best recommendation concerning the long-run performance of new issues is to consider entering the new-issue market carefully with the perspective of our information hierarchy. That is, when you are thinking about buying a new issue, your decision should rely heavily on your current assessment of economic and market optimism. Above-average returns, in exchange for above-average risks, are available in optimistic markets. Conversely, during a bear market the new-issue market is not the place to invest.

New Listings

In this section we examine the usefulness of knowing that a company has decided to list its stock on the New York Stock Exchange (NYSE). To be eligible for NYSE listing, a company must have a minimum of $2.5 million in pretax earnings, $14 million in net tangible assets and $14 million in publicly held common stock representing at least 800,000 shares spread among 1,800 round-lot shareholders. Needless to say, not all companies can qualify by these criteria. Also, in any one year the number of new listings is relatively small. In 1970, only 68 new companies were admitted to NYSE trading. One could reason, however, that the decision to list on the NYSE represents the pinnacle of management optimism. Following this train of thought, news that a company has applied for NYSE listing might indicate that the shares of these select companies offer an opportunity for above-average future rates of return.

Several researchers [1, 56, 119, 120, 121, 168] have examined the pre- and post-listing behavior of stocks on the NYSE. The consistent pattern that emerged may be summarized as follows:

- When measured from a time three to six months before the application date to the application date, these stocks performed significantly better than the market. Such price advances are doubtless a factor in the subsequent decision to list the security.
- During the time span covering the application date, the approval date, and the listing date, these stocks continue to have some significantly better-than-average price appreciation.
- When the period measured is one day, one month, or one, three, or five years from the listing date, the rate of return for these stocks is, on average, *below that for the general market*.

We conclude from these studies that stocks which have recently moved their trading to the NYSE do not, on average, represent a likely source of above-average returns.

Secondary Distributions

Any offering of publicly owned stock after its new-issue offering is termed a "secondary distribution." Because the size of such offerings swamp the exchange's auction process, secondary distributions are organized off the floor. The sellers are typically institutional investors or the trusts or families of the company's founders. The reasons for such sales are as varied as the reasons for any sale. But, the fact that these sellers consist of knowledgeable investors, who are sometimes presumed to have superior information, and the fact that *they* are selling, is viewed by many as a portent of bad times.

Under the 1969 Tax Reform Act, foundations must pay out each year a small percentage (initially pegged at 4⅛ percent in 1972 and slated to rise to 5½ percent by 1975) of their assets in grants. Stock sales by foundations to raise funds for these payouts have caused increased activity in the secondary market. Since many foundations are now required to sell stock, many observers reason that they will sell their worst stock. Thus, some people look on secondary distributions as an early-warning indicator of poor future performance.

A detailed study has been made of 345 secondary distributions by Myron Scholes [147] at the University of Chicago. A short-term effect of a secondary offering on the relative (that is, with market comovement removed) performance of these 345 stocks is shown in Figure 15–1.

By tracing the average relative performance from 26 days before the offering to 14 days after, it is clear that secondary distributions are followed by an abrupt drop in the market price of approximately 2 percent. The size of this percentage drop is obviously not large. Even a small percentage decline, however, can have a substantial impact on the investor. An expected 2 percent drop, relative to the overall market, in a 30-day period slices off a sizable percentage of a 10 percent or 12 percent hoped-for annual rate of return. On the other hand, if you already own such a stock, and decide to sell it, the sales commissions plus the post-distribution price dip leave you with approximately the same asset value.

To study the long-term effect of secondary offerings, Scholes traced the monthly performance of 1207 stocks for 18 months preceding and following these sales. These longer-term results are shown in Figure 15–2.

Clearly, the market, on average, interprets a secondary distribution as a signal that "something" is wrong with the stock. As hypothesized

FIGURE 15–1
Relative Pre- and Post-Secondary Distribution Performance of 345 Stocks

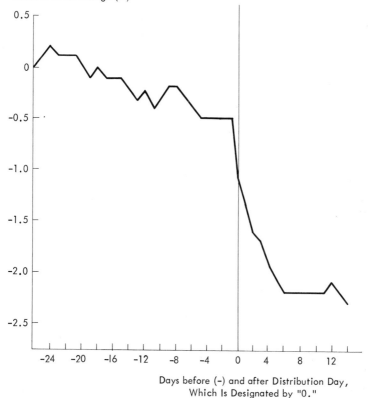

Relative Price Change (%)

Days before (-) and after Distribution Day,
Which Is Designated by "0."

Source: Scholes [147] and Brealey [13].

by Scholes, when the distributions were not registered with the SEC (and the 20-day waiting period was thus avoided), the market's reaction was, on average, more "surprised" and hence more sudden and severe. This difference between the performance of registered and nonregistered distributions is shown in Figure 15–3.

Scholes also classified pre- and post-secondary distribution performance by the kind of seller. These interesting differences are shown in Figure 15–4.

These data indicate that individuals typically sell after a substantial rise, and that the market does not react to this "news." While firms and officers also sell their own stock after a substantial rise, the market clearly interprets this "information" as a signal to sell and adjusts the

FIGURE 15–2
Relative Performance of 1207 Stocks before and after Distribution
Relative Price Change (%)

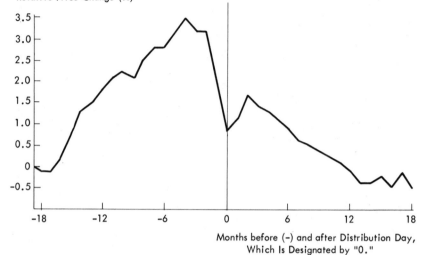

Months before (-) and after Distribution Day,
Which Is Designated by "0."

Source: Scholes [147] and Brealey [13].

FIGURE 15–3
Comparison of Registered and Nonregistered Secondaries
Relative Price Change (Percent)

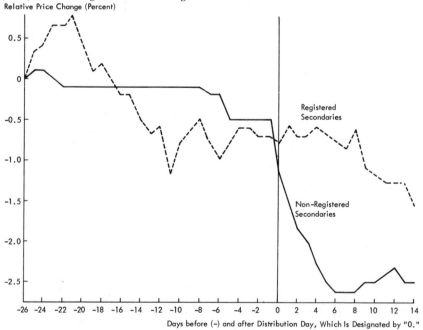

Days before (-) and after Distribution Day, Which Is Designated by "0."

Source: Scholes [147] and Brealey [13].

FIGURE 15–4
Comparison of Secondaries by Type of Seller
Relative Price Change (Percent)

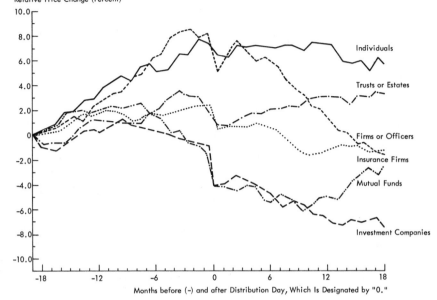

Source: Scholes [147] and Brealey [13].

relative price downward. As one might expect, mutual funds and investment companies tend to unload their poor performers, and the market
interprets this information in a way that adjusts the price still lower.

Whether because of superior analysis or a self-fulfilling prophecy, as
reflected by their publicized sale, mutual funds and investment companies
sold stocks that were destined to exhibit relatively poor performance.
This bodes well for the forecasting ability of such professionals. What
should not be overlooked, however, is the cost an institution must bear
to attract a market for a large secondary distribution. If the size of the
offering forces a seller into the secondary market, all commission costs,
and any discount, are borne by him. Commenting on Scholes research,
Brealey remarked "this provides some reassurance that these firms are
able to distinguish overvalued securities, but it also vividly illustrates
that the discount needed to sell the stock together with the 2 percent
commission combine to rob the seller of just about all of the benefits
of his superior judgement." [13, p. 94]

To know whether the price drops that are observed after large secondary distributions are the result of the sellers' wisdom, or the market's

assumption of their wisdom, does not alter the result—large secondary distributions, on average, precede price declines. This research should not be construed as an automatic sell signal. One should, however, avoid buying such stocks, and should reassess any existing holdings of such shares in terms of his or her investment objectives.

Odd-Lot Transactions

Suppose you were asked to rank various classes of investors in terms of their "closeness" to important information. You would probably begin such a list with corporate insiders, closely followed by market professionals. The last entry on such a list would likely be the small amateur investor. Given such a list, there is a temptation to attribute the above-average rates of return to the informed, presumably skillful investors, and conversely, the below-average returns to the relatively unskilled and uninformed amateurs. Intuitively, such an explanation of the varying degrees of market performance makes sense.

The odd-lot theory is based on the assumption that odd-lot trading (transactions involving less than one-hundred shares) reflects the sentiments of small, presumably amateur, investors. Further, this theory holds that these odd-lot investors are consistently the below-average performers. This odd-lot theory raises four questions:

1. Do odd-lot investors behave differently than round-lot investors?
2. Do odd-lot investors have performance measurably different from that of their round-lot counterparts?
3. Do aggregate odd-lot statistics forecast market movements?
4. Do odd-lot statistics on individual stocks forecast the movements of those stocks?

Odd-Lot versus Round-Lot Investor Behavior.   The odd-lot market is relatively small in size. Odd-lot volume on the NYSE in 1970 totaled 186 million shares, or only 5.8 percent of the market's total volume. Furthermore, both odd-lot trading volume and its overall value have been declining. The 1970 odd-lot volume was off 23 percent from the 1969 level, making it the lowest since 1963. In addition to lower odd-lot market activity in recent years, the odd-lot customers have sold more shares than they have purchased in nine of the last ten years. These figures do not say anything about the relative performance of the odd-lot and round-lot groups, only that they differ widely in size and the trend of their activity.

Studies of odd-lot investors reveal several behavior patterns that distinguish them from round-lot investors in terms of *when* they buy and sell. With surprising consistency odd-lot investors wait for what they consider to be "buys." This is evidenced by their tendency to enter the market when prices are at an interim low relative to former levels.

Reflecting an unplanned investment approach, odd-lot investors then tend to "cash in" after an interim market rise. The tendency for this money not to reenter the market is evidence that odd-lot investors feel "richer" by the rise and use their profits for other expenditures. This increased spending for goods and services could impart some degree of stimulus to the economy and support the theory that net odd-lot sales portend increased economic activity.

Odd-Lot versus Round-Lot Market Performance. The odd-lot theory holds that the market tends to decline after odd-lotters buy and to rise after they sell. In terms of what we know about *when* odd-lotters trade, the odd-lot theory would hold that the market *continues* to decline after they buy, and *continues* to rise after they sell. If this pattern is true, it would appear that odd-lotters, on average, do a remarkably poor job of market timing.

D. J. Klein [91], at Michigan State University, has compared the rates of return from the 20 most-sold and most-bought odd-lot stocks. Regardless of the period measured, the odd-lotters' purchases yielded a lower rate of return than the stocks they sold. This conclusion has been subsequently confirmed by Stanley Kaish [80]. While the studies of aggregate performance differences have not been as numerous or definitive as one would like, and there is some countervailing evidence of no differences (see [13, p. 134]), we can conclude that odd-lot investors are relatively unsuccessful in both timing and investment selection.

Odd-Lot Trading Rules. There is widespread belief that useful trading rules can be developed from odd-lot statistics. (Odd-lot short-interest trading rules are discussed later.) Some strategies based on odd-lot statistics (see [86, 87]) have shown outstanding performance. The problem with these strategies is that they have been "fine tuned" on historical data. Indeed, *if* the future is like the past, they should prove extremely useful. But, without some *reason* why things like filters of odd-lot sale/purchase ratios *should* continue to work, we are skeptical.

Odd-Lot Information—A Conclusion. The market performance of small investors, as reflected by odd-lot statistics, seems to be below average. The evidence that the small investor behaves differently, and profits less, has also spawned apparently useful market indicators. We feel, however, that the *most important* lesson to be gained from the odd-lot research is an understanding of *why* odd-lotters fail—so that you can avoid their poor results.

The generally inferior performance of the small investor can be attributed to several factors. The small investor's tendency to enter and leave the market at the wrong time reflects fragmented asset management and an impulsive response to the market's products. If the small investor's decisions were made in the context of other financial decisions and in terms of reasoned objectives and goals, this pattern would cease to exist. One explanation of why many investors "enter the market at the wrong time, with the wrong product, only to leave at the wrong time," is what Robert Dunwoody at duPont Walston, Incorporated calls the "greed-hope-fear-hope cycle."

The cycle usually begins when people have a little "extra" money. This extra money is often available at the top of an expansionary economic phase. The person who has been out of the market throughout this expansion has been exposed to stories of others' successes. He feels he has missed out and also wishes to invest successfully—*greed*. Seeing a glamour stock below its recent high, he takes the plunge, precisely at the time the odd-lot theorist says he enters the market. He *hopes* his stock will go up, without stopping to consider how much, how soon, or at what risk. If it does not go up, he rides it down, ever hoping that it will go up again. Finally, seeing the stock descend and afraid that it might go still lower, *fear* motivates him to sell at a loss, precisely at the time the odd-lot theorist says he leaves the market.

With his money safely out of the market, he sits on the sidelines. Then, according to the odd-lot theory, prices rise and he starts hoping again. This time he *hopes* the price will go back down so he can buy the stock at its prior low level. He then remains on the sidelines until his friends start talking about their profits, and the greed-hope-fear-hope cycle repeats itself.

The decline in the number of odd-lot investors over the last decade probably reflects the chronic and growing disenchantment of the small investor. We can conclude that the small investor, as represented by odd-lot volume, has withdrawn from the market.

Short-Interest Positions

Another contrary-opinion approach to stock selection and market timing is based on short-interest statistics. Short sales are made by people who expect the market to do down. In a regular securities transaction, you buy first and sell later. In a short transaction, you sell first and buy later. This is accomplished by borrowing stock through your broker and selling it at the current market price. The proceeds of the sale are then held as collateral for the loan of the stock. When you want to close the short position, you must replace the borrowed stock. This is done by buying an equivalent number of shares at the current market price. If you sold the borrowed stock (that is, the stock you are "short") at $100, and you can later cover the shortage by buying the stock at $90, you would have a $10 profit (before any intervening interest on your loan and replacing any dividend income).

Market technicians know that *eventually* each short position must be closed out with a purchase.[1] Hence, they reason, an increase in outstanding short interest represents an increase of potential demand that serves as a downside cushion. Conversely, followers of this system reason that a reduction in short interest reflects a reduction of latent demand and makes the market weak.

To assess the usefulness of short-interest information, it is necessary to answer three basic questions:

1. Do short-interest traders consistently attain above-average performance?
2. Can short-interest statistics be used to predict general market movements?
3. Can short-interest statistics be used to predict the movements of individual stocks?

Performance of Short-Interest Traders. The use of the word "trader," which implies a short-term, in-and-out speculator, appropriately describes most short sellers. SEC statistics show that most short positions are held for only about two weeks. In view of the general long-range upward trend of stock prices and difficulties inherent in predicting such short-term movements, one would expect short sellers to do *worse than average.* This would be so *unless* they time their decisions so that they tend to sell short before market declines and move into "long" (the opposite of short, which is the way most investors come into the stock market) positions before market advances; or alternatively, *unless* they can skillfully select individual stocks that will experience short-term declines!

---

[1] Short sales "against the box" are not replaced by market purchases. The term "against the box" means against stock held in a safe-deposit "box." For a full description of this trading strategy, and when it might be used, see Cohen and Zinbarg [20].

Thomas Mayor [117], after studying the short-interest transactions in 14 popular stocks between 1962 and 1966, concluded that short sellers, on average, had absolutely no market timing ability and, as a result, incurred large losses. We conclude from this evidence that one should not pay interest on borrowed stock to take a position against a generally upward market trend, unless he is extremely confident that a price decline is imminent. The poor performance of short-interest speculators does not, however, bear on the question of their behavior's serving as a market predictor. Regardless of their success or failure, the asserted cushioning effect from short-interest profit-taking in a price decline is a separate issue.

Short-Interest Market Indicators.   Several researchers (see [13, 117]) have reported that the aggregate *level* of short interest is not correlated with market *levels*. But, because the level of short interest fluctuates with the market's overall volume, a better relative measure of this activity is the ratio of short interest to average daily volume as published by *Barrons*. Studies (see [13, 69, 148, 149]) of the correlation between this short-interest ratio and the market reveal a slight relationship—as predicted by proponents of the short-interest indicators. It is difficult, however, to apply such information profitably to trading strategies.

A successful application of the short-interest ratio, illustrated by Cohen and Zinbarg [20], is reproduced in Figure 15–5. Buy and sell signals are generated when the ratio moves above 1.75 or below 0.75—as indicated by the horizontal lines so labeled at the bottom of the graph.

Two points should be emphasized about the Cohen and Zinbarg illustration. First, note how sensitive the buy and sell signals would be to even slight changes in the "signal points." Secondly, without a clear cause-and-effect relationship, one should be cautious, as Cohen and Zinbarg remind us, about inferring that these bands will be useful for individual stocks, or will be as useful in the future as they were in the past.

Short-Interest Stock Indicators.   To test the usefulness of short-interest statistics for predicting the movement of individual stocks, Randall D. Smith [157] studied the performance of portfolios of NYSE and AMEX stocks that were selected according to the short-interest theory. Smith found that the portfolios picked on the basis of short-interest statistics favored extremely volatile stocks. This is easily explained by the proclivity of the short-interest trader for quick action. We would expect a portfolio of such stocks to amplify the market's movement. Indeed, Smith found that the stocks selected by using short-interest statistics as a guide had widely fluctuating profits and losses. But, the overall performance of

FIGURE 15-3

Short-Interest Indicators 1945–1966

1941–43=10

ratio scale

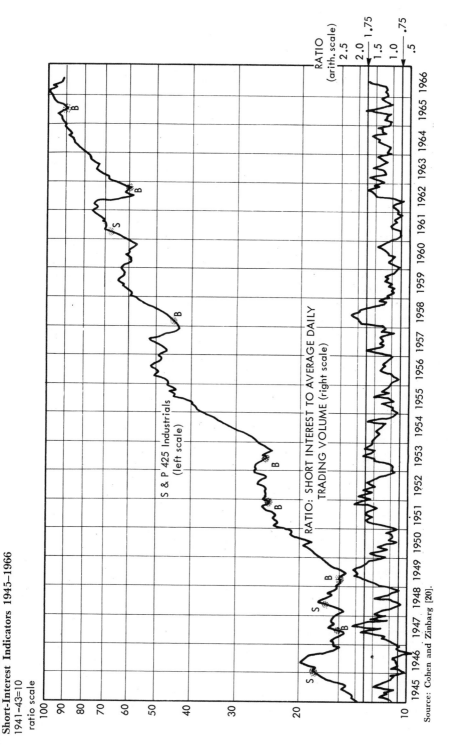

S & P 425 Industrials
(left scale)

RATIO: SHORT INTEREST TO AVERAGE DAILY
TRADING VOLUME (right scale)

RATIO
(arith. scale)

Source: Cohen and Zinbarg [20].

149

stocks picked by the rules of the short-interest theory was the same as that for randomly chosen stocks with similar risk.

Odd-Lot Short Sales

Many people who reason that both odd-lot transactions and short sales are plausible indicators reason that together—odd-lot short sales—they would provide a useful, but quite different, indicator. The logic behind this indicator is that small investors are usually not short sellers. When the small investors do move to the short side they feel *strongly* that the market is going down. On the assumption that the little guy is always wrong, this clear indication of small-investor pessimism is interpreted as a sure sign that a market bottom is near.

As further testimony to the conclusion that small investors do not obtain dependable advice, (or if they do, shun it in favor of their intuition), odd-lot investors *do*, with remarkable consistency, sell short at market lows. Manown Kisor and Victor Niederhoffer [90] demonstrated this phenomenon by contrasting the odd-lot short-sales ratio with the general level of the market between 1960 and 1969. Their results, reproduced in Table 15–2, show that the "little guy" who sells short has consistently misjudged the market.

TABLE 15–2
Relation between Levels of Odd-Lot Short-Sales Ratio and Changes in Market Index over Subsequent Month, 1960–1969

Odd-Lot Short-Sales Ratio	Number of Occurrences	Percentage of Occasions That Market Rose	Average Market Change (by percent)
0.0–1.0.	1222	56.1	0.2
1.0–2.0.	652	71.0	1.1
2.0–3.0.	181	63.0	0.4
3.0–4.0.	65	67.7	1.8
4.0–5.0.	43	72.1	2.3
5.0–6.0.	35	88.6	3.3
Greater than 6.0.	50	96.0	6.1

Source: Kisor and Niederhoffer [90].

Confirmation of the regularity with which swelling, odd-lot short sales signal the end of bear markets came in 1970. During April and May, when the Dow Jones Industrial Average plunged to a six-year low of 631.16, odd-lot short sales swelled abnormally, correctly signaling the end of the 1969–1970 bear market.

Again, small-investor behavior constitutes an unplanned, highly emotional response to what is incorrectly perceived as the time and the way to enter the market. It appears that these investors watch from the sidelines until they are overcome by the desire to participate, and then, starting late, they try to make as much as they can, as fast as they can. But, as stated earlier, impulsive forays into the market too often produce losses.

chapter
16
Econometric Forecasts

Taking into account the research examined thus far, one concludes that we have a "generally" efficient capital market. A perfectly efficient market would be one in which, at any point in time, the market price of a stock fully reflects all available information about that stock. If this theoretical characterization were true, it would be impossible for an investor to utilize *any* available information to predict extraordinary stock price movements. According to this theory, any information an investor might possess is, at that instant, already reflected in stock prices.

Paul Samuelson, the Nobel Prize winning economist and presidential adviser from M.I.T., was the first author to offer the efficient market explanation for what researchers had been observing. In his classic 1965 paper, "Proof That Properly Anticipated Prices Fluctuate Randomly," Samuelson [146] provided the theoretical framework for this efficient market school of thought. His contention was enhanced as a result of subsequent work by Benoit Mandelbrot [110, 111]. With the perfectly efficient capital market model thus established as a bench mark for investigation, researchers began to interpret their findings about stock market behavior in terms of this theory.

In December 1969, Eugene Fama of the University of Chicago presented a paper to the 28th annual meeting of the American Finance Association. In it he reviewed the recent research on the behavior of stock prices in terms of efficient capital market theory. In a general sense, Fama related this research to the theory in three areas: the "case against the technician," the "case against the fundamentalist," and "hope for the insider." His general conclusion was that ". . . the evidence in support of the efficient market's model is extensive, and (somewhat unique in economics) contradictory evidence is sparse." [**44,** p. 416]

Only in one area, where insiders have access to information that others do not, did Fama, as expected, find instances that investors possess *useful* information. Even so, Fama stated that "there is no evidence that deviations from . . . the efficient market's model permeate down any further through the investment community. For the purposes of most investors the efficient market's model seems a good first (and second) approximation to reality." [**44,** p. 416]

The research summarized thus far concludes that data on recent price and trading volume has failed all reputable tests of its usefulness for predicting future stock prices. We can conclude that such price and volume information is fully reflected in any stock's price at any point in time. The stock market is efficient at processing such price and volume data. Thus, for price- and volume-based technical analysis, the stock market behaves according to the efficient capital market theory. Any hopes of being able to predict future price movements from historical price and volume information are destroyed by the efficient readjustment action of the market itself.

Much evidence also questions the usefulness of earnings-based fundamental security analysis. In terms of efficient capital markets, the question becomes whether or not the market is so efficient that at any point in time it fully reflects all available fundamental information. If so, then the steady stream of publicly available fundamental information, such as earnings and dividends, is immediately fully reflected in a stock's price. Thus, an individual who possesses such fundamental information enjoys no advantage, because the information has already been absorbed into the stock's price through the market's ability to adjust immediately to all available information. If the stock market is truly an efficient capital market, in both the technical and fundamental sense, then neither technical nor fundamental information can be useful to the investor! While the new science of investing has succeeded in uncovering several instances of market inefficiencies which point to inordinately profitable investment strategies, the ever-pervasive force is the market's "general" efficiency.

Here, then, is the way academic researchers see the stock market. *It is impossible for you, or the skilled professional, to utilize most publicly available information to select stocks which will be more profitable than comparably risky stocks chosen on a purely random basis!* These findings are indeed counter to most people's intuition and to what investors believe. But our investment intuition has been derived from market folklore that, until recently, has never been subjected to scientific inquiry.

Today, many investors, as well as some Wall Street professionals, are reluctant to discard their "childhood" beliefs in the light of an overwhelming body of evidence gleaned from scientific investment research. To those investors who believe in Santa Claus:

'Twas the night before Christmas,
and all through the land
the investors were sleeping,
their heads in the sand.
Then from journals obscure
there arose such a clatter!
Maybe someone should ask,
"Is something the matter?"

Yes, something is the matter. Most investors haphazardly manage a fragmented pool of assets with irrational, ill-timed decisions. We know that price changes in individual securities can be traced to the public's reaction, first, to the market as a whole; secondly, to the basic industry; thirdly, to the industry subgroup; and lastly, to those characteristics that distinguish the particular company from its competitors. Even a sound, well-managed company cannot pass through a weak stock market or adverse industry conditions with its stock unaffected. Yet, few people adequately consider stock market (economic) and industry factors *before turning to the relatively insignificant company factors!* The more rational approach would be to *begin* with a careful assessment of the relatively more important factors—likely economic changes and their impact on the securities markets and on particular industries.

A branch of economics called econometrics seeks to do this via mathematical models programmed into electronic computers. Econometrics is a relatively new and promising field. In fact, in 1969 the first Nobel Prize for economic science was awarded jointly to Ragmar Frish of Norway and Jan Tinbergen of the Netherlands for their work in econometrics. Unfortunately, 1969 was a rather embarrassing time to receive an award for econometric forecasting. Disappointingly, the most popular and widely followed econometric models of the U.S. economy provided their creators with poor results.

Something Went Wrong

In mid-November of 1966, the Wharton Econometric Model forecast that the nation's 1967 gross national product would be $794 billion.

The actual level attained in 1967 was $794 billion! But, by mid-1968 this and other highly touted models' predictions for that year started to go wrong. An economic slowdown had been predicted for the second half of 1968. Something went wrong! The slowdown never materialized. At the forecast time for the following year in the latter months of 1968, the consensus of economic statisticians contributing to the American Statistical Association's annual forecast was for a 1969 GNP of $922 billion. Something went wrong! This forecast was not only $11 billion below the mark, but it also erroneously predicted an expanding economy by year-end with relatively minor inflationary pressure.

Business Week commented on the ability of econometricians to predict the 1969 economy as follows:

Going back over the record it is almost impossible to find a satisfactory projection. At best, there are some examples of partially successful forecasts. For example Irvin Schweiger, a professor at the University of Chicago, and for years a forecaster, said early last December that "GNP will total $933 billion in 1969," seemingly a perfect forecast. But he also said that "prices will rise a little less rapidly than in 1968 and will decelerate slowly during the year"—bad forecast.

Another leader in the forecast derby, Walter Heller, chairman of the Council of Economic Advisors under President Kennedy, came very close to estimating the dollar output of the economy. He even saw "higher prices accounting for a bit more than half the increase." But Heller incorrectly projected a slower first-half than a second-half. [180, p. 36]

And so went the predictions of the nation's foremost economists as the economy headed into the 1969–70 "mini-recession."[1] Something had gone wrong!

In a lecture in 1973, Solomon Fabricant, N.Y.U. economist and a member of the senior research staff at the National Bureau of Economic Research, offered the following assessment of econometric models:

Some of you may be wondering whether these models really mark a big step forward in the art of forecasting. I am afraid that I must say "no," or at any rate "not yet." Tests of the forecasts made with the models indicate that they are little better, and often worse, than the so-called "naïve" projections. [17, p. 22]

---

[1] Though 1969–70 was never labeled a recession by the National Bureau of Economic Research—whose definition is "a period of decline in economic activity which is at least as long, deep, and widespread as the shortest and mildest such episode that has been historically recognized as a recession"—by the popular "two consecutive quarters of no real growth" definition, it was a recession.

It is helpful to classify economic or econometric forecasts into three categories:

* Monetarist Forecasts,
* Keynesian Forecasts, or
* Leading Indicator Analysis.

Monetarist Forecasts

Some of the most interesting, and encouraging, work with econometric models has been reported by Burton Malkiel, Richard Quandt, and William Baumol at Princeton's Financial Research Center. After much careful research along the lines reported here, they concluded that "technical analysis is akin to astrology . . ." and characterized people who analyze earnings as "alchemists." [152, p. 43] Having thus discarded the traditional forms of investment analysis, Malkiel et al. turned, with other Princeton researchers, to the study of basic economic factors that might be related to stock prices. Following the monetarist view as expressed by Milton Friedman [51] and Beryl Sprinkel [158, 159], two other Princeton researchers, Kenneth Homa and Dwight Jaffee [72], had already shown that, if one could predict the money supply, he could attain above-average investment returns. In the words of Professor Malkiel, "the trick [in applying the Homa-Jaffee findings] is to estimate what the Federal Reserve will do about the money supply in the next quarter." [152, p. 43] Reasoning that changes in the money supply were largely dictated by the decisions of Federal Reserve chairman Arthur Burns, Homa and Jaffee tried to model Dr. Burns to predict *his* behavior. This approach and other less inventive ones have, as yet, proved to be poor indicators of changes in the money supply.

Keynesian Forecasts

The monetary theorist's approach to econometric model building is sometimes termed "outside in." That is, the theoretical underpinnings for their models describe how an "outside" change in the money supply translates itself "into" changes in the economy and/or stock market. This is in contrast to the "inside out" approach of the Keynesians. The Keynesian models start "inside" the economy and work their way "out" to such measures as GNP and the Dow averages by aggregating estimates of the behavior of each of the various economic sectors. One such sector in the Wharton Econometric Model is automobile demand. The size of this economic sector is forecast by an equation that combines projections of such things as after-tax income, prices, unemployment, consumer attitudes, and interest rates.

Leading Indicator Analysis

Another group of forecasters, who are sometimes grouped with the econometricians, rely on statistics prepared by the National Bureau of Economic Research (NBER). Each month, the NBER updates a host of economic statistics and reports this information in the *Business Conditions Digest,* a monthly publication of the U.S. Department of Commerce. Based on whether changes in these statistics have tended to precede, accompany, or follow changes in past economic cycles, the NBER classifies each of them as a leading, coincident, or lagging indicator.

The NBER maintains records of our economic activity dating back to 1871. The Bureau's records show that, since that time, changes in stock prices have tended to precede changes in business conditions. Since 1871, our economy has reversed itself 41 times. On 34 of these occasions, changes in stock prices have led the turn in business conditions. On two of the 41 occasions, the change in the stock market coincided with the change in the business cycle. And, as if to show that the stock market refuses to move consistently over time, on five occasions the turn in stock prices followed the turn in the economy.

The NBER publishes reams of statistics on various economic indicators some of which have *tended* to signal turns in the general health of our economy. But the two questions regarding the predictive value of these indicators are:

- Do NBER indicators accurately portend the course of the *business cycle?*
- Do any NBER indicators predict changes in the level of the *stock market?*

The answer to both questions is a very qualified "yes." While the NBER statistics have historically tended to lead such changes, the important variables are "what constitutes a significant change in the indicator" and "what is the lead time?" Owing to the complexity of our economy, these two problems—distinguishing between true and false signals on the basis of their size, and accurately predicting in which month the signaled change will occur—cannot be solved in such a way as to furnish precise answers.

Success in combining NBER indicators into a leading index for the stock market has been claimed by Jesse Levin [95] and several forecasting groups that will not divulge their secret approach. Unfortunately, their failure to quantify either signal size or lead time prevents subjecting their boastful claims to rigorous analysis.

The most extensive, and successful, publicized effort to combine published economic statistics into a stock market forecaster has been made by Professors Baumol, Malkiel, and Quandt at Princeton. Such forecasts, which we call "marketometric" forecasts because they are designed to predict the behavior of investment *markets* rather than *economic* sectors, are based on a combination of seven economic variables. These include: forecasted consumption (from the University of Michigan's consumer sentiment index); anticipated investment (as measured by new orders for durable goods); government expenditures (as reflected by new defense obligations); the interest rate on AAA corporate bonds; anticipated labor disruptions (as portended by data on expiring labor contracts); anticipated unemployment; and projected consumer prices. When Baumol et al. tested a predictive scheme based on these inputs they found that their return was roughly half again as much as that from a buy-and-hold strategy.

Commenting on the usefulness of economic indicators which have tended to lead price movements, Brealey has stated that

> The strong upward trend in stock prices . . . has imposed a heavy penalty on those who have erred in attempting to predict cyclical movements [from leading indicator analysis] and . . . it is not surprising that there have been quite long periods when such mechanical schemes . . . would have produced for their followers less favorable results than those of a buy-and-hold policy. Neither is it surprising that apparently minor changes in the decision rules could have resulted in the disappearance of profits on the remaining occasions. Equally, therefore, a combination of the same decision rule and minor changes in the economic relationship could result in losses rather than profits.
>
> This sensitivity to minor changes in the behavior of the variables could be crucial to the value of such decision rules. Although the investor may well feel that the broad nature of stock market cycles and the relationships to other economic series will persist in the future, it is difficult to believe that they will endure in detail. For example, the changing role of monetary policy in government economic management may well affect the relationship between money supply and stock prices. [12, p. 35]

Seasonal Trends?

There are also many myths about seasonal market trends. According to these beliefs, it is prudent to make timely purchases of securities of companies with definite seasonal market patterns, such as those that make soft drinks, air conditioners, and agricultural machinery, so as to benefit from seasonal stock price fluctuations. Julius Shiskin, at the University of Chicago, has conducted an exhaustive study of seasonal price movements [153]. Shiskin found that any apparent seasonal effects were so weak that their influence on stock prices would be negligible at best. Further, he reported that the weak seasonal patterns that he detected tended to shift over time and could not be used for the development of profitable trading rules. Brealey, in reflecting on the lack of seasonal patterns, has reminded us that Mark Twain was correct when he observed that "October is one of the peculiarly dangerous months to speculate in stocks. The others are July, January, September, April, November, May, March, June, December, August, and February." [12, p. 30]

So Where Does This Leave Us?

What is the wisdom of relying on leading stock market indicators that (1) have not been very reliable in the past, and (2) you suspect will be no more reliable in the future because of changing variables? On balance, the three kinds of econometric models have been characterized by much *promise* and marginal *performance*. The hard fact is that, to date, no econometric model has satisfactorily predicted the turning points in our economy or stock market. Investors must realize that processing mathematical equations by means of electronic computers does not mean that these equations, or the input assumptions, will be completely accurate. Model building is a detailed and rigorous science. The computer merely does the lengthy calculations and adds not a whit to the researcher's wit. When one builds a model, all of the assumptions must be stated explicitly. When models go wrong, it is possible to dissect them and find out which assumptions were invalid. Through this valuable learning experience and redesign, econometric forecasting models should soon be providing extremely useful projections. At the present time, econometric forecasting does not offer investors a prediction panacea.

Conclusion

Man's age-old dream has been to predict the future. In ancient Rome the haruspices, wearing star-studded, tall, pointed hats and clad in robes decorated with mystic symbols, professed to foretell the future by interpreting animal entrails. Today, both government and business base their forecasts on increasingly more scientific, reliable, and complex econometric models. The Federal Reserve, Council of Economic Advisers, and Commerce Department each make their own econometric projections. Similarly, large corporations, such as IBM and General Electric, use forecasting models that they developed themselves. Moreover, a host of universities and private consulting firms are working on econometric forecasting procedures.

Our conclusion is that econometric and, more importantly, "marketometric" forecasting is in its infancy. Born from the age-old desire to know, understand, and predict, this young science of econometrics brings together sophisticated analytical tools and dedicated researchers. Their skill and effort will, within the next decade, undoubtedly lead to a quantum jump in our comprehension and application of this newest branch of the new science of investing.

chapter
17
Inside Information

Certain insiders are required to report their security dealings to the Securities and Exchange Commission. These include exchange specialists, substantial owners (more than 10 percent), directors, and corporate officers. Notably excluded from SEC monitoring are persons who are relatives of these insiders, as well as various employees, or banks, that might have access to the same confidential information. While this definition has some obvious shortcomings, the fact is that monitoring the stock transactions of every insider's friends and relatives would be inconceivably difficult. To protect against the possibility of abuse by secretly informed outsiders, the law governing insider trading goes beyond persons directly monitored by the SEC.

The law holds (see *SEC* v. *Texas Gulf Sulphur Co.* and *SEC* v. *Cady, Roberts & Co.*) that anyone who trades on the basis of nonpublic information becomes a de facto insider. Both lawsuits, which set important precedents, involved parties who were clearly "insiders." The *Texas Gulf Sulphur* case involved the actions of company officials. In the *Cady, Roberts* case a broker's partner was a director of the company. The outcome of both cases made it clear, however, that an insider is *anyone* who has access to confidential information. This means that a person who is given a confidential tip by a bona fide insider becomes, upon receiving the tip, a de facto insider.

Public versus Private Information

A landmark test case concerning the use of nonpublic information sprang from the events of June 21, 1966. Sometime after 2:00 P.M.

161

on that day, it was alleged that institutional salesmen from Merrill Lynch began advising certain privileged institutional clients that Douglas Aircraft would soon report disappointing earnings. This information had come to Merrill Lynch in confidence on June 20 in connection with a proposed underwriting. Within less than 11 trading hours, and still prior to public disclosure of the disappointing earnings, it was alleged that 13 privileged clients placed orders to sell 199,400 shares of Douglas Aircraft stock. (The hearing examiner later held that 12 firms sold a total of 154,000 shares for more than $13.3 million on the basis of tips from Merrill Lynch salesmen.)

The significance of the Douglas Aircraft–Merrill Lynch situation does not lie in the alleged improprieties of the parties. (Merrill Lynch settled its part of the case on November 26, 1968, and without admitting any wrongdoing, agreed to certain sanctions. The charges against the institutional investors who allegedly acted on the information supplied by Merrill Lynch culminated in an SEC hearing examiner's decision on June 26, 1970.) The significance of the case is its importance as a legal precedent applicable to investors acting on tips.

In a landmark decision, SEC hearing examiner Warren E. Blair used the term "tippee" to refer to persons who, through a corporate insider, become aware of confidential information. Blair held that the rules governing corporate insiders should be extended to tippees. He held that it was the responsibility of *anyone* receiving "material inside information" from insiders either to disclose the information publicly, or to refrain from trading on it. Applying this extended concept of an insider, Blair held that the 12 firms that allegedly received information from Merrill Lynch and acted on that information, violated the SEC disclosure requirements.

Recognizing the magnitude of a ruling enlarging the definition of corporate insiders to include tippees, the SEC spent more than a year reviewing Blair's decision. In July 1971, the SEC reaffirmed Blair's opinion that a person who acts on a tip violates the law if he has reason to know that the information was not made public. To make its position even stronger, the SEC ruled that people who use information that *innocently* comes into their possession are in violation of the law if they have reason to know that the information was intended to be confidential.

The position of the SEC that the rules governing corporate insiders extend to tippees poses a particularly onerous problem for anyone who receives a tip. The SEC has held, for example, that an investment adviser violated the law when he heard about the drop in Douglas's earnings at a luncheon, verified the accuracy of the information with several sources including Merrill Lynch, and then acted on it. The examiner held in this case that the adviser did not first ascertain (as he should have) whether the information he had heard, and subsequently verified, was public knowledge.

Clearly, in the matter of insider information, the SEC is moving in the direction of the consumer's interest. It is imperative to the free and orderly working of a competitive stock market that all parties have equal access to all factual information. The SEC decision on the responsibilities of tippees clears the air on a vital point—*all parties to transactions must have access to the same material facts!* If you buy or sell securities knowing something that the other party to the transaction cannot know, you are in violation of federal law. If your broker gives you some inside information, and you act on it, you are *both* in violation of federal law.

It is doubtful that the significance of the preceding point can be overemphasized. This rule obligates all publicly owned companies to insure that disclosed changes in material facts are widely disseminated. If information is disclosed to one analyst, it must be made *equally* available to all analysts! It is unlawful for anyone to profit from material facts unless those facts are *public knowledge*. This, in turn, means that all investment advice must be restricted to *analysis* of public facts.

The law notwithstanding, when you decide to buy a share of stock, two groups of people already have access to confidential information. The management of the company knows, or certainly should know, more about that company than you. Similarly, when your order reaches the floor of a stock exchange, the specialist in the stock you want to buy has nonpublic information on standing buy and sell orders at specific prices. Thus, two important questions are

- Do either corporate insiders or specialists use their privileged information for extra profit?
- Do any of their actions give *us* useful information?

Corporate Insiders

Of all people, corporate insiders are in the best position to interpret company-related information, the competitive forces in their industry, and how impending economic predictions will influence the future price of their stock. These insiders also have access to confidential information.

This does not mean, however, that corporate insiders use either their ability to analyze public information, or their access to private information, for personal profit. There are two deterrents to such insider profiteering. First, there is the moral obligation of corporate officers to meet their fiduciary responsibilities. Secondly, the SEC restrictions against insider trading constrain insiders who might otherwise neglect their moral and fiduciary obligations.

Needless to say, in spite of the moral and legal deterrents, there have been many well-publicized allegations of misconduct by corporate insiders. These periodic actions by the SEC against alleged violators remind the public of both the possibility of insider misconduct and the importance of SEC-enforced legislation to prevent it. We should remember, however, that stories of alleged corruption, or errors in judgment, tend to assume headline importance. We should be careful not to generalize from these cases. It is not enough to focus on the headline cases and assume that they represent the visible tip of a giant iceberg.

Do corporate insiders profit from expert analysis or proprietary information? Several researchers (see [37, 178]) have studied the general question of whether corporate insiders have better-than-average foresight in their investment decisions. If insiders make the right decision regarding their company's stock more often than outsiders, they could be using their general understanding of the company and/or inside information for personal profit. The consensus of this research is that there is very little speculation by insiders on short-term price fluctuations of their company's stock, but the results of transactions by corporate insiders do provide above-average returns. This means that corporate insiders can, on average, forecast the future price of their stock accurately.

The number of insider transactions is probably a better measure of insider sentiment than the total volume of shares traded in such transactions. Insider trading volume could be easily swamped by big outsider transactions. Hence, the consensus of insider opinion is best reflected by the number of trades. Donald Rogoff [144] studied the relationship between the number of insider trades and subsequent stock performance in his doctoral dissertation at Michigan State University. Rogoff defined a "consensus" as existing when the difference between the number of buyers and sellers over a given month was at least two. For example, if during a particular month one insider sold, while three bought, the difference would indicate an insider consensus existed in that month. Using this measure on 98 stocks between 1957 and 1960, Rogoff found 108 increases (relative to the market six months hence) after insider consensus and 54 decreases. Of the 210 occasions of sale consensus, 98 preceded advances and 112 preceded declines.

We can infer from Rogoff's research that, on two out of three occasions when insiders were motivated to purchase their company's stock, it subsequently advanced ahead of the market. The common fear that insiders unload their holdings before declines was not substantiated by Rogoff's research. In a study of insider activity during 1963 and 1964, James Lorie and Victor Niederhoffer [106], at the University of Chicago, found stock market performance almost identical to that reported by Rogoff after insider consensus to purchase. In this study, consensus preceded advances (relative to the market six months hence) 36 times and preceded declines 19 times. Lorie and Niederhoffer, however, found a stronger tendency than did Rogoff for insider sales to precede declines: Of the 124 sales consensus points, 81 preceded declines and 43 preceded advances. Thus, the research by Rogoff, and Lorie and Niederhoffer, clearly reflects insider foresight.

Shannon Pratt and C. DeVere [139] have taken the issue of insider trading a step further and have studied the profitability of 52,000 insider transactions between 1960 and 1966. They defined an insider consensus as three or more transactions of one kind and none of the other: that is, three or more sales and no purchases, or three or more purchases and no sales. The comparative performance for 36 months following such insider activity is shown in Figure 17–1. Notice that, one year after a consensus of insider sales, those stocks had an average return of 9.6 percent. This is a respectable rate of return and reflects the general market expansion during the period covered by the study. The results following insider purchases, however, are almost too good to be true. Stocks purchased by three or more insiders during one month appreciated 27.1 percent after a year had passed. Further, there was an obvious long-run difference between the performance of the two groups.

We can conclude that corporate insiders can successfully forecast the future of their companies and that they profit from this superior forecasting ability. It should be emphasized, however, that they do not abuse such ability or knowledge by excessive trading.

The important question is whether *we* can use the actions of corporate insiders as indicators? Insider transactions of publically traded stocks are reported to the SEC. After approximately a one-month clerical and printing delay, a complete record of these transactions is available in the *Official Summary of Security Transactions and Holdings*. Studies of the usefulness of these published reports have provided encouraging results.

FIGURE 17-1
Performance of Stocks Experiencing Unusual Insider Activity—No Lag

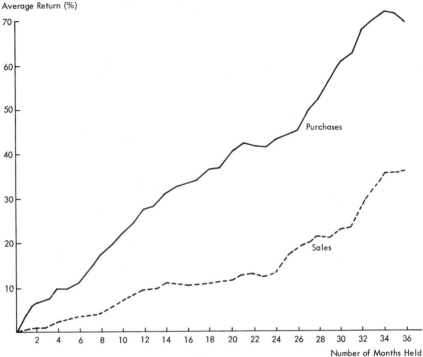

Average Return (%)

Purchases

Sales

Number of Months Held

Source: Pratt and DeVere [139] and Brealey [13].

Robert Hamanda [68] studied the relationship between total trading volume and market-level changes. His findings suggest insider opinion is a leading indicator of which direction the market will take. At the level of the individual stock, Pratt and DeVere found that imitating insiders' behavior one or two months after the record of their actions was published *still allowed one to achieve above-average performance.*

We can conclude, therefore, that corporate insiders have special ability and/or inside information which makes them better-than-average forecasters, and that they, in turn, profit from these forecasts. What is surprising, however, is the discovery that the advantage of being a corporate insider is largely available to anyone who reads the *Official Summary of Security Transactions and Holdings.*

chapter
18
The Specialist's Book

The specialists who maintain the markets in securities on the floor of a stock exchange know the size and prices of standing buy and sell orders. Under the rules of the exchange, this information is known only to the specialist. The existence of such private information raises several important questions:

- Can the information in a specialist's book be used for personal profit?
- Is the information used for personal profit?
- Can *we* profit from an understanding of the mechanics of the specialist's book?

The answer to each of these questions is *yes!* There is evidence that specialists profit from information that, under the rules of the exchange, is known only to them. Understanding how they profit from the information in their books can be important to investors.

The Specialist System

Specialists received much adverse publicity from Richard Ney's best-selling book *The Wall Street Jungle* [127]. Ney, an actor turned investment adviser, documented many instances of specialist abuse, but was apparently unaware of the research in this area. It is not our purpose to pass judgment on the specialist system but instead to understand how it bears on our investment decisions. This is done by outlining the specialist's job and looking at the relevant research.

The New York Stock Exchange is a private, recently incorporated, association with 1,366 members. Memberships in the Exchange, or "seats," are bought and sold much like stock. The price for membership varies with the economic outlook. The highest price ever paid for an NYSE seat was $625,000 in 1929, reflecting the frenzied days that preceded the great crash. The lowest price paid in modern times was $17,000 in 1942, when Wall Street's future was quite uncertain. With the Dow Jones Industrial Average nearly reaching 1,000 in 1966, 1968, and 1969, NYSE seats sold for about $500,000 during those years. With Wall Street's future uncertain, when the Dow crossed 1,000 in November 1972, Exchange memberships sold for $180,000. During 1973, seats sold as low as $72,000.

For this sum of money (plus an initiation fee of $7,500 and annual dues of $1,500), a member is entitled to transact business on the Exchange floor. The rest of the world must pay commissions to members for exchange services. The trading floor contains many different posts: fixed locations where specialists maintain markets in their assigned stocks. Over one fourth of Exchange members are specialists, and these are organized into some 70 business units.

Serving in a different function, about half of the Exchange members are associated with member firms dealing with the public. Since public investors are excluded from the Exchange floor, member firms transact business as agents for the public and charge a commission for this service. The remaining members roam the Exchange floor. They are called "two dollar" brokers and trade for their own account without standard commissions or, for a small member-to-member fee, they will assist member firms in executing orders from investors.

The Historical Accident

The specialist system is an historical accident. One story is that it all started in 1875, when a member fractured his leg. With his broken leg, the hapless broker could not move around the Exchange. Perched on a stool where Western Union shares were traded, he found he could transact business for friends. By knowing what various people wanted to do, he could make a few dollars trading Western Union and, at the same time, make the market more orderly. According to the story, the idea caught on, and the Exchange found it convenient to have a member stationed at each stock post to specialize, for a fee, in that stock. The specialist, in effect, became a bookkeeper for other brokers wishing to leave orders with him or to trade with him directly.

This specialist system holds the potential for conflict of interest. On the one hand, a specialist is a broker's broker who receives a commission for the business he transacts. In this capacity he is charged with obtaining the best possible price for the brokers he represents. On the other hand, he is allowed to trade for his own account. In his official capacity of maintaining an orderly market in a stock, a specialist is supposed to stand ready to buy for his own account if no one else wants to buy, or conversely, sell from his own account if no one else wants to sell. Thus, he is always ready to buy or sell. Specialists provide this market liquidity, in the words of the Constitution of the New York Stock Exchange "in so far as reasonably practicable."

When You Buy Stock . . .

When an investor decides he (or more likely "she") would like to buy, say, 100 shares of Avon Products, what happens? Purchasing stock generally begins by placing an order with an account executive of a member firm. This broker then transmits the order to his firm's New York office where it is telephoned to the firm's clerk at the Exchange. This clerk transmits the customer's order to the firm's Exchange member (or one of its members if the firm has more than one seat) who, by right of membership, can transact the purchase on the floor.

Each stock listed on an exchange is traded at a specific trading *post* on that exchange's trading floor. To purchase this 100 shares of Avon Products at the market price, the member broker must walk to the post where Avon Products is traded. The broker then moves into the "crowd" around the Avon specialist, who maintains the market in Avon Products. As the member enters the "crowd," he (only one woman is currently an NYSE member) will ask for a quote on 100 shares of Avon. Let's say the quote is "115 to a quarter." This quote represents the bid-asked range for the stock. This means that someone stands ready to buy 100 shares of Avon Products at $115 a share and someone stands ready to sell 100 shares of Avon Products at $115.25 a share. The buyers and sellers are $0.25 apart.

One of two things can happen. The Exchange members who comprise the "crowd" can buy and sell among themselves without intervention by the specialist. Alternatively, they can transact their business with the specialist. If two floor brokers are at the post, and one holds an order to buy at the market, while another holds an order to sell at the market, they could transact the trade directly between themselves at the middle price of 115⅛. In that case, each does $0.125 better than if he had dealt with the specialist. Often, no compatible buys and sells can be arranged directly between floor brokers, so the specialist will consummate the trade. In either case, an Exchange reporter notes the transaction. This information is then transmitted to the Exchange's computer and on to the quotation tickers and terminals in brokerage house offices across the nation.

Types of Orders You Can Leave with the Specialist

The market price of a stock is established through the dynamics of supply and demand as representatives of buyers and sellers meet on the Stock Exchange floor to carry out their customers' orders. When opportunities present themselves, all members may also trade for their own accounts. The most common type of customer transaction is a *market* order. Between 75 percent and 85 percent of the orders transacted on the New York Stock Exchange are said to be market orders, although such data are not made public. A customer who places an order to buy or sell "at the market" thereby authorizes the Exchange member who represents him to execute his order at the best possible price when the order reaches the post.

In addition to market orders, there are two other important kinds of buy and sell orders: limit and stop orders. Limit orders, like market orders, may be to buy or to sell. With a limit order, however, execution of the order is limited by a specified price. Suppose, for example, that General Motors is selling at $82, and an investor decides to purchase GM if its price is *at or below* $81. In this case the investor will place a buy-limit order at $81. When the floor broker receives the order, he will attempt to execute it. If GM's price is at or below $81, the buy-limit order becomes a market order and it is executed. However, if GM's price is above the buy-limit order when it reaches the Exchange floor, the buy-limit order is left with the specialist to enter into his book of pending transactions. Thus, such orders in the specialist's book are standing offers to buy at some price below the current market price. Similarly, sell-limit orders in the specialist's book are standing offers to sell when the stock's price rises to the "limit" set by the customer's order.

Stop orders, sometimes called stop-loss orders, are the opposite of limit orders. Stop orders to sell specify some price *below* the current market price, while stop orders to buy specify a price *above* current market. Stop-loss orders to sell are used by investors who wish to curtail losses by being "stopped out" if their stock's price moves down. Stop-loss orders

to buy (an order to buy at a price above the current market) are sometimes used by holders of short positions to cut off further loss if the
price moves up. The pending and unexecuted limit and stop orders comprise what is known as the specialist's "book." The understanding of
how the specialist's book works not only clarifies the kinds of orders available to investors, but also provides insight into how specialists use this
information for personal profit.

A Look at the Specialist's Book

The "specialist's book," the mechanics of which are not known by most
investors, lies at the heart of the Exchange. (Market orders are executed
immediately at the current price, either with or without the specialist,
and are not entered in the specialist's book.) A typical format of a specialist's book appears in Figure 18–1. The left side is used to enter the names
of people who want to buy and the prices they are willing to pay. The
book's right side contains the names and order prices of people who want
to sell. Notice that the higher prices appear at the bottom of the book.

Suppose that a given stock's current market price is somewhere between $45 and $46. There are four nonmarket orders that can be placed
with the specialist. First, "buy-limit" orders, the most common, are stand-

FIGURE 18–1
Format of Specialist's Book

45	Buy	Sell	45
1/8			1/8
1/4			1/4
3/8			3/8
1/2			1/2
5/8			5/8
3/4			3/4
7/8			7/8
46	Buy	Sell	46

FIGURE 18–2
Sell-Limit Order Placement in Specialist's Book

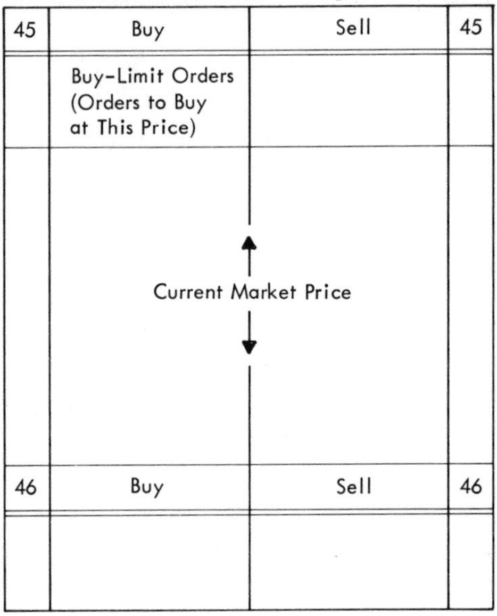

45	Buy	Sell	45
Buy–Limit Orders (Orders to Buy at This Price)			
	Current Market Price		
46	Buy	Sell	46

ing offers to buy at some price below the current market. The investor who reasons "if **XYZ** ever gets down to $45 it will be a good buy" can place a buy-limit order in the specialist's book at $45. It will appear in the upper left part of the page until executed, as shown in Figure 18–2.

Being able to leave an away-from-the-market order with the specialist is a convenience to customers and certainly to floor brokers who need not frequently check back to make sure of this order's execution. This important service also draws orders into the market and provides liquidity. This off-market demand information, which is the secret preserve of a stock's specialist, is a useful indicator of the stock's strength or weakness.

If an investor reasons that "when **XYZ** goes to 46 I want to sell it," he can place a "sell-limit order." These orders appear on the lower right side of the specialist's book as shown in Figure 18–3.

An investor might wish to hold his stock as long as it goes up in price, but is not willing to ride down a decline. He can place a "stop-loss" order to sell at a price that is below the current market price. This order to sell at a price that is below the current market price is recorded in the upper right side of the specialist's book. Under Exchange rules a

FIGURE 18–3
Sell-Limit Order Placement in Specialist's Book

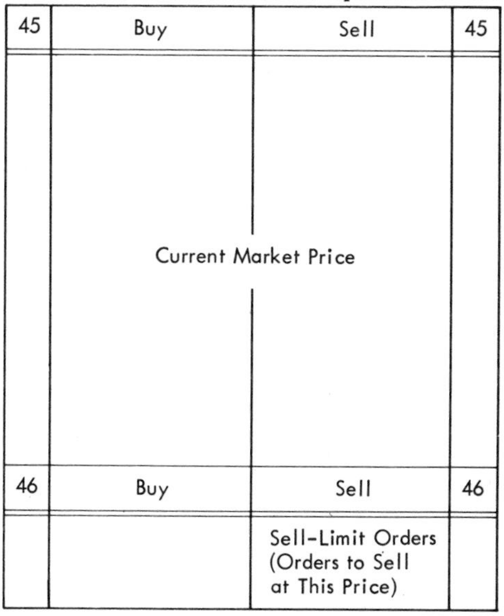

45	Buy	Sell	45
		Current Market Price	
46	Buy	Sell	46
		Sell-Limit Orders (Orders to Sell at This Price)	

stop-loss order does not become effective until another transaction takes place at the same price or less. When this happens, the stop-loss order becomes a market order. The investor cannot be assured, however, of selling his stock at the exact price designated by his stop-loss order. If the market "falls out of bed," the stop-loss order is executed at whatever price the specialist can obtain after it becomes a market order. In some cases the actual selling price is much below the "stop" price.

Finally, the specialist's book also contains orders to buy stock at a price above the current market price. Who would want to buy stock above the current market? Suppose you held a short position in a volatile stock. In holding a short position you are betting that the stock's price will *go down*. How can you insure your bet? You can place a "stop order to buy." If the stock's price runs up, your "stop-buy" will become a "market-buy," and the necessary shares will be bought to cancel out your short position. These stop-buy orders are recorded in the lower left side of the book. Thus, the specialist's book, when complete, looks like Figure 18–4, with buy and sell orders above and below the current market price.

To illustrate the actual use of a specialist's book, Figure 18–5 shows hypothetical entries for XYZ stock. The left side contains the pending

FIGURE 18–4
Arrangement of Orders in Specialist's Book

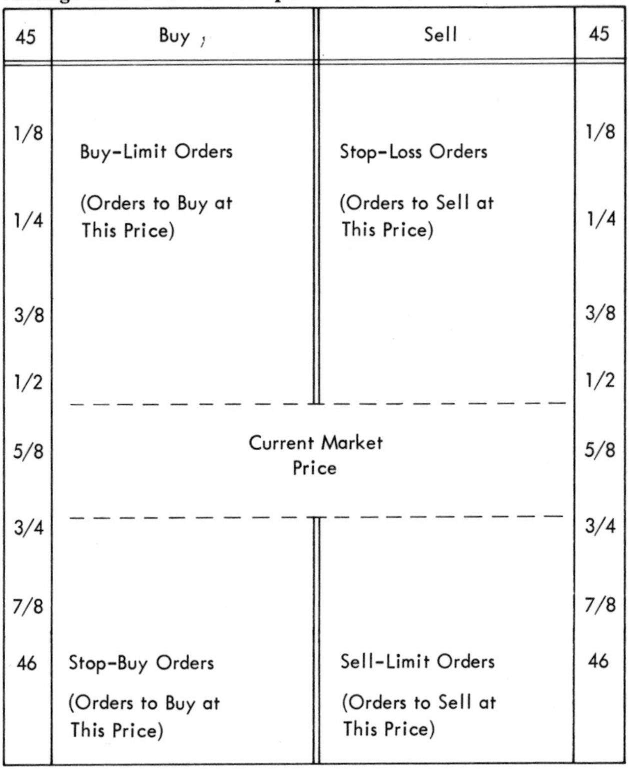

45	Buy ,	Sell	45
1/8	Buy–Limit Orders	Stop–Loss Orders	1/8
1/4	(Orders to Buy at This Price)	(Orders to Sell at This Price)	1/4
3/8			3/8
1/2			1/2
5/8	Current Market Price		5/8
3/4			3/4
7/8			7/8
46	Stop–Buy Orders (Orders to Buy at This Price)	Sell–Limit Orders (Orders to Sell at This Price)	46

bids, with the lowest bids at the top of the page. The right side contains the pending ask prices of sellers. Orders are entered in the book in sequence as received. Each entry denotes the number of round lots (that is, 100-share lots) and the member who placed the order. Total supply or demand at each price level can be added up and shown in the book as illustrated.

Suppose a broker asks the specialist for a quote on XYZ stock. The specialist consults his book and quotes the highest bid currently below the market (buy-limit order) and the lowest above-market ask (sell-limit order). These prices represent the current bid-ask spread for investors willing to trade this stock. If no limit orders exist at a given price, the specialist may quote for his own account. In this illustration, the quote for XYZ stock would be 45 bid and 45⅛ asked; a market order to buy would be executed at 45⅛, and a market order to sell would be

FIGURE 18–5
Hypothetical Specialist's Book for XYZ Stock

45	Buy		Sell		45
	6–Mason 3–Simon 5–Adams 4–West 8–Neal 8–Brown	34	3–Miller—Stop	3	
1/8			2—Fox	4	1/8
1/4			4—Edwards	4	1/4
3/8			1—Smith	1	3/8
1/2			2–Gates 2–Hill 2–Abbott	6	1/2
5/8					5/8
3/4			4–Owen	4	3/4
7/8	2–Hayes—Stop		1–Hodge	1	7/8
46	Buy		Sell		46
	5–Wilson—Stop		6–Garson 4–King 2–Harris 3–Brent	15	

executed at 45. These bids and asks will not change until all limit orders are filled at one of these prices.

Thus, many *limit* orders in the specialist's book, at least over the short run, serve to stabilize price movements. On the other hand, *stop* orders on either the buy or sell side tend to add momentum to the short-run trend of a stock's price. Since stop orders are the less frequent type, this destabilizing effect of accelerating price "runs" is not generally as strong as the stabilizing effect of limit orders. Bad news, however, will occasionally cause a sudden price drop. Stop-loss orders to sell would add to the dumping of stock in such a case. To reduce such market instability, exchanges occasionally suspend the privilege of placing stop orders.

chapter
19
Clues from the Exchange

Under Stock Exchange rules, the contents of a specialist's book are kept secret. Thus, in making a market, the specialist has access to information that is not available to *anyone* else. If one individual has a monopoly on certain information, the efficient capital market theory holds that investors at large cannot efficiently process that information and thereby neutralize its investment usefulness. Clearly, specialists have monopolistic access to vital trading information that other people, even members on the Exchange floor, cannot see. Theoretically, at least, it *is* possible for specialists to use this information for personal profit.

While it is clear that specialists have unique information in their books, the question remains whether they actually use it to practice profitable investment strategies for their own accounts. This question may be answered, in part, by determining whether price changes for successive trades of NYSE stocks behave according to the random-walk model.

Resistance and Support

The tendency for a stock's price to cluster at particular levels is termed resistance and support by stock market technicians (cf. Edwards and Magee [38]). In economics, the same phenomenon is known as the "Taussig Penumbra," honoring the renowned Harvard University professor, F. W. Taussig, who introduced the concept in 1921 [165]. There are two versions of this clustering phenomenon: congestion and reflection. Congestion implies that a stock's price remains within a particular range for an inordinately large number of transactions. Reflection implies that price levels exist from which a price change in one direction is much more likely than a price change in the other direction.

If a reflection barrier is above the stock's current price, it is called a resistance level. Upon rising to this resistance level, the stock's price would be deemed more likely to turn down again than to be able to penetrate the reflection barrier. If the barrier is below the current price, it is called a support level. Let's explore the general issue: Is there any evidence that stock prices do tend to cluster between support and resistance levels?

In 1962, M. F. M. Osborne brought his training as an astronomer to bear on this issue of stock price clustering. He studied the fractional portion of closing prices for an across-the-market[1] sample of NYSE stocks. Osborne reported: ". . . a pronounced tendency for prices to cluster on whole numbers, halves, quarters, and odd one-eighths in descending preference. . . ." [**136**, p. 287] This means, as we might *intuitively* expect, that stock prices are more likely to close at whole numbers than at odd one-eighth fractions (for example, $12\frac{1}{8}$, $12\frac{3}{8}$, $12\frac{5}{8}$, $12\frac{7}{8}$). Such clustering is *not* consistent with the random-walk model. Thus, the phenomenon technicians refer to as resistance and support might furnish some explanation for the observed price clustering.

Osborne probed this issue further. He studied what he called the "partially reflecting barrier" aspect of resistance and support. He hypothesized that if stock prices moved within reflecting barriers, then their highs and lows would tend to cluster near such barriers. That is, if a stock's price is reflected back down as it rises to whole number levels, we should find the number of daily highs ending in $\frac{7}{8}$ fractions significantly greater than would be expected on a chance basis. Similarly, if prices are reflected back up as they sink to whole numbers, we should find too many daily lows with $\frac{1}{8}$ fractions.

Osborne investigated this line of reasoning. He found that more daily *highs* were at the $\frac{7}{8}$ and $\frac{3}{8}$ fractions than daily lows at the same fractions. Conversely, he found more daily *lows* at the $\frac{1}{8}$ and $\frac{5}{8}$ fractions than daily highs. He interpreted these findings as evidence of price clustering and reflection barriers. Whole number and half-number price levels acted as partially impenetrable barriers. Thus, many stocks had daily highs of $\frac{7}{8}$ or $\frac{3}{8}$ because they were unable to reach the "barrier" price level. Conversely, clustering of lows was observed at price levels just above integers and halves, as at $\frac{1}{8}$ and $\frac{5}{8}$, exhibiting support for

---

[1] Stock market data can be collected in two ways: "sequentially" or "across-the-market." A sequential sample is data on a particular stock collected over time. An across-the-market sample records data on a group of stocks during a single time period. Thus, an across-the-market sample can be drawn from *one* financial page of a newspaper.

sinking prices above these popular price levels. Thus, as stock prices move either up or down toward whole or half numbers there is a tendency for price *reversal* or, in a sense, for resistance or support.

Osborne's curiosity caused him to test if stocks tended to trade at "favorite" whole number prices. For example, is AT&T more likely to trade at 55 than 53 just because people like numbers ending in "5" better than numbers ending in "3"? Of the ten possible digits (0–9) than can occur in the units position of a closing stock price, Osborne tested for unequal occurrence rates. His results, however, showed no tendency for prices to cluster at "favorite" prices [136]. Thus, at the non-fractional price level, no "round number favoritism" forms of nonrandomness were apparent, even though "favorite fractions" were discovered.

In 1964, Victor Niederhoffer, then a promising young honors student in Harvard's Department of Economics, elaborated on Osborne's work in his bachelor's thesis [128]. The portion of Niederhoffer's thesis dealing with stock price clustering—which later drew academic attention (see [129, 130, 132])—confirmed Osborne's results for a much larger sample of stocks.

These early studies provided evidence that, for the fractional price movements of concern to a specialist, *all is not random*. The conclusions from these studies, however, had to be refined. For instance, there was academic concern that testing data from across-the-market samples could not distinguish between different clustering tendencies contingent on the price level of a particular stock. In particular, Osborne's conclusion of "a pronounced tendency for prices to cluster on whole numbers" was based on an across-the-market sample including stocks at many price levels. Suppose, however, that only higher-priced stocks actually cluster at whole numbers. Such clusters could have produced Osborne's results, although his general conclusion would really be true only for high-priced stocks. In any case, researchers set about two tasks: first, devising a theoretical explanation of how the specialist "maintains a fair and orderly market" in a stock which would explain the observed results (see [67, 132]) and secondly, confirming Osborne's and Niederhoffer's limited experimental evidence on stock price clustering (see [67]).

What Could Cause Clustering and "Reflection" Barriers?

Unfortunately, explanations of stock price clustering must be reached deductively because "outsiders" cannot examine the causative process of price movements on the Exchange floor itself. Specialists who execute buy and sell orders on stock exchanges are prohibited under Section 11(b) of the Securities and Exchange Act and NYSE Rule 115 from divulging their "books" to the public. Without access to these records, our theoretical explanation of the clustering phenomenon must be conjecture, which we then seek to verify by what we observe.

To explain price clustering at whole numbers and even fractions, we can advance a conjecture. Suppose that limit orders placed with the specialist occur most frequently at whole numbers, and secondarily at halves or quarters. Human decision makers are known to prefer round numbers (see [84], pp. 187–188). If this conjecture is true, empirical transaction data should disclose clustering of stock prices at whole numbers and, to a lesser degree, at even fractions ($\frac{2}{8}$, $\frac{4}{8}$, $\frac{6}{8}$). Research already cited has shown this to be the case.

This situation presents a lucrative trading opportunity for specialists. Suppose, for example, that the price of our hypothetical stock in Figure 18–5 rises from $45\frac{1}{8}$ to $45\frac{3}{4}$. Higher prices are shown reading down the page in the specialist's book. For such a price rise to occur, all sell-limit orders in the range $45\frac{1}{8}$ to $45\frac{3}{4}$ would have to be executed. Furthermore, since buy-limit orders must be set *below* the current asking price ($45\frac{7}{8}$ after this rise), the buy side of the specialist's book would contain very few buy-limit orders in the $45\frac{1}{8}$ to $45\frac{3}{4}$ range immediately after such a quick rise.

Now the specialist has his trading opportunity. A small cluster of sell-limit orders at 46 and a large cluster of buy-limit orders at 45 would remain. *If* the specialist now sold for his own account, he would push the market back toward the bids at 45 (buy-limit orders) about which he—and *only* he—knows. The specialist can then execute his own buy-limit order at $45\frac{1}{8}$ to cancel his earlier sales. He would make up to a $\frac{3}{4}$ point profit. Conversely, the specialist could reverse the market after declines. By buying stock and placing his own sell-limit order an eighth point below some cluster of sell-limit orders waiting in his book, the specialist has a unique opportunity for "insider" profit. If this technique is indeed practiced, an examination of actual stock trading data will reveal a tendency for prices to reverse after rising to the $\frac{7}{8}$ fraction, and conversely to reverse after declining to the $\frac{1}{8}$ fraction.

What are the facts? Osborne and Niederhoffer, as already reported, developed evidence that stock prices behave as conjectured above. The telltale signs of specialists' trading patterns are like the footprints of foxes in the snow leading to and from the hen house. These "tracks" constitute residual evidence of the feast "inside." Hypotheses of this kind can be tested statistically. The number of various fractional prices observed are compared with the number expected. For example, 8 fractional prices are possible—whole numbers, and ⅛ through ⅞. This fractional classification is displayed in Table 19–1, which shows the frequency of these various fractions for 752 closing prices of a particular stock.

TABLE 19–1
Observed and Expected Frequencies of the Whole Number and Fractional Parts of 752 Closing Prices of Consolidated Cigar Corporation (Oct. 1, 1962–Sept. 27, 1965)

Frequencies	Whole Number	¹/₈	¹/₄	³/₈	¹/₂	⁵/₈	³/₄	⁷/₈
Observed.........	167	34	140	64	138	62	95	52
Expected.........	94	94	94	94	94	94	94	94

The observed frequencies for the 8 possible fractions of 752 closing prices of Consolidated Cigar Corporation are recorded in the first row of Table 19–1. The issue is whether the observed frequencies are compatible with those expected if each fraction is equally likely. Each fraction would be expected to occur about 94 times, or its one-eighth proportion of the 752 closing prices in this illustration. Using a statistical test, it

TABLE 19–2
Occurrence of Clustering in the Fractional Parts of Closing Prices for 764 Stocks Classified by Average Price Range

Average Price Range	Statistically Uncertain Clustering of Fractions	Statistically Significant Clustering
0–9.............	30	66
10–19............	59	77
20–29............	42	78
30–39............	33	105
40–49............	15	100
50–59............	9	64
60–69............	7	33
70–79............	1	22
80–99............	1	12
100–999..........	1	9
Total...........	198	566

is possible to measure the odds that fractional closing prices favor certain fractions. In this illustration, the tendency for prices to close frequently at whole numbers, and to a lesser degree at ½s or ¼s, is clear. Our conjectures about price clustering and specialist behavior are supported.

The statistical findings for 764 major stocks, classified by price range, are summarized in Table 19–2. For example, of the 120 stocks tested which were in the $20–$29 average price range, the tendency for unequal proportions of fractions was statistically significant 78 times and uncertain 42 times. In all, 566 of the 764 stocks exhibited significant clustering. The clustering at whole numbers is more pronounced for higher-priced stocks. In sum, there can be no doubt of this clustering tendency. Furthermore, this "playing the fractions game" is more evident with high-price stocks, for which ⅛ of a point is a lesser percentage of the total price.

Reflection Points Above and Below Whole Number Prices

If limit orders in the specialist's book tend to cluster at whole numbers, as the evidence indicates, we have theorized that it is possible for specialists to use this information for personal trading profits. That is, when a specialist sees a cluster of limit orders, frequently at a whole-number price, he can push the price toward the cluster by trading for his own account. Then, as the market price nears the cluster of *pending* transactions, the specialist can *execute his own order ⅛ point away, producing up to a ¾ point profit!* Furthermore, profits are possible in either direction depending on the balance of orders, which is known only to the specialist and already "on the book."

By examining daily stock market data, we can determine whether specialists *actually* use this technique and run their stocks up and down between full-point or even half-point reflection barriers. That is, if specialists use the privileged information in their "books" to practice the trading scheme outlined, we would expect an unusually large number of intraday highs to occur with ⅞ fractions. Similarly, we would expect an unusually large number of daily lows to occur at ⅛. If, however, the practices of the stock specialists do not create reflection points above and below whole number prices, then equal numbers of daily highs and lows at both ⅛ and ⅞ should prevail.

Again, Osborne's and Niederhoffer's evidence confirms that reflection points exist around whole number prices. But more comprehensive research is also available on this point. One way to study this characteristic of stock price behavior is to count the number of daily highs and lows at ⅛ and ⅞. If the number of highs at ⅛ equals the number of lows at ⅛, their ratio will be 1.0. However, if prices tend to reverse after falling to a ⅛ fraction, then there would be more lows than highs at ⅛. Dividing the number of highs at ⅛ by the number of lows would then produce a ratio consistently less than 1.0. Similarly, if prices tend to reverse after rising to a ⅞ fraction, then the highs-to-lows ratio would be consistently more than 1.0 for the ⅞ fraction. Table 19–3 shows the ratios of (1) the number of daily highs with ⅛ fractions to lows with ⅛ fractions, and (2) the number of daily highs with ⅞ fractions to lows with ⅞ fractions. The table lists a representative portion of the stocks studied as part of this author's doctoral dissertation. As surmised, these data verify the existence of reflection tendencies at whole number prices.

Our *ad hoc* theory of stock price clustering hypothesized that reflection points exist around whole number prices. If a stock declines to a ⅛ fraction, it tends to bounce back up. Thus, the ratios of intraday highs to lows at the ⅛ fraction would be less than 1.0 and at the ⅞ fraction would be greater than 1.0. A cursory inspection of Table 19–3, drawn from this author's 1966 doctoral dissertation [67], looks extremely consistent with this theoretical prediction.[2] Notice that the column showing ratios of highs to lows for ⅛ fractions is dominated by ratios of less than 1.0. Similarly, the ratio of highs to lows for ⅞ fractions are overwhelmingly greater than 1.0.

A closer look at the data in Table 19–3 also reveals some interesting differences between stocks, and hence, their specialists. Note, for example, Homestake Mining Co. Its ratio of highs to lows with ⅛ fractions is 0.38—the lowest on this page of computer output. Similarly, its ratio of highs to lows with ⅞ fractions is 2.15—the highest on the page. At the other extreme, the Hazeltine Corporation has ratios of 0.96 and 1.01—indicating no tendency price reversals at particular fractional levels.

These findings were tabulated by price range for all stocks tested. Results are summarized in Table 19–4. This comparison of ratios clearly supports the reflection-at-whole-numbers hypothesis. For example, intraday lows at the ⅛ fraction exceeded intraday highs at ⅛ for 646 of the 781 stocks shown. The reflection phenomenon, however, is markedly

---

[2] It should be emphasized that while these conclusions are based on a study of 790 stocks that was completed in 1966, the findings have been reaffirmed on a smaller sample, using data through the second quarter of 1973.

TABLE 19–3
Ratios of Highs to Lows for ⅛ and ⅞ Fractional Prices (tabulated by stock)

Stock	H-⅛	L-⅛	Ratio	H-⅞	L-⅞	Ratio	Price
Gustin Bacon Mfg.	63	94	0.67	95	79	1.20	19.
Halliburton Co.	48	70	0.69	86	51	1.69	47.
Hallicrafters Co.	103	75	1.37	115	120	0.96	9.
Hammond Organ Co. . . . . . ˙	69	73	0.95	129	94	1.37	24.
Hanna, M. A. Co.	63	77	0.82	116	58	2.00	35.
Harbison Walker Refrac.	47	75	0.63	85	65	1.31	37.
Harris Intertype Corp.	51	51	1.00	69	40	1.72	47.
Harsco Corp	58	90	0.64	104	78	1.33	36.
Harvey Aluminum, A.	92	98	0.94	88	89	0.99	20.
Hayes Industries, Inc.	73	109	0.67	100	54	1.85	27.
Hazeltine Corp.	109	114	0.96	90	89	1.01	15.
Heinz, H. J. Co.	41	53	0.77	85	47	1.81	44.
Helene Curtis Ind.	84	91	0.92	97	75	1.29	21.
Heller, W. E. & Co.	102	72	1.42	138	112	1.23	14.
Hercules Powder Co.	58	90	0.64	117	74	1.58	42.
Hershey Chocolate Corp.	53	67	0.79	115	59	1.95	34.
Hertz Corporation.	41	95	0.43	107	64	1.67	41.
Hess Oil & Chemical	85	110	0.77	105	88	1.19	13.
Hewlett-Packard Co.	63	112	0.56	103	65	1.58	23.
Hilton Hotels Corp.	81	90	0.90	105	92	1.14	20.
Hoffman Electronics	85	99	0.86	91	86	1.06	8.
Holt Rinehart & Winst.	35	48	0.73	61	43	1.42	30.
Homestake Mining Co.	43	113	0.38	101	47	2.15	47.
Hooker Chemical Corp	65	75	0.87	77	60	1.28	40.
Household Finance Corp.	25	41	0.61	65	50	1.30	55.
Houston Lighting & Power.	36	66	0.55	89	46	1.93	63.
Howe Sound Co.	86	76	1.13	88	67	1.31	12.

Source: Hagin [67].

more pronounced in higher-priced stocks. For example, very few stocks priced above $30 failed to exhibit this tendency. At these higher prices, it is apparently more conscionable or just easier for the specialist to prac- tice the profitable trading strategy we have outlined.

Examination of daily closing prices and intraday highs and lows re- vealed that the majority of stock market transactions occur at popular fractions and whole numbers, and that reflection points exist around these price levels—even in lower-priced stocks. These findings lend credence to the *ad hoc* theory which asserts that the books of stock spe- cialists contain valuable short-term trading information. Similarly, it is apparent from this research that specialists actually can and do use this information for personal gain. The inequity is obvious. In a nation with 31,000,000 consumer-investors, a small group of specialists on the New York and American Stock Exchanges have access to privileged informa-

TABLE 19–4
Ratios of Highs to Lows for ⅛ and ⅞ Fractional Prices
Tabulated by Stock Price Range

Stock Price Range	Ratio of Highs to Lows at ¹/₈		Ratio of Highs to Lows at ⁷/₈	
	Less Than 1	More Than 1	Less Than 1	More Than 1
0–9.	60	59	60	57
10–19.	90	43	28	108
20–29.	102	17	8	112
30–39.	132	6	3	135
40–49.	108	6	2	113
50–59.	70	2	0	73
60–69.	40	0	0	40
70–79.	23	0	0	23
80–99.	12	1	0	13
100–999	9	1	0	9
Total	646	135	101	683

tion. Convincing evidence reveals that these specialists use their privileged information for an extremely profitable personal trading scheme, within their exchange-defined province of "maintaining an orderly market."

Equal Information for "Almost" Everyone

The specialist system is a curious anomaly. Evolving legal theory holds that *all* parties to a stock transaction must have equal access to information. Yet, the exchanges foster the untenable situation whereby specialists, who are free to trade against the public for their own accounts, have "more equal" material information. Further, there is convincing evidence that information in the specialist's book is used for personal profit.

In addition to the material information on supply of and demand for stocks, specialists also receive *advance* notice of news items likely to affect stock prices. The NYSE's "telephone alert" procedure was established in 1967. Compliance by news sources with this procedure was reaffirmed in December 1971 when Merle S. Wick, a vice president of the NYSE, urged the presidents of the approximately 1,400 companies listed on the Big Board to notify the exchange "before the release is made to the press services," of any information "which might reasonably be expected to affect the market price of the company's listed securities."

Mr. Wick's letter further asserted that forewarning the exchange of material news is "recognized as an important step to provide fairness to all those participating in the market." [193]

The NYSE seems to equate the need to maintain fair and orderly markets with allowing specialists an unfair competitive advantage over the public. Unquestionably, the market-making mechanism must buffer temporarily unbalanced buy or sell orders triggered by news announcements. The NYSE's system for accomplishing this buffering, however, has many inherent flaws.[3]

What Investors Should Do

It is tempting to inveigh against the inequities of the specialist system. Our thesis is, however, that the new science of investing allows us to extract our own *private* information from public knowledge. From our analysis of the specialist's book and the clustering phenomena we can conclude that a stock is much more likely to rise to the next ⅞ fraction than the whole number. Similarly, we can conclude that the probability of a stock's falling to the next ⅛ is much more likely than its falling to the whole number. Hence, if certain orders are placed at these fractions, *one stands a better-than-average chance of improving purchase and sale prices.*

---

[3] The authors believe the current flaws in market mechanics will soon be eliminated through automation. We have devised a plan, to be included as part of a future publication, for an automated central market place called IT (Instantaneous Transactions).

part II

applying the new science to personal investing

A KNOWING WHAT TO EXPECT

chapter
20
A Performance Bench Mark

The element of the new science of investing that has so far had the most significant impact on professional investing has been the so-called beta revolution. Beta, properly called the beta coefficient, is a mathematical expression of the degree to which a stock, or a group of stocks, moves with the overall market. Seeded by the ideas in John von Neumann's and Oskar Morgenstern's seminal 1940 book, *The Theory of Games and Economic Behavior* [170], the beta measure of comovement was brought to fruition by Harry Markowitz. Now labeled "the father of the beta," Markowitz began his search for a quantifiable measure of risk while a doctoral student in economics at the University of Chicago. After much careful research, Markowitz formalized the concept in a 1952 paper [113] and later elaborated on the idea in his own, now classic, book, entitled *Portfolio Selection: Efficient Diversification of Investments* [112], which was published in 1959.

While Markowitz's concept was attracting little public attention, it was generating widespread academic interest. By 1968, the *Financial Analysts Journal* listed a bibliography of 253 articles and papers, and 89 books and pamphlets on the subject. Curiously, however, in spite of Wall Street's fanatic search for the newest ideas, the notion of beta was not really noticed by the investment profession until 1971. Even then, it was literally forced upon the investment community by the banking industry, which used it to show the public the length of the risk pendulum on which go-go money management swings.

To illustrate the suddenness with which the beta revolution overtook Wall Street, Chris Welles began an outstanding article in the September 1971 issue of the magazine *Institutional Investor* with " 'If you had told me six months ago that Wall Street would go crazy over something called a beta coefficient,' says a somewhat flabbergasted security analyst, 'I would have said you were totally off your rocker. But, by God, that's what's happened.' " Describing the revolution's unexpected assault on the Wall Street fortress, Welles noted "an obscure statistical term which has lurked quietly and innocuously for 20 years in abstruse, equation-filled scholarly journals, the beta coefficient over the past year, with remarkable force and suddenness, has staged a massive assault on the real world of investing." [**172**, p. 21]

Unfortunately, like much of the research that emanates from universities, the beta concept was not, and in many cases is still not, well understood by many investment professionals. On the other hand, as in the case of most of the concepts of the new science of investing, it is rare to find a professional who really understands the beta concept who does not also believe in its usefulness.

Without minimizing the significance of the voluminous beta research, it is fair to say that the concept is relatively simple. Beta is simply a measure of market risk. We know that some portion of a stock's price movement can be explained by the movement of the market as a whole. By comparing a stock's, or a portfolio's, volatility over a period of time with the volatility of a representative market average, it is possible to specify how this investment has reacted to overall market fluctuations. Since such volatility is remarkably stable over time, beta measures based on past behavior are reasonably reliable indicators of future volatility.

The beta calculation can be thought of as a comparison of the market's movement with a stock's, or a portfolio's, overall movement. The calculation begins by assigning a beta equal to 1.0 for the fluctuations of some representative market index. If a stock, or a portfolio, has a beta equal to 2.0, it means that it has been twice as volatile as the overall market index. Similarly, if a stock or a portfolio has a beta of 0.5, it means that it has historically been only half as volatile as the overall market. But beta does more than just designate the portion of an investment's price movement that can be attributed to changes in the overall market: it tells us the degree to which an investment, or a portfolio, has *amplified* or *dampened* the market effect.

Beta theorists correctly hold that a price change is made up of beta (the market-related movement) and "everything else." The basic industry comovement, the subindustry comovement, and the movement attributable to the company contribute to "everything else" and are labeled "alpha" by the beta theorists.

According to the beta theory, there are two ways to attain above-average performance. One way is to forecast overall market moves and adjust your beta accordingly. That is, you can *double* the market's appreciation with a 2.0 beta in an up market. Risk's double-edged sword, in beta terms, means that a 2.0 beta in a down market will give you double the market loss.

The other way to secure better-than-average performance, according to the beta theory, is to obtain a high alpha. That is, derive your performance from something other than the fact that you have ridden the market's coattail. Unfortunately, while beta—the historical amplification or dampening of market comovement—tends to be persistent over time, alpha does not!

In summary then, beta is a mathematical measure of an investment's historical sensitivity to the overall market. Because such sensitivity tends to persist over time, beta is a reasonable estimate of an investment's *future* sensitivity to overall market movements. Readers should be cautioned, however, not to become enamored with the wizardry of mathematics and a computer's ability to calculate beta to several decimal places. When asked to comment on the calculation of beta to *two* decimal places, Professor Merton Miller at the University of Chicago's business school offered a succinct "Fooey!"

Placed in its proper perspective, the beta coefficient serves two important functions. It can be used

- to dissect past performance records to determine the portion of the return that can be explained by market comovement, and
- to predict the degree to which a stock's future performance can be expected to dampen or amplify the market's overall movements.

One obvious shortcoming of beta analysis is the problem of how to handle the undissected alpha. We know, for example, that a rate of return is derived as follows:

Rate of Return	=	Market Sensitivity	+	Basic Industry Sensitivity	+	Industry Subgroup Sensitivity	+	How the Company Distinguishes Itself from Its Competition
		Beta				Alpha		

In spite of notions like the random walk, efficient capital market, and beta, some people outperform the market. Yet, when many people "play the game," some *must* win. Being the growth winner does not necessarily imply that the investment selection process was responsible for the winning results. Even if all mutual funds, for instance, were to select their stocks in a completely random fashion, some mutual fund would still outperform all others. Investors hear much about so-and-so's "expert performance." But how much is luck, as in roulette, and how much is attributable to skill? A comparison of the investment performance which *should* occur, and the results which actually *do* occur, holds the answer.

The Performance Bench Mark

What investment results would you expect from an experiment that randomly selected thousands of separate portfolios, each containing exactly 25 stocks chosen from an eligible list of many stocks? You would expect these portfolios to have different results. Although each portfolio would tend toward the market's average performance, some portfolios would, by chance, do better than others. Such differences can be represented by a bell-shaped, or "normal," curve. The performance results one would expect from the purely random selection of many portfolios are shown by such a curve in Figure 20–1.

Understanding what is expected to happen from purely random portfolios is very important in interpreting modern stock market research. Such "no skill," random investment selection provides a bench mark against which to measure the investment results actually obtained by "skilled professionals." The performance of most random portfolios is expected to cluster around some average. Purely by chance, some portfolios are expected to perform very well. Others, by chance, are expected to provide comparatively poor results.

The Consumer-Investor's Viewpoint

The efficient capital market theory states that, at any moment in time, a stock's price fully reflects everything known about that stock. According to this theory, no publicly available information can be used to predict future price movements accurately. If this concept of stock market behavior is correct, the performance attained by even "skilled investors"

FIGURE 20–1
Expected Distribution of Performance for Many
Separate, Random Portfolios

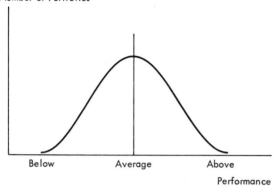

Number of Portfolios

Below   Average   Above

Performance

will not differ significantly from the performance attained by the totally unskilled, or random, selection depicted in Figure 20–1.

The efficient capital market theory questions the value of the investment management profession. An industry based on the value of investment advice is braced against the weight of research evidence concluding that much advice is useless. This careful assessment of the value of investment advice—both inside and outside the investment profession—is destined to impact dramatically on the future of the investment industry. In the decade ahead, knowledgeable consumer-investors can facilitate many needed changes.

Unfortunately, the apparent complexity of Wall Street frightens away many would-be consumer advocates. But, anyone intimidated by the rigorous techniques of modern stock market research should also remember that very few consumers actually understand the detailed chemical formula of DDT. In fact, the average citizen cannot even recite what "DDT" stands for. This does not preclude him, however, from studying the differing opinions of experts, debating DDT's benefits and dangers, and coming to well-reasoned conclusions.

As our society grows more complex, involved and interested citizens must assume an increasingly responsible role in "finding out" about such things as breakfast cereals, drug hazards, DDT, the SST *and* the efficient capital market theory. In most such cases, the consumer will be faced with situations where the "experts" disagree. Indeed, if this were not the case, there would be nothing to debate. Choosing solutions would be simple. But when there is debate, while it is not an infallible rule, the consumer advocate should ask, "who has the vested interest?"

The research reported in this book was conducted largely by university professors. As a group, it is fair to say that university scholars have no vested interest in maintaining the status quo on Wall Street. Meanwhile, if we look at the batting average of traditional Wall Street research it is 0 for 3—having struck out on theoretical, statistical, and historical tests.

Actually, the three methodological approaches cited above are not easily separable. Yet, of the three, the contention by academic researchers that the traditional approach of Wall Street's "experts" has *historically failed* to achieve results that are better than mere chance is *intuitively* the most difficult to accept. This historical failure is, of course, the capstone to the case against the existence of "experts." Is it historically true that the time-honored approaches of investment professionals have not beaten the market? What about the fact that some people *did* outperform the market? Can this apparent contradiction be explained?

What Performance Should Be

Suppose the performance of portfolios selected by investors is compared with the performance of portfolios put together by purely random selection. Such a comparison could yield one of several different outcomes. A result that would clearly support the efficient capital market theory would be if no significant difference existed between the investment returns attained by actual investors and the returns attained by purely random selection. If such were the case, investors could just as well have used *darts* rather than advisory services for their investment selections. Of course, deducting the cost of darts for tax purposes is a little more suspect than deducting expenses for advisory services!

Another possible outcome of our performance comparison experiment might be that the *average* performance of actual investors would again equal the average return attained from random selection, but that results of actual investors would *cluster more* around that same average performance. This would mean that fewer real investors would end up with investment returns as extreme as the performance results attained by random portfolio selection. This possible case is shown in Figure 20–2.

What could cause the possible comparative performance depicted in Figure 20–2? These results—the same average performance, but with less variations in the performance of actual investors—could be attained if investors could not accurately forecast the market, yet did an especially

FIGURE 20–2
Possible Performance Outcome of Random Selection
of Portfolios Compared with Actual Investor Portfolios
Number of Portfolios

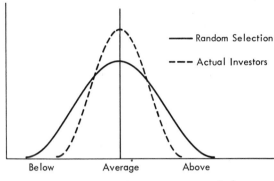

good job of protecting against performance swings (a rather unlikely assumption). While the investors in this hypothetical case could not beat the market average, they successfully defended against the risk of much deviation from this level of average performance.

Let's review another, more plausible, potential outcome of our performance comparison experiment. Suppose, in practice, investors do *not* diversify or spread their investments around as much as by purely random selection of 25 stocks for a portfolio. The investor who buys only computer-related companies puts "all of his eggs in one industry basket." The investor who "understands" the oil industry or "likes" airlines tends also to diversify *less* than random selection. In these cases his portfolio contains an extremely high degree of industry risk. His portfolio performance results would be characterized by wider deviations about the average value than randomly selected, and more diversified, portfolios. This possible experimental observation is represented in Figure 20–3.

The bell-shaped curve drawn with the solid line in Figure 20–3 again represents the expected performance results from many, purely random portfolios. The dashed line shows the more widely varying investment results of *less* diversified actual portfolios. The dashed-line portfolios do not "hug" the vertical line of average performance as much as the random portfolios. This is so because undiversified portfolios are relatively more subject to wide swings in performance due to special circumstances, caused by industry or company factors. Thus, actual investor results would be fanned out in both the good and bad directions. This experi-

FIGURE 20–3
Performance Comparison for Little
Diversification
Number of Portfolios

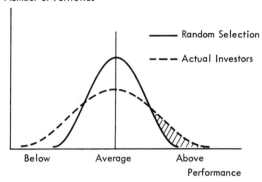

mental outcome would occur if actual investors tended to prefer the
more volatile (hence, widely varying) stocks and/or diversified less than
the random portfolios by confining portfolio stock selections to a few
industries.

Notice that in Figure 20–3 many investors perform *better* than they
would have performed if they had relied on random selection. This better-than-random performance is shown in the cross-hatched area on
the right side of Figure 20–3. Unfortunately, by tending to select risky
stocks or to diversify inadequately, many investors would also perform
worse than the results attained by random selection. In fact, in our hypothetical situation, the number of actual investors doing worse than
random might exactly counterbalance the number of investors who
appear to have done better than random. As we will see in the next
chapter, such apparently "good" performance by some investors is "all
a matter of risk." The gamble for high returns carries the concomitant
risk of high losses. In this case, the actual investors simply chose to take a
more risky course of action than random selection. In our experiment,
which forces each investor to pick exactly 25 stocks for his portfolio, the
possible outcome shown in Figure 20–3 would indicate that investors
concentrated their 25 selections in a few industries and/or selected high-
volatility stocks. Their average performance is shown as no better nor
worse than random performance. Rather, it is more widely varying, and
hence risky, around that average.

chapter
21
It Is All a Matter of Risk

The success of some investors is one of the most heart-warming things about the stock market. In the face of the efficient capital market theory, which holds that it is difficult to have more knowledge than that already processed by the market, some people *do* perform. Unfortunately, there are many misconceptions about performance. The public is often not aware of the implications of this performance and the *risk* involved in trying to attain it.

Consider, for a moment, the chance that a blue-chip stock, like General Motors or American Telephone and Telegraph, would have of either doubling or halving the value of one's investment in the next year. The risk-reward structure that is inherent in blue-chip securities is usually more balanced than that found in something like "Fly-By-Night Electronics, Inc." If "Fly-By-Night" boomed, it could conceivably double your investment next year or sooner. If things went badly for "Fly-By-Night," you could lose substantially in a few months. Some stocks are simply more risky than others. Generally, the potential for extraordinary gain is accompanied by the potential for extraordinary loss.

How to Perform—Maybe

Imagine two hypothetical fund managers, one who invests in stocks of mature companies traded on the New York Stock Exchange and one who invests smaller amounts of money in a large number, say 300, of highly speculative stocks of small companies. Now, suppose we go back to the mid-1960s and consider the performance we would have expected from each fund manager. In the rapidly expanding economy of the mid-

1960s, phenomenal successes materialized in some small, unknown firms. Perhaps as important, investors zealously rewarded "growth" with increasingly rich stock price valuations.

As we would expect, during this period the price increases in the highly speculative stocks far outpaced the gains returned by mature blue-chip securities. With 20–20 hindsight, we would *expect* any fund manager who invested his clients' money in highly speculative stocks during the middle and late 1960s to have had a "performance" record that far outpaced the record of a fund manager who concentrated on less glamorous securities. Notice, however, that merely reporting the *performance* of these two fund managers is not fair. The issue of performance cannot be separated from the issue of risk.

The Story of Fred Carr

The preceding example of two fund managers' differing performance is not as artificial as one might imagine. Once upon a time there was a mutual fund manager named Fred Carr. Carr's investment philosophy was to specialize in what he called "emerging growth companies." In fact, his Enterprise Fund ". . . made itself famous by specializing in tiny OTC companies with thin capitalizations that nobody ever heard of, that have a way of roaring up like skyrockets and down like punctured balloons. . . ." [**81,** p. 33] In our rapidly expanding economy Fred Carr was golden! He bought Kentucky Fried Chicken at an adjusted price of $3.50 and watched it go above $50. He acquired a position in Republic Corporation at $5 and later sold above $60. In fact, Fred Carr's Enterprise Fund was the only mutual fund to rank among the nation's top 25 performers for *6 straight years.* In 1967 alone, the value of Enterprise shares jumped 116 percent, followed by another 44 percent gain in 1968. Carr was a "star" in the performance arena.

There was only one thing wrong with Carr's performance. It ended. Fred Carr was playing one of the most risky "games" a money manager can play. In the latter half of 1969, our red-hot economy slowed down. Carr's "emerging growth companies" led the slowdown. As the hot air burst from his balloons, the value of the Enterprise Fund tumbled. Enterprise Fund finished 1969 with a performance that failed to match the Dow Jones Industrial Average, and 1970 was worse. Did Enterprise Fund really *perform?*

It's All a Matter of Risk—What's Risk?

There are several different types of risk: business risk, market risk, interest-rate risk, liquidity risk, and purchasing-power risk. Further, these basic risks can be magnified by leverage, or the use of borrowed money. Both the type and amount of risk varies greatly between one investment and another. Yet, whether the investment decision is to hold cash or to gamble with very speculative stocks, it will involve some form of risk.

Business Risk. Not all firms that issue bonds remain solvent long enough to repay their obligations. Not all firms that issue stock reward their investors with profitable performance. Many factors may affect the profitability or ultimate solvency of an enterprise. When an investor purchases a company's securities, he shares the risk of the future prosperity or solvency of the business.

An investor assumes little business risk in United States government bonds or the bonds of broad-based, well-financed, blue-chip corporations like AT&T. It is very doubtful that these institutions will, in the foreseeable future, lack the capacity to pay their obligations. It is important to realize, however, that all profit-seeking enterprises face some degree of business risk.

The extent of business risk depends on a variety of factors which may be either exogenous or endogenous to the enterprise. Exogenous factors, which are not under the control of the company's management, nevertheless can influence earning power. Such factors include competition, changes in demand, government policies, etc. The very important endogenous elements are subsumed under the elusive rubric of "management," with the firm's future dependent in part on management's ability to guide the organization successfully in a changing environment. Because every business faces uncertainty with regard to its future earning power, the investor assumes similar business risk when he invests in a company.

Market Risk. As we have seen, the fortunes of the overall market have a significant impact on the performance of individual securities. In the short run, the market effect coupled with investors' collective judgment on a given firm's industry usually outweighs the significance of business risk alone. It is clear that a great company in a bad securities market makes a poor investment.

Interest-Rate Risk.   Most investments provide current income such as bond interest, stock dividends, rents, etc. Overall return is augmented or lessened by the difference, either positive or negative, between the selling price and the purchase price. The relative desirability of an investment's current income varies over time. Fluctuations in the interest rate (the rental charge for money) reflect changing supply of and demand for this "commodity." Furthermore, the desirability of an investment reflects its adjudged future ability to pay income or provide capital gain.

If interest rates rise, a bond paying a fixed return will be relatively less desirable than other alternatives until its price falls to a new level in equilibrium with comparable investments. Thus, bond prices fall as interest rates rise. The value of current dividends or rents is similarly diminished if alternative investments begin to pay more.

An important related factor is the maturity date of the investment. Short-term bonds will not fluctuate much in price because the fixed-sum loan repayment lies in the not-too-distant future. As long as the repayment is assured (reflecting elements of company or market risk), the bond price will not drift far from the solid anchor of a fixed final payment. Long-term bonds maturing in 20, 30, or even more years, however, can swing substantially in price when interest rates change.

Ownership securities are usually assumed to have an infinite life as they do under the law. Buildings and other real property typically also have long life. Accordingly, stocks and other investments with an anticipated long life span are subject to substantial interest rate risks. Stock or real estate price swings, however, are often somewhat mitigated by simultaneously changing *expectations* of future income and future value, whereas bonds are much more certain in regard to future income payout and principal repayment. If interest rates rise, but future dividends or rents are expected to rise as well, the asset's price may not drop at all. Interest rate risk in stocks may be offset by rising *expectations about the future.*

Liquidity Risk.   Liquidity is the degree to which an investment can be quickly converted into cash. Liquidity risk, therefore, is the possibility of sustaining a loss from current value just by the process of converting or "liquidating" the asset into cash. There is the further risk in some investments of not being able to liquidate at any price.

For the average investor, a few hundred shares of an NYSE company can be considered a highly liquid holding. But an institution holding 100,000 shares of even a large company will have a perceptible impact on the market when it desires to sell as, indeed, it also does when it buys. Mutual funds sometimes find that a major portion of their holdings cannot be liquidated without significant reduction in value, such as 5 percent, just from the process of liquidation. Investors who hold or buy "letter stock," which carries transfer restrictions, sometimes find absolutely no market at all when they wish to liquidate such positions.

Purchasing-Power Risk. We hear a lot about inflation these days, and its threat to certain investors is indeed serious. It is startling to realize, for example, that the purchasing power of the 1940 dollar had shrunk by 1973 to under $0.40.

Economists attribute our inflationary spiral to various causes. The champions of industry like to blame inflationary pressures on "wage push" inflation. They contend that sharp increases in labor costs push prices higher. Conversely, as we might expect, labor union economists blame our inflation spiral on a "profit push" tendency of Big Business to raise the prices they set. Other economists attribute the inflationary malady to "demand pull" inflation resulting from too much money chasing too few goods. As this process continues, demand pulls prices up. Still others contend that the government's deficit spending lifts price levels by boosting consumption pressures faster than the available supply of goods and services can grow to meet the accelerating demand. Whatever the cause, inflation means that, as an investor, you are like Alice in Wonderland: "If you want to keep in the same place you must run. If you want to go someplace else, you must run twice as fast."

Consider the investor who puts $10,000 in a bank a 5 percent interest and plans to spend his principal and $500 of interest income after one year. During severe inflation, while this investor's money is *earning* 5 percent a year, the purchasing power of the principal and accumulating interest is *losing* nearly 5 percent a year. In terms of purchasing power, capital has been preserved but not increased. Moreover, income tax is due on the interest income, further reducing the apparent return on investment. Indeed, "to get ahead, you must run even faster." But, how can an investor achieve desirable *real* returns without incurring undue risks?

How Much Risk for "You"?

An investment manager is likely to ask the following question: "Is your investment objective to ensure the safety of your principal or to aim for capital appreciation?" The investor stereotype connoted by the phrase "widows and orphans" exhorts a prudent money manager to exhibit paramount concern for the safety of the investor's principal. On the other hand, the stereotype described by "wealthy young bachelor" will exude the opposite response from many money managers. Most of us, however, fall neither into the "widows and orphans" nor the "wealthy young bachelor" category. We are interested in investments which offer both protection of principal and a high potential for capital appreciation.

It is a fact of life that one must incur risks in order to get the opportunity to make profits. Becoming a better investor requires *using your own risk preferences* to select among available investment alternatives. But how *should* this personal attitude toward risk affect investment choices? What has the blend of modern research on risk and stock price behavior discovered that is useful in the process of investment decision making?

When one considers the wealth of exciting stock market research that has emerged in the last decade, perhaps the most far-reaching has been the explicit integration of concepts of risk and uncertainty into the framework of investment analysis. Yet, before reviewing this recent research, we should first briefly define what is meant by risk.

While most people are not overtly aware of the process, they are continually selecting among alternative decisions on the basis of the risk involved in attaining their objectives. The somewhat classic example of risk-return preferences is provided by contrasting insurance with gambling. When a person buys insurance he decides to avoid the risk of uncertain events. By paying insurance premiums, an individual accepts a loss in the amount of the premium for the certainty that he will be insured against further loss. When people purchase insurance they are choosing it over other investment alternatives. Contrast this purchase of insurance with placing a $2 bet on a long shot at the horse races. This two-dollar gambler is risking the loss of his relatively small wager against the slim chance that he will win big. In effect, he has made a very risky investment.

Similarly, if one selects a career in government civil service, income is almost assured to remain within certain limits. On the other hand, a motion picture actor chooses to be subject to extremes in compensation. There is a small probability that an actor will earn a phenomenal salary. But there is also a high chance that he will earn extremely little. The actor's "return" is highly variable.

Selecting risk in the stock market is somewhat like selecting among alternative risks in occupations. Some stocks' prices tend to remain relatively stable. Others, like motion picture acting, offer highly uncertain returns. *Risk* is related to the *uncertainty* of the investment and the possibility of outcomes that adversely affect the investor's objective.

Volatility, Uncertainty, and Risk

When an investor makes a decision to buy or sell a particular stock, his action impacts on the dynamics of demand and supply for the stock. This action can, but does not have to, cause the price of the stock to move up or down. As investors' confidence fluctuates, so will stock prices. Thus, the uncertainty of investors at large is reflected in something that can be measured—the volatility of stock price changes. While J. P. Morgan reminded us (when asked what the market will do) that, "it will fluctuate"—not all stocks fluctuate the same.

Would you feel "safer" in a stock that typically had daily price changes of 0.5 percent or one that had wide daily swings of as much as 10 percent? Intuitively, most investors would feel an extra margin of safety in a stock that experienced relatively stable price movements. Indeed, this "intuition" is borne out by modern research. It is correct to conclude that the stocks that have been volatile in the past will continue to be volatile in the future. This means that a security analyst can *predict* which stocks will be volatile—and therefore risky—from an analysis of historical data.

Modern research has also concluded that a stock selected from a particular *risk* category (for example, the stocks of large NYSE firms) cannot be expected to behave much differently than the average of the group! After analyzing such data, Brealey has concluded:

. . . in any year approximately 50% of high-grade stocks will provide their owners with a return that differs by less than 12½% from the group average, and 75% of these stocks will provide their owners with a return that is within a range of 25% either side of the average. Such figures are very rough, indeed, but they do suggest that, unless dealing costs are very low, the majority of stocks at any one time offer very limited opportunities for even the most able investor to increase his profitability by trading. They therefore raise serious questions about the advisability of a very active trading policy. For the same reason, any investment organization that expects its research staff to comment on, or to generate, a constant flow of suggestions is probably inefficiently structured. [12, p. 41]

This evidence shows not only that the stable stocks tend to remain stable, but also that there is surprisingly little variance in the performance of portfolios composed of stocks with similar risk characteristics.

chapter
22
Predicting Risk

Intuitively, it seems correct that risk persists over time and is predictable. It is logical that a well-diversified, conservatively financed, mature company that has exhibited low risk in the past would continue to exhibit low risk in the future. If this premise is correct, one could study the riskiness or variability of a stock's past price behavior and then predict its future riskiness. Yet, brokers talk very little about risk. Therefore, how much risk should *you* take—and when?

Several scholars have studied the role of risk. One outstanding contribution was Shannon Pratt's doctoral dissertation at Indiana University in 1966. Pratt's research concerned the relationship between risk and rate of return on common stocks. He asked, "Is the investor who is willing to assume a greater risk in his investments compensated for such risk by a higher *average* return? Will an investor who continually seeks risky investments be rewarded for such an investment strategy or will he be destroyed by losses?" As a step in the research, Pratt investigated the question at hand: Will stocks that are the most volatile (hence risky) in one time period persist in being the most volatile in the next period?

To test this question, Pratt hypothesized the existence of five investors, each with differing attitudes toward risk. Pratt wanted to observe what would have happened if five such investors selected the stocks in their portfolios purely on the basis of their price volatility (that is, risk) over the prior three years. Using as many as 992 stocks and 372 portfolio selection (buy and sell) dates, Pratt devised the following experiment: First, he arrayed all of the stocks which might be included in the portfolio, say 992, on the basis of risk. Stocks with the least risk were put at the top of the list, and those with the highest risk were put at the bottom of the list. Pratt divided this list of stocks into five groups designated "A" through "E." Thus, the stocks in group A comprised the lowest-risk group, while the stocks in group E comprised the highest-risk group.

Pratt confined his hypothetical investors to choices among stocks purely on the basis of historical risk (that is, volatility). Thus, the most conservative investor would select a portfolio composed of stocks that had been the least risky in the past (group A). Similarly, the investor with the highest-risk posture would select stocks for his portfolio only from group E, which showed the highest variability in the past. By dividing his sample into five, equal-size groups, one fifth of the stocks were assigned as possible portfolio stocks to each of his five hypothetical investors.

Pratt's findings support our intuition. Portfolios composed of stocks which had been less variable in the preceding three years produced fewer losses. Table 22–1, which has been abstracted from Pratt's dissertation, shows that an investor's probability of gain tended to increase as he held portfolios with stock which had greater historical variability. Pratt also confirmed that volatility (hence risk) does persist over time.

TABLE 22–1
Subsequent Returns Received from Portfolios of Stocks
Selected on the Basis of Prior Volatility

	One-Year Return (by percent)	Three-Year Return, Annual Rate (by percent)
Investor A	9.8	10.8
Investor B	11.0	12.8
Investor C	11.2	13.5
Investor D	11.2	13.6
Investor E	10.9	13.2

Source: Pratt [138, p. 82].

Risk and Return—A Balancing Act

Why do investors incur risk? Risks are undertaken because investors expect to be rewarded accordingly. Even gambling can be explained on the basis of rewarding people for their risks. While the "rewards" derived from Las Vegas generally are not monetarily sufficient, most gamblers would testify that the excitement derived from the casinos is sufficient extra "compensation." Investors, however, expect to be compensated monetarily for risks which they voluntarily assume.

This raises another question that has been carefully researched: Is it true that investors are compensated according to the risks that they assume? Conceptually, we should be able to define an entire spectrum of investments on the basis of risk.

Consider, for example, the difference between common stocks and bonds of a particular enterprise. Common stocks, the inherently more risky investment, have historically yielded higher *average* rates of return than bonds, which are, of course, the inherently safer investment vehicle.

Are investors compensated for risk? Yes! As we would suspect, modern research has shown that investors who are willing to assume higher levels of risk will, in general, and assuming fairly long investment periods, receive higher average returns. Shannon Pratt and other researchers reviewed here have validated the proposition that people are rewarded with higher returns when they are willing to hold more risky portfolios. Recall that Pratt's experiment sought to compare the returns from five progressively more risky sets of portfolios. The returns attained from these portfolios are shown in Table 22–1 for both one-year and three-year holding periods.

Are investors compensated *enough* for risk? In addressing this question, researchers are interested in the relationship between risk and return on common stocks. One *possible* relationship is shown in Figure 22–1. The graph shows that an investment of "no risk" should offer some

FIGURE 22–1
Relationship between Risk and Expected Return
If Expected Return Increases *Proportionately* with
Risk

Risk

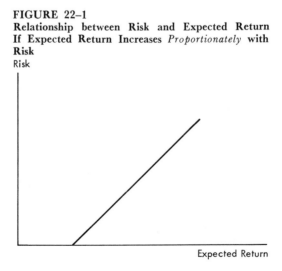

Expected Return

rate of return. In that case the investor's expectation of the outcome is assured with certainty, by the definition of "no risk." As the investor accepts more risk, he expects higher returns. Here, an investor would be willing to move to progressively more risky investments, if for each move he was compensated by a *proportionate* increase in his expected return. Hence, the relationship is represented by a straight line, with expected return increasing uniformly as the risk level rises.

Some economic theorists have suggested, however, that moving to progressively higher risk positions past some point is *undesirable*. If this is so, a rational investor could be enticed to assume such high risks only if he had the hope of attaining an *extra* margin of expected return as he entered into increasingly uncertain investments. If that suggested relationship held true, the risk-return diagram would look like Figure 22–2. As risk increases, larger and larger returns must be available as a necessary incentive to invest.

FIGURE 22–2
**Relationship between Risk and Expected Return
If Increases in Risk are Compensated by *More
Than Proportional* Increases in Expected Returns**
Risk

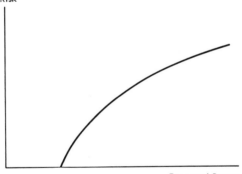

Expected Return

The actual behavior of investors does not follow either of these "rational" descriptions. Pratt's research showed that, as an investor moved to more risky investments, he generally did expect a higher return. But the expected extra returns were, contrary to our intuition, *not commensurate* with the increased amounts of risk. This relationship is shown graphically in Figure 22–3. A miserly additional return results from substantially increased risk. Looking at the expected return per unit of additional risk, it does not appear that investors are fairly compensated for their willingness to assume high-risk postures!

FIGURE 22–3
Relationship between Risk and Expected
Return Showing That Increases in Risk
Are *Not* Compensated by Proportional
Increases in Expected Return

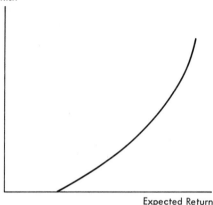

Why doesn't high-risk investment result in proportionately higher return? The stock market is made up of people. People, it turns out, are
very poor estimators of long-odds bets. Analysis of the behavior of bettors
at the horse races, for instance, reveals that people overbet the long shots.
This proclivity extends broadly throughout human behavior. We favor
the underdog. The result in the stock market is that many investors seek
high return through high risk. As in other markets, this excessive competition lowers the return for all.

Substantial evidence in support of this phenomenon has been provided
by William Sharpe in several outstanding pieces of research. In one of
these studies Sharpe [150] was concerned with the performance of 34
mutual funds between 1954 and 1963. Naturally, there were differences
among the results of the various mutual funds. As we have mentioned,
however, the investor tends to be sold on "performance," with little regard for "risk." Sharpe was interested in the relationship between the
performance of the various mutual funds and the differences in risk assumed by them. He found that 70 percent of the difference in rate of
return between funds could be explained solely by their different
riskiness!

In 1967, George Douglas [36] in his doctoral dissertation at Yale University provided additional support for this finding. The same results
were also reported by Fred Arditti [3]. In effect, each of these scholars
was confirming that the higher the risk, the higher the *average* return.

Of course, any particular high-risk portfolio might do very well or very poorly. The long-term *average* return of such portfolios did, however, exceed the average performance of less risky portfolios.

Through all of this research the recurrent question arose: Are investors compensated *enough* for the risks that they assume? Upon reinspection of Table 22–1, one gets the rather uneasy feeling that the increasing returns are *not commensurate* with the increasing level of risk. In fact, investor E's portfolio produces a *lower* average return than investor D's portfolio. Is this indicative of something meaningful about risk? Various statistical tests applied by Brealey to data from these earlier studies tended to confirm that increasing levels of risk do not provide sufficient additional return [**12**, p. 49–51]. Brealey concludes, although with less than absolute statistical certainty, that rate of return "premiums received on high-risk stocks have tended, in retrospect, to be inadequate." [**12**, p. 54]

Conclusions for the Investor

The goal of an investor is to maximize the rate of return from his assets *for a given level of risk*. Evidence supports the conclusion that increased risk (at least among stocks of the quality listed on national exchanges) generally does produce increased average return. Happily, the risk level of a stock is highly predictable—it corresponds to its price volatility in the recent past. Unfortunately, however, it also appears that high-risk securities do not proportionately compensate the investor for his extra risk.

This research does not mean that investors seeking high rates of return may not, on occasion, find them. It means, in fact, that higher risk, more volatile stocks are more likely to produce higher *average* returns. However, such risky stocks, by definition, are most likely also to provide *wide variation* (up and down) from the average results of such risk-oriented portfolios. Further, it is seriously questionable whether the extra *average* returns of a risk-stock strategy compensate adequately for the increased likelihood of wildly varying results.

Stated simply, it is easy to find risky stocks which, with luck, will do better than average. But the "performance" that results is overwhelmingly the direct result only of risks taken—risks possibly unjustified by hoped for extra return. It takes little investment skill to produce "performance" in bull markets when picking high-risk securities is the only technique used. True performance measurement, therefore, must consider risk.

part II
applying the new science to personal investing

B BALANCING PERFORMANCE AND RISK

chapter

23
How About "Superior" Performance?

"Superior" performance has been a two-edged sword. First, the traditional approach to seeking a higher-than-average return has been to buy speculative stocks. The evidence indicates, however, that speculative stocks subject investors to *undue* risks. (Alternative investment approaches that can provide comparable returns—with less risk—are discussed in Section C, "Analyzing Alternative Investment Instruments.") Secondly, most good portfolio "performance," when it occurs, can be traced directly to inherent riskiness. These two points—that speculative stocks tend to be overbet long shots not offering returns commensurate with their risk, *and* that portfolio riskiness largely dictates subsequent performance— raise serious questions about the ascendance of Wall Street's "stars." This chapter focuses on performance. To understand and measure portfolio results properly, however, we need to discuss them in terms of statistics—not hunches or intuition.

Statistics—The Antithesis of Intuition

The word *statistics* connotes bewildering volumes of numbers arranged in imposing tables describing virtually anything from births to deaths. This interpretation reflects use of the word *statistics* to describe numerical facts or data, for example, the "statistics" on this year's Rose Bowl game. On Wall Street, especially to the old-timers, a statistician is one of the faceless drones who compile charts, tables, and graphs in a windowless office.

To the majority of college and university students today, the word *statistics* has a far different connotation. To them, it is usually a one-

213

semester obstacle between matriculation and graduation. As these students know, present-day statisticians do not spend their time compiling almanacs. Modern statistics is a vital tool of scientific inquiry. Statisticians often must evaluate the reliability of conclusions drawn in the face of uncertainty. So, while classical statistics involved the development and presentation of *descriptive* data, modern statistics is additionally concerned with problems of *statistical inference.*

An illustration simplifies this *shock* word—inference. When a researcher avoids making generalizations based on his calculated measures, he is only *describing* what has been observed. For example, the statement "in 1973 the Jones Growth Fund was the top performer with a gain of 19.38 percent" merely uses a statistic to describe observed fact. Suppose another researcher measures the growth in inches during 1973 for all first-grade students in a large city and reports "Mrs. Jones' class grew up most with a gain of 9.14 percent." Would you *infer* from this descriptive statistic that Mrs. Jones *selected* faster growing children? No! You would expect some natural variations, even in group growth rates. With purely random assignment of first-grade students to teachers, one class would still have to be the "growth winner."

Statisticians summarize such variations in *frequency distributions.* A frequency distribution is a tally of each occurrence, in this case first-grade classes' growth in inches. This procedure is shown in Table 23–1. A *histogram* shows the growth data on first-grade children graphically, as in Figure 23–1.

TABLE 23–1
Hypothetical   Distribution   of
Growth   Rates   for   First-Grade
Classes

Growth in Inches	Tally (frequency)
2	11
2¼	⊞
2½	11 ⊞
2¾	1111 ⊞
3	⊞ ⊞
3¼	1 ⊞
3½	⊞
3¾	111
4	1

The data in Figure 23–1 confirm our expectation that first-grade classes did not all grow by the same amount. The purely random assignment of children to classes naturally results in classes with *differing* growth

FIGURE 23–1
Histogram of Growth Data

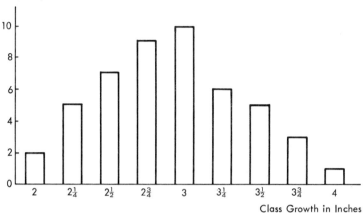

Frequency of Occurrence

Class Growth in Inches

rates. We *expect* some variations. But we have no reason to *infer* that these differences stem from anything but chance! In a statistical sense, the different average growth rates between random classes would not be "significant."

Let's examine our earlier descriptive statistic: "In 1973 the Jones Growth Fund was the top performer with a gain of 19.38 percent." Can you *infer* from this statistic alone that Jones selected better-performing stocks? No! As in the example of growing first grades, some variation in growth rates would occur even if every mutual fund selected its stocks on a purely random basis. A statistician is interested, therefore, in the more important question: Was the performance of the Jones Growth Fund *significantly better* than the performance of other mutual funds, or could such performance be explained by chance alone? After all, if every fund manager merely threw darts, some fund would "perform" best.

What Does a Statistician Need to Know?

Consider the histograms shown in Figure 23–2, which compare the hypothetical performance or rate of return of 30 different mutual funds. In Case A, it "looks like" the return of one fund is *significantly* better than the returns of all others. In Case B, it "looks like" the "best" fund is merely best because of natural variations. The fund's position as "Number One" should not be inferred to have any significance.

FIGURE 23–2
Illustration of Visually Apparent Significant Differences

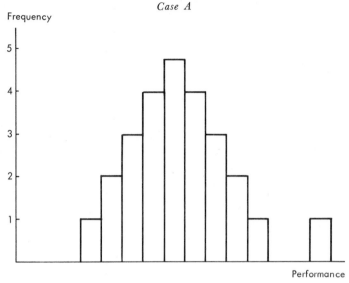

Case A

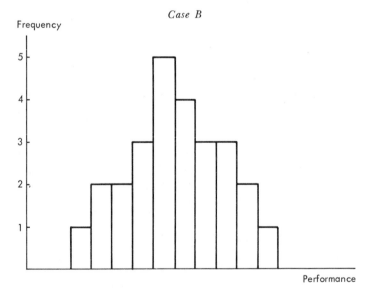

Case B

In a world anxious to eulogize "winners" and among a nation of scorekeepers, it is easy to attribute more to being "Number One" than is deserved. Applying statistical inference to such problems permits modern researchers to estimate whether certain results are "significant" or merely a chance occurrence.

Let's Look at a "Star" Performer

In their excellent book, *The Money Managers*, Gilbert Kaplan and Chris Welles included a chapter entitled "Fred Mates: The Risky Ride of a Super-Swinger." The Mates Fund, which started in July 1967, stepped into the limelight in early 1968. Kaplan and Welles reported that Fred Mates' mutual fund "rocketed from nowhere to rack up, as of December 1968, a spectacular gain of 153.5 percent. Mates was widely hailed as the new boy-wonder, the reigning genius." [**81**, p. 60] The interesting explanation of Mates' genius is that in December of 1968 he held 300,000 shares of an *extremely speculative* stock called Omega Equities. Omega's *tenfold increase in price in the three months* preceding December 1968 accounted for $6.8 million of Mates' $31 million port-folio. Mates was short-lived as the reigning genius. Before the year was out, the SEC charged Omega with "deceptive and manipulative con-duct" and suspended trading in the stock. As a result, Mates could not assign a market value to his holdings "just two weeks before he would have walked away with the top prize" in the "performance derby." [**81**, p. 61]

Such journalistic homage in popular stock market literature perplexes a modern statistician. *As long as the market goes up,* funds invested in the most speculative stocks would be expected to win the "performance derby." Should we applaud and reward the fund managers who place clients' money in such risky investments? No, because it is unfair to talk about performance without talking about risk!

Let's Define a "Winner" Before We Play the Game

An experiment is easily conducted for comparing stocks traded on the New York Stock Exchange to those on the American Exchange. The largest percentage gainers and losers on each exchange are listed in daily and weekly newspapers. Almost always, the rising ASE stocks will gain more as a group than their NYSE counterparts. Importantly, however, the ASE losers will also virtually always lose more. Similarly comparing the *performance* of high-risk portfolios with the performance of low-risk ones is like comparing apples and oranges. Without measuring "risk," there is no common denominator for return comparison.

Investment theoreticians advise grouping investments into portfolios which provide the maximum expected return with the minimum amount of risk. A portfolio is considered "optimal" if, at any point in time, the anticipated rate of return is the highest obtainable for a particular level of risk. Alternatively, a portfolio is similarly considered "efficient," if its risk is the lowest possible for a given rate of return. This ideal optimization recognizes a "trade-off" between return and risk. In reality, this investment Nirvana of maximizing returns for a given level of risk, or minimizing risk for a given return, proves elusive.

Donald Farrar, now at the University of Pennsylvania after heading the massive 1969–71 SEC report on institutional investors, studied the relationship of risk and return for his doctoral dissertation at Harvard University in 1961. Farrar's research extended Markowitz's work and applied risk-return analysis to the study of mutual fund performance. Essentially, Farrar wanted to determine whether some mutual funds were actually able to provide lower risks for given returns or, alternatively, higher returns for given risks. It was wonderful news for the mutual fund business when Farrar concluded that "professional portfolio managers are capable of providing a substantially higher expected yield, at little or no extra risk, than could be obtained by the random selection of assets." [45, p. 76]

It was not long after Farrar reported this encouraging evidence on mutual funds that Irwin Friend and Douglas Vickers, of the Wharton School of Finance, pointed out two flaws in Farrar's research methodology. In essence, Farrar's analysis focused on what would have happened in the past. His research showed that mutual funds held portfolios in September 1956 which, if they had held them during the *preceding* ten years, would have provided returns higher than those from a group of randomly selected stocks with the same risk. Past returns, however, are little correlated with future returns. In discussing Farrar's work, Friend and Vickers remarked, "only in a trivial sense is there any interest in the ability of management to choose stocks which performed well in terms of past average return or past average risk . . . . [The investor is interested in] *future* returns and the risk associated with that return." [53, p. 396] In the debate on mutual fund performance, Farrar's dissertation provided much useful data on the nature of risk, but care should be taken not to accept this inference that portfolio managers do better than random selection.

The First Challenge to Mutual Fund Performance

The first comprehensive study of the mutual fund industry, released as the now-classic Wharton School *Study of Mutual Funds* prepared under the supervision of Irwin Friend, appeared in 1963. The startling conclusion of this study was that, on the average, mutual fund performance "did not differ appreciably from what would have been achieved by an unmanaged portfolio consisting of the same proportion of common stocks, preferred stocks, corporate bonds, government securities, and other assets as the composite portfolios of the funds." [52]

It is difficult to reconcile this conclusion of the 1963 Wharton Study with the fact that over 800 mutual funds now operate in the United States. These funds purportedly provide the average investor with both diversification and the best attainable professional investment management. Mutual funds pool the money of numerous fund shareholders and invest it according to the fund manager's discretion within broad guidelines. For this management service, a mutual fund manager will generally receive a fee approximating or exceeding one half of 1 percent annually of the total assets in the mutual fund. This "management fee" is paid over and above certain expenses incurred in operating the fund, such as commissions, legal services, stock certificate custody, etc.

In the face of the 1963 Wharton Study, mutual funds have grown extensively, and some investment managers continue to be paid phenomenal compensation. Obviously, the public refuses to believe that unmanaged portfolios could do as well as "expertly" managed investments. (Importantly, the 1963 Wharton Study does not deny the possibility of making money with mutual fund shares. All it questions is whether investors get something of *value* for their management fee. To provide an actual bench mark against which to measure the *value* of investment management, we must know statistically how well an investor should expect to do by merely selecting stocks with a dart board.)

The Chicago Studies

The foundation research on the stock market's overall rate of return was conducted by Lawrence Fisher and James Lorie [49] at the Center for Research in Security Prices at the University of Chicago during the mid-1960s. Under a grant from the brokerage firm of Merrill Lynch, Pierce, Fenner, and Smith, Inc., the Center for Research in Security Prices undertook the horrendous job of collecting extensive monthly data (such as prices, dividends, splits, etc.) on all NYSE stocks traded between January 1926 and December 1960. These data, together with more recent daily data on all NYSE stocks, plus a wide variety of national economic statistics, were then keypunched and stored on computer-readable magnetic tape.

This data-collection task was enormous. Consider, for example, the difficulty of assigning the "value" of a "dividend" consisting of a quart of whiskey (that's one way to reduce inventory) given to shareholders in the 1930s. After much patience and financial backing, the Center for Research in Security Prices completed this much needed data file that a few years earlier was only a researcher's dream.

Fisher and Lorie were the first to use this data. They were interested in determining the historical rate of return on portfolios consisting of all NYSE common stocks. In all, Lorie and Fisher studied what would have happened if one had held all stocks traded on the NYSE during 22 different, but overlapping, periods between January 1926 and December 1960. Most of the rates of return they reported were greater than 10 percent compounded annually, however, the rates ranged from minus 48 percent to plus 17 percent.

In a subsequent article, Fisher published the results of an elaborate investigation into the outcomes of *random* investments in common stocks. In his earlier work, published jointly by Fisher and Lorie, *all* stocks were studied in composite for the specified periods. Fisher's subsequent investigation sought to determine how well an investor would have done by holding *individual* NYSE stocks. The stocks selected were randomly chosen, as were the buy and sell dates (that is, as though the investor had thrown darts at stock listings and calendars as the basis for his decisions). Fisher enumerated, by computer, the investment results for multiple combinations of purchases and sales of individual common stocks for which data were available. For the 1,715 common stocks in his study, 56,557,538 combinations of stocks and holding periods were tabulated. These results (allowing for brokerage commissions) are shown in Figure 23–3.

Figure 23–3 reveals that annual rates of return showed a marked central tendency, or "normal" grouping about the average. Taking brokerage commissions into account, Fisher reported that "seventy-eight percent of the time common stocks yielded a positive net return. Over two thirds of the time the rate of return exceeded 5 percent . . . [and] the median rate of return was 9.8 percent. . . . Nearly one fifth of the time the rate of return exceeded 20 percent per annum, compounded annually." [48, pp. 153–154]

Other facts among Fisher's conclusions are worth noting. The variability of rates of return is much greater for short-term investments than it is for long-term investments. On the average, the probability of a gain on a long-term investment was greater than 78 percent. Furthermore,

FIGURE 23-3
Frequency Distribution of Rates of Return on Investment in Each Common Stock
Listed on the New York Stock Exchange, 1926–60, Using All Possible Combinations
of Month-End Purchase and Sale Dates (based on 56,557,538 cases).

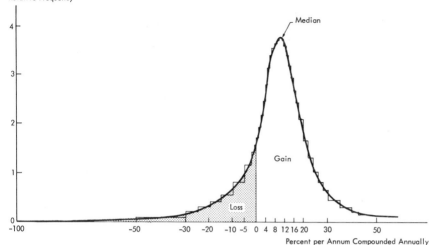

Source: Fisher [48, p. 154].

the "long-term" holding of more than one stock at a time would have
led, on the average, to a positive return far more than 78 percent of
the time and, in fact, would have led to returns at a rate greater than
9.8 percent per annum substantially more than half the time. [**48**, p.
159]

The significance of Fisher's work should be emphasized. By investing
in the most random, haphazard fashion imaginable, *an investor would
have profited 78% of the time.* If an investor had held a portfolio of
many stocks, he would be expected to have profited even more often.
Further, Fisher has shown that risk, or the variation in rates of return,
is much greater for short-term investments. Investments held several years
were much less likely to produce absolute losses. Fisher also derived that
the average rate of return, compounded annually, for NYSE common
stocks was almost 10 percent per annum. Using stock price charts, fundamental analysis, or Ouija boards, an investor could have expected to
do this well!

Some Things to Remember

The decision to invest large sums of money is often approached in
a naïve fashion—by both individuals and institutions. There seems to

be a general feeling that *any* level of return can be attained by merely searching out the appropriate stock. This feeling gave rise to "go-go" money management and a plethora of ill-conceived investment strategies. This "I can get high returns too" attitude is fostered by the loudly acclaimed "successes" of those who gamble and win.

The moral is to know the odds of the game. Chances are you will move with the market. And the market's odds, in the long run, are stacked in your favor, unlike Las Vegas, state lotteries, or even New York's Off Track Betting system. You can exaggerate this market movement, either up and down, by investing in the "swinging" (literally) stocks. Overall, the odds are that you will win. But the hardest thing to remember when you win is that winning should not automatically be attributed to genius. Fisher's stock market tests, using random selection, average almost 10 percent returns, with a winner more than three times out of four. Should such "performance" be labeled investment genius? Investors should know the various odds and pick the "game" they want to play. The results of risky games go both ways. If investors win, they should not cry "genius." If they fail, they should not cry tears.

Southern Californians, for example, watched the American Football League's star pass receiver, Lance Alworth, become a "millionaire" (off the field) in a few short years. Starting with an interest in the Minnie Pearl Fried Chicken franchises, Alworth's early investments snowballed with the late 1960s franchise boom. Riding the crest of this speculative wave, he formed the "million dollar" Lance Alworth, Ltd.—ostensibly as a vehicle to manage other athletes' money—and purchased an interest in several "swinging" franchises. These included a chain of dry-cleaning stores, called 60-Minute Systems, and four franchises of Royal Inns of America hotels in Atlanta and in Florida. Alworth did so well that he announced his retirement from pro football to devote full time to his *financial* affairs.

Shortly thereafter the franchise bubble burst, and Alworth subsequently filed for bankruptcy. After his highly speculative fiasco, Alworth's almost classic quotation appeared in Neil Morgan's Aug. 11, 1970, column in the *San Diego Evening Tribune:* "I think my worst mistake was that I had too much faith in the American economy."

Remember that in seeking higher and higher rates of return one assumes higher and higher risks. When the "American economy" slowed down by a mere 2 percent shrinkage of the nation's gross national product in real terms, Lance Alworth lost 100 percent of his assets. He cannot blame the economy for such an excessive and leveraged risk posture.

The famous economist, John Maynard Keynes, noted that "the game of professional investment is intolerably boring and overexacting to anyone who is entirely exempt from the gambling instinct; whilst he who has it must pay to this propensity the appropriate toll." Keynes was correct. Investors should know the odds. If craps players win, they are inclined to say, "the table was hot." Unfortunately, few investors ever bring themselves to say, "I'm not doing anything; it's the market that's hot." Instead, when investments work out, it's their genius![1]

The parallel of gamblers and investors who play in risky securities is apt. It doesn't require investment genius to engage in risky speculations. Performance must be interpreted in the light of risk to be meaningful. But remember, if your four-year investment performance record is "Up 20 percent, up 40 percent, up 20 percent, down 50 percent"—you're *even!* On the other hand, if you plod along with a "mere" 10 percent compounded annual return, you will gain, after four years, almost half again (+46.41 percent) the money you started with.

Hit 'Em Again—Harder—Harder

In 1965, Friend and Vickers, who were both major contributors to the Wharton Study two years earlier, published another study of mutual fund performance. They compared the performance of the common stock portfolios of 50 mutual funds with the performance of 50 randomly selected common stock portfolios over a six-year period. (Mutual fund performance data are more readily available, and therefore more subject to scrutiny, than the actual results of other "professional" investors). Friend and Vickers reported "for the six-year period as a whole, from the end of 1957 through 1963, the random portfolios experienced a slightly higher average return than the mutual funds." [**53**, p. 398] Friend and Vickers concluded that "there is still no evidence—either in our new or old tests, or in the tests so far carried out by others—that mutual fund performance is any better than that realizable by random or mechanical selection of stock issues." [**53**, p. 412] These results prompted Friend and Vickers to remark that their results "raise interesting questions about the apparent inability of professional investment management on the average to outperform the market." [**53**, p. 413]

---

[1] If your gambling instincts extend to the casinos, this author recommends as an excellent guide to casino games: Allan N. Wilson, *The Casino Gambler's Guide* (New York: Harper and Row, 1965). For the famous treatment of the game "Twenty-one," see Edward O. Thorp, *Beat the Dealer* (New York: Vintage Books, 1966.)

One segment of Friend's and Vickers' research, however, raised more questions than it answered. They reported that their first year's data revealed mutual fund performance significantly better than results from their randomly selected portfolios. Did this mean that mutual fund managers did do better than the "dart board" during that period, or could something else explain the results? It so happened that the variability of returns for mutual funds was consistently higher than the variability of the randomly generated portfolio returns. The mutual funds were, on the average, inherently more risky than the randomly generated portfolios. In such a case we would *expect* the mutual funds to outperform the random portfolios in a year characterized by a sharp upward movement in the overall stock market. Indeed, this seemed to explain this facet of their findings. More important, however, was the recognition that *risk* must thereafter be factored into measurements of *performance*.

chapter

24
Performance versus Risk

Jack Treynor, the editor of the *Financial Analysts Journal,* was the first to publish a performance measure of mutual funds which included that vital ingredient—risk [167]. He devised a way to compare the distinctive risk "characteristics" of different mutual funds. Prior to his research, investigators noted that rates of return for mutual funds typically show wide variations from year to year. The problem was, as it is to a lesser degree even today, to devise a stable risk-related measurement to include in the measurement of "performance." Treynor approached the problem by showing the remarkable stability of a fund's "characteristic line," which can be used to measure risk.

Suppose we plot the rate of return history of two portfolios over the past ten years. The horizontal axis records the rate of return for the *general* market, while the vertical axis records the return for each fund. Notice that the line—called the characteristic line—which is fitted to the points describing our two funds in Figure 24–1 provides two quite different pictures.

Drawn in this way, Treynor's "characteristic lines" allow comparison of these two funds on both their rates of return and their historical *risk* over the past ten years. *The slope of Treynor's characteristic line gives a graphic measure of the fund's volatility in relation to the general market.* Notice that a steeply sloping characteristic line (such as that of Fund A) means that the historical rate of return for the fund has magnified the general market's rate of return. By contrast, the slope of Fund B's characteristic line is less steep than that of Fund A. A characteristic line such as Fund B's indicates a lesser sensitivity to general market fluctuations. Fund B carries a lower component of general market risk. Trey-

FIGURE 24–1
Characteristic Lines Representing Different Historical Risk Postures

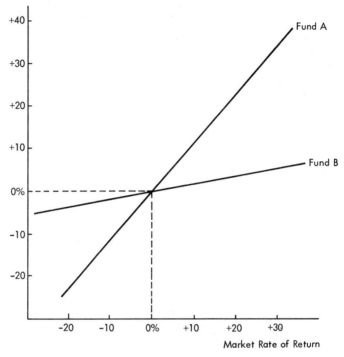

Portfolio Rate of Return

Market Rate of Return

nor observed, "the slope-angle of the characteristic line obviously provides a more refined measure of a fund's volatility than the usual categories of 'balanced fund,' 'stock fund,' or 'growth fund.' " [**167**, p. 66] Treynor reported further that "the range of volatility observed in actual practice is enormous." He found, for example, that a 1 percent change in the rate of return of the Dow Jones Industrial Average was often accompanied by changes in rates of return of certain funds that were more than twice as large.

Besides comparing the historical risk posture of two funds, the characteristic line discloses other performance information. Notice that the slopes of the characteristic lines for Fund X and Fund Y in Figure 24–2 are identical. The volatility, or risk, of the two funds is the same. Fund X's characteristic line, however, lies *above* the characteristic line for Fund Y. This means that Fund X has historically demonstrated consistently higher return than Fund Y—in good years and bad. Thus, Treynor's "characteristic line" reflects both distinctive ingredients of a fund's performance history—return *and* risk.

FIGURE 24–2
Characteristic Lines Representing Identical Historical Risk
Postures with Different Average Rates of Return

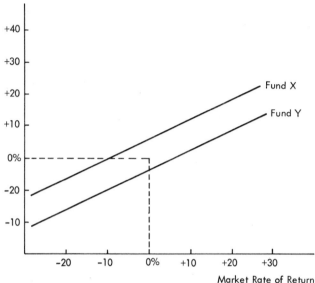

In his now-classic paper, Treynor used this graphic technique to compare the performance of 54 mutual funds. He noted that, over a ten-year period (1954–1963), roughly 80 percent of the funds studied maintained a constant posture toward risk. By and large, these funds did *not* shift to more speculative investments when they felt optimistic. Similarly, they did not get less speculative when there was reason to be pessimistic. Such a policy produces fund returns in any year that are largely determined by the general market.

Putting the Pieces Together

This evidence asserts that the search for undervalued common stocks which can be expected to yield consistently better-than-average returns may be futile. Sharpe set out to test this observation by dissecting the causes underlying the performance of 34 open-end mutual funds. Sharpe utilized a ratio, similar to the one devised by Treynor, that measured the "reward per unit of variability." Like Treynor's measure of performance, Sharpe's statistic described the reward provided to the investor for assuming risk. Sharpe was able to confirm large differences among the mutual funds in the way they rewarded their investors for assuming risk. Further, Sharpe's research showed that "past performance appears to provide a basis for predicting future performance, especially when measured with the Treynor index." [**150**, p. 131]

It would be more useful, however, to discover the underlying *cause* of observed differences in mutual fund performance. If, for example, elaborate and expensive security analysis is useless, the mutual funds which spend the *least* on research should show the best net performance records. In Sharpe's words, "the only basis for persistently inferior performance would be the continued expenditure of large amounts of a fund's assets on the relatively fruitless search for incorrectly valued securities." [**150**, p. 121] Conversely, if security analysis is worthwhile, funds spending the most on such research should have records of better net performance. After much careful investigation, Sharpe reported that "the results tend to support the cynics: good performance is associated with low expense ratios." [**150**, p. 132]

Next, Sharpe compared the 34 mutual funds in his study with the Dow-Jones Industrial Average by using his reward-to-variability performance measure. Sharpe's reward-to-variability ratio overcomes the problem of the popular "performance derby," which generally reports only on returns. A portfolio of volatile AMEX stocks, for instance, should not be expected to perform the same as a portfolio of stocks drawn from large companies on the NYSE. Volatile stocks can be expected to have more dramatic upside performance in good markets and, correspondingly, worse downside performance in weak markets. Nor should the reader be deluded into reasoning that one can reap phenomenal profits on highly speculative stocks merely because "the market goes up more than it goes down." A single bear market undoes a lot of previous "performance." *Remember,* if your four-year record is "up 20 percent, up 40 percent, up 20 percent, down 50 percent!," *you're even!*

Using a *realistic* measure of performance, Sharpe reported that, in terms of a reward-to-risk ratio, the odds were "greater than 100 to 1 against the possibility that the average mutual fund did as well as the Dow-Jones portfolio from 1954–1963." [**150**, p. 137] Sharpe traced the cause of this remarkably bad mutual fund performance to differences between their *gross* and *net* performance. Sharpe had hypothesized that if the security analysis practiced by Wall Street professionals was indeed useless, their *gross* performance before fees and expenses would equal that attained from random selection of securities with similar risks. If his hypothesis is correct, it means that, counter to our intuition, the investment companies which have spent the largest amounts on security selection in fact will provide the worst *net* performance! After much careful study, Sharpe reported ". . . all other things being equal, the smaller a fund's expense ratio, the better the results obtained by stockholders." [**150,** p. 137]

In the spirit of open debate, Sharpe closed his paper with the following remarks.

Further work is required before the significance of this result can be properly evaluated. But the burden of proof may reasonably be placed on those who argue the traditional view—that the search for securities whose prices diverge from their intrinsic values is worth the expense required. . . . Fortunately many who hold this view have both the means and data required to perform extensive analysis; we will all look forward to their results. [**150,** p. 138]

Sharpe's research is not presented here as conclusive fact. No academic research is devoid of statistical qualification. The essential point, however, for anyone truly interested in understanding the securities markets, is that the quality of evidence adduced by the academic community is the highest attainable. On the other hand, high-quality support for "professionals" is almost entirely nonexistent.

The Experts Do Not Always Agree

It is only fair to mention that not all scholars agree with the 1965 research findings of Friend and Vickers or those subsequently reported by Sharpe in 1966. Also, unwarranted generalizations should not be inferred from these investigations. On the other hand, one should be careful to base his reasons for agreeing, or disagreeing, with this research on facts, not on intuition or the irrational beliefs often cited as reasons for blindly disregarding this research.

What follows is the essence of a recent cocktail party conversation with a professional money manager. He mentioned that he detested accounting, statistics, and mathematics, and had always steered clear of anything involving numbers. This statement of "qualifications and interests" was followed by his emphatic assertion that statistical inference could be used to prove "anything." Finally, he stated that academe's "mud-throwing" at the mutual fund industry was nonsense, because "those professors probably never invested a dime." And, it is easy to criticize someone unless you've tried "doing it yourself."

It might be true that Ralph Nader is incapable of building a safe automobile. This does not, however, invalidate the movement begun by Ralph Nader when he contended that the automobile industry was negligent in providing the public with safe automobiles. Similarly, it is enough for researchers to show that the performance from random selection is no better than from mutual funds. They need not also provide the performance that the professional mutual fund managers cannot! Market professionals should not try to discredit this research with irrational statements about the "real-world" experience of the researchers. My acquaintance at the cocktail party was guilty of saying, in one breath, he "didn't understand," and in the next breath, he "didn't believe."

Some competent researchers do not believe that the evidence in Friend's and Vickers' 1965 paper is conclusive because of certain limitations which, in the tradition of academic research, were disclosed by the authors. Kalman Cohen and Jerry Pogue, at the Carnegie Institute of Technology, published a paper in 1967 [217] which questioned the conclusiveness of these findings. It should be carefully noted that the challenge to Friend's and Vickers' research is an academic one, and as Cohen and Pogue emphasized in a later paper, they took "no position in the controversy regarding mutual fund versus random portfolio performance." [22, p. 190] Their criticism of Friend's and Vickers' research was that it was not powerful enough to condemn the performance of all mutual funds. Their criticism was restricted to the relevance of the findings and they offered no counter evidence that mutual funds could indeed outperform random selection.

A similar article was published in 1968 by Richard West [173], an economist for Cummins Engine Company. West attacked the methodology used by Sharpe to conclude that funds with relatively high rates of return also showed relatively high risk. In effect, West presented an imposing argument that Sharpe's results could have been influenced by his data which spanned the strong bull market period of the 1950s and early 1960s. Yet, like the work of Cohen and Pogue, West's paper served only to challenge the methodology employed. Neither critique offered any evidence contrary to the growing evidence that mutual fund performance is no better than that achievable by totally random selection.

The Case Against "Professional" Management Grows Stronger

By 1968, the case against professional management's ability, as typified by mutual fund results, was growing stronger—yet there were several unanswered questions. The 1963 Wharton Study, and subsequent research by Friend and Vickers, did not adequately relate performance differences to risk. Treynor and Sharpe were concerned with risk, but their work was not sufficiently comprehensive. A study was needed analyzing the performance of a large number of mutual funds. Fortunately, investors did not have to wait long.

In 1968, Michael Jensen built upon the theoretical models derived by Treynor and Sharpe. Jensen devised a measure for comparing fund performance across "different risk levels and across differing time periods irrespective of general economic and market conditions." Jensen used this measure to evaluate the "ability of the portfolio manager or security analyst to increase returns on the portfolio through successful prediction of future security prices. . . . [76, p. 389] In seeking evidence of portfolio managers' predictive ability, Jensen studied the performance of 115 open-end mutual funds in the period of 1945–64. Jensen's measure of performance tested the managers' ability to forecast market behavior as well as price movements of individual issues. His findings are summarized as follows.

It is important to note . . . that the mutual fund industry (as represented by these 115 funds) shows very little evidence of an ability to forecast security prices. Furthermore, there is surprisingly little evidence that indicates any individual funds in the sample might be able to forecast prices. . . .

The evidence on mutual fund performance . . . indicates not only that these 115 mutual funds were *on average* not able to predict security prices well enough to outperform a buy-the-market-and-hold policy, but also that there is very little evidence that any individual fund was able to do significantly better than that which we expected from mere random chance. It is also important to note that these conclusions hold *even* when we measure the fund returns gross of management expenses (that is, assume their bookkeeping, research, and other expenses except brokerage commissions were obtained free). Thus on average the funds apparently were not quite successful enough in their trading activities to recoup even their brokerage expenses.

The evidence . . . indicate[s] . . . a pressing need on the part of the funds themselves to evaluate much more closely both the costs and the benefits of their research and trading activities in order to provide investors with maximum possible returns for the level of risk undertaken [76, pp. 414–15].

In a subsequent study, Jensen reported

. . . mutual fund managers on the average are unable to forecast future security prices. [76, p. 170]

. . . it appears that on the average the resources spent by the funds in attempting to forecast security prices do not yield higher portfolio returns than those that could have been earned by equivalent risk portfolios selected (*a*) by random selection policies or (*b*) by combined investments in a "market portfolio" and government bonds. [**76**, p. 170]

[Even though] analysts . . . operate in the securities markets every day and have wide-ranging contacts and associations in both the business and the financial communities . . . the fact [is] that they are apparently unable to forecast returns accurately enough to recover their research and transaction costs . . . [**76**, p. 170]

So Where Do We Stand?

A long series of research studies dating from 1963 has validly sought to measure the performance of mutual funds. While the methodology has differed somewhat, the conclusions unanimously cast serious doubt on the "management" ability of mutual funds. Their performance has been no better than could be attained through random stock selection. Despite some debate on research technique, no substantial evidence verifies that mutual funds can, as often implied, perform better than chance.

In a still more recent study, John O'Brien evaluated the performance of 119 funds during the ten years covering 1959–68. He reported that: "On the basis of the observed results . . . it is concluded that there are no more managers than predicted by chance occurrence either exceeding or failing to exceed the rate of return predicted for them based upon the level of uncertainty they assume." [**134**, p. 102]

Where, then, is *any* evidence to be found that mutual fund managers, whom investors employ with the hope of getting professional results, can indeed do their job? A modern student of the stock market can find no reliable evidence which disagrees substantively with the common outcome of the research we have discussed: Stock market professionals hired by the public, with all of their resources, contacts, "insider information," jargon, techniques and analysis do not perform any better than would be expected on the basis of pure chance!

How Much Evidence Is Enough?

Certainly one of the most extensive research studies of mutual fund performance and that of other institutional investors was published in August 1970 by three faculty members of the Wharton School. In this study Irwin Friend, Marshall Blume, and Jean Crockett reported on the performance of 299 leading funds for the years 1960 through 1968. These researchers reported that

The overall annual rates of return on investment in 136 mutual funds [essentially all the larger, publicly owned funds for which data were available] averaged 10.7 percent for the period January 1960, through June 1968 (9.0 percent for the period January 1960, through March 1964, and 12.8 percent for the period April 1964, through June 1968). Unweighted investment in *all* stocks listed on the Big Board in the same periods would have yielded 12.4 percent (7.0 percent in the first part and 17.8 percent in the second).

. . . .

When funds were classified by fund size, sales charges, management expenses, portfolio turnover, and investment objectives, no consistent relationship was found between these factors and investment performance properly adjusted for risk. To the extent that a relationship exists between performance and sales charges, the funds with the lowest charges, including the "no-load" funds, appear to perform slightly better than the others.

. . . .

The apparent absence of any consistent relationships between the nonrisk characteristics of mutual funds and their investment performance suggests that, for the industry as a whole, there may be *no* consistency in the performance of the same fund in successive periods [55, pp. 19–21].

Here, then, is the unvarnished truth! These findings were produced by researchers with no vested interest in whether or not the public utilizes professional investment advice. A brief look is appropriate at a sample of the criticisms Wall Street professionals have directed at Friend's 1970 study.

" 'Based on newspaper accounts, the study is totally irrelevant to the investor's needs,' declares C. Grady Green, vice president of Van Strum and Towne Co., investment adviser to the five Channing Funds."

"Richard A. N. C. Johnson, portfolio manager of the Dreyfus Fund, objected to Friend's device of comparing fund performance with a hypothetical average of all NYSE stocks since no investor could actually buy a cross-section of the Big Board in real life."

This author does not agree with Mr. Green's comment that this kind of research is "totally irrelevant to the investor's needs." Indeed, it is a thesis of this book that much useful research conducted by university scholars is unjustly criticized by the "insiders" who foster their own best interests by a "head-in-the-sand approach" to the stock market of the 1970s. Mr. Johnson's criticism that "no investor could actually buy a cross-section of the Big Board" in no way reflects on the merits of Friend's research. Instead, the criticism should be directed at the mutual fund industry for not providing consumers with a minimal cost, totally diversified, and unmanaged fund of all Big Board stocks. In Friend's words:

The performance analysis gave no indication that higher sales charges, management costs, or trading expenses are consistently linked with performance either above or below that of random portfolios. Because no clear payoff results from higher management and trading expenses, a new type of mutual fund and minimal management and trading may be desirable. Such a fund would resemble the fixed or semifixed trusts of former years. These trusts deliberately duplicated the performance of all NYSE stocks or of some other broad range of investments.

This new kind of fund would provide, at a minimal cost, the risk diversification which seems to be the most important continuing service rendered by today's mutual funds. The larger this fund might be, the smaller would be the relative management expenses, and the easier it would be to duplicate the performance of the entire market. Such large funds would become sufficiently well known to the investing public for their shares to be sold at commission rates appreciably lower than the sales loads now charged by mutual funds [55, p. 23].

Facing overwhelming research evidence, the mutual fund industry, and "professional" money managers in general have several alternatives which investors should anticipate. They can drastically alter their management policies and dispense with the unsuccessful and expensive search for the "yellow-brick road." Or, they can attempt to discredit academic research by claiming that it is "irrelevant." But it is not. Investors should realize that what *does* appear to be irrelevant is much of the traditional investment advice which market professionals provide.

chapter

25

To Diversify or Not

In the last chapter (Performance versus Risk) we examined some very startling evidence. In Chapter 21 (It Is All a Matter of Risk) we saw that investors who try for a higher-than-average rate of return generally do so by choosing high-risk investments. Chapter 22 showed that the expected rate of return from most high-risk stocks is not enough to offset the extra risk of such holdings. Thus, investors seeking higher-than-average returns should carefully consider the risk-reward alternatives of investment instruments other than risky stocks—a strategy we will apply in Chapter 29 (Bonds and Hedges) and Chapter 30 (Puts and Calls). The preceding chapter showed that, when risk is measured with performance, 70 percent of the apparent "performance" of professionally managed portfolios, such as mutual funds, is explained by the risk level of the underlying investments. Therefore, the degree to which any portfolio outpaces a general market rise is largely dictated by risk which, in turn, is the degree to which the portfolio can be expected to outpace the market in the other direction during a downturn. This chapter discusses the technique of reducing risk through diversification.

Broadly speaking, there are two categories of investors—those who prefer to concentrate, and those who prefer to diversify their holdings. Investors who concentrate their assets in relatively few investments typically reason that they can better focus their attention on a limited group of stocks. Conversely, other investors reason that it is difficult to do a reliably better-than-average job of investment selection. Members of this group typically diversify their holdings over a wide variety of stocks so as to achieve approximately the market's average rate of return.

The "If All of Your Eggs Are in One Basket, You Can Watch Them" Investor

If concentration is the gospel of some professional money managers, Gerald Tsai has been its apostle. Gerald Tsai (pronounced sigh!), who was born in Shanghai, came to the United States in 1947 to attend Wesleyan University in Middletown, Connecticut. He later transferred to Boston University and, after graduation, worked briefly in the research department of Bache & Co. Tsai then moved to Boston's Fidelity Management and Research Company where, in 1958, he was placed in charge of the Fidelity Capital Fund. The subsequent "performance" of the Fidelity Capital Fund was phenomenal. Tsai's credo was *concentration!*

During this era, Tsai received much publicity from the press as Wall Street's "Star" and "Wonder Boy." He was even thought by some to possess mystical powers of the Orient which allowed him to glimpse the future of high-flying growth stocks. By the mid-1960s, this aura surrounded every move Tsai made. In this irrational climate, a rumor that "Tsai is buying" caused waves of enthusiasm and a frantic rush to acquire what Gerald Tsai, in his eminent genius, was acquiring. By generating such demand for the stocks he selected, Tsai's "genius for picking stocks" became somewhat self-fulfilling and appeared impeccable.

The journalistic license of news media augmented Tsai's mystique. For example, *Newsweek* described Gerald Tsai as "something of a mystery man" who "radiates total cool" and remarked with awe on his "black, impassive gaze." In 1966, Tsai left Fidelity to start his own mutual fund. With his mystical image and reputation, and specific philosophy of investment concentration, Tsai hoped to attract $30 million of initial investment. On *the first day* of Tsai's Manhattan Fund, the underwriters provided Gerald Tsai with *$270 million* of the public's money to invest in a market which was then bubbling up to all-time highs.

Tsai's modus operandi during his years at Fidelity has been summarized as follows:

Tsai's specialty was the big glamour stocks such as Xerox and Polaroid which generally had been considered too speculative for anyone but private traders. At a time when broad diversification was the prevailing philosophy, Tsai concentrated his portfolio in a small handful of these glamour issues. Though all responsible money managers bought on fundamentals, Tsai freely admitted that he traded by the charts. He would establish positions with dramatic snatches of tens of thousands of shares. Then, watching the technical progress of his holdings very carefully, he would dump his positions with equal suddenness. . . . His annual turnover generally exceeded 100 percent, an almost scandalous level, then unparalleled among other institutions. [81, p. 84]

When Tsai initiated the Manhattan Fund in 1966, he quite naturally intended to run it with the same modus operandi he used at Fidelity.

Tsai began 1968 with $500 million in a group of 40 stocks which looked like a typical Tsai portfolio for any time in the previous ten years: lots of data processing (Control Data, IBM); electronics (Collins Radio, General Instrument, Itek, Raytheon, Teledyne); office equipment (Burroughs, National Cash Register); along with touches of conglomerates (Gulf & Western, Walter Kidde, LTV); some oils, and his long-time loves, Polaroid and Sperry Rand. [81, p. 87]

To aid in the collection of "technical information" Tsai surrounded himself with almost every conceivable gadget.

To facilitate his chartist maneuverings, he built an elaborate trading room with a Trans-jet tape, a Quotron electronic board with the prices of relevant securities, and three-foot-square, giant loose-leaf notebooks filled with Point-and-Figure charts and other technical indicators of all of his holdings. Adjoining the trading room was erected "Information Central," so aswarm with visual displays and panels that slid and rotated about that it resembled some Pentagon war room. Three men were hired to work full time maintaining literally hundreds of averages, ratios, oscillators, and indices. . . . [81, p. 86]

From the material covered thus far, you should be able to make a few observations about the Tsai investment philosophy. First, Tsai's 1968 investments were concentrated in high-risk glamour stocks. We would expect stocks in this risk category to do very well in up-markets, and very poorly in down ones. Secondly, many of the specific stocks which Tsai had selected could be expected to have large components of industry comovement[1] and market-based volatility. They were concentrated in similar industries which were all particularly sensitive to the overall mar-

---

[1] As discussed in Chapter 10—What Causes Price Movements?—industry comovement refers to those aspects of an industry which have the same stock-price implications for *all* stocks within the industry. For example, a government announcement that tighter gasoline price controls were forthcoming would be expected to affect the prices of *all* oil stocks in roughly the same way.

ket. Hence, Tsai's portfolio could be expected to do extremely well in a rapidly expanding economy accompanied by a rising market. But, during a general market downturn, we would expect his portfolio to experience a severe decline—unmitigated by meaningful diversification.

The technique by which Tsai hoped to prevent such downside disaster was his mystical use of charts. Yet, the wealth of evidence summarized in previous chapters dismisses the technical gadgetry Tsai placed in his "Information Central" as being nothing more than an expensive electronic Ouija board. Finally, then, we are left with Tsai's dark eyes and mystical oriental powers. This book cannot refute such powers. It is one thing to challenge the shibboleths of Wall Street, but quite another to challenge 3,000 years of oriental mysticism! Nonetheless, this author is not a great believer in so basing investment decisions.

Scientific research leads us to predict that Gerald Tsai's philosophy of concentration would do well in a rapidly expanding economy, subject to periodic disastrous downside performance. The problem was even worse in Tsai's case because, by purchasing a significant percentage of the outstanding shares of a few stocks, he pushed their price to the high-water mark, where comparatively little buying demand was left. The inevitable followed:

. . . in 1968, without warning, Jerry Tsai collapsed as the aura of the big glamour stocks, upon which his entire market philosophy was based, abruptly ended. While the Dow Jones Industrial Average was up 5 percent, and many other performance mutual funds were up 30 and 40 percent, Tsai's Manhattan Fund, which he had started to loud fanfare in 1966 after leaving Fidelity, was actually *down* 7 percent, the worst record of any of the 310 funds in the Authur Lipper survey of mutual fund performance. Superman had been confronted with a giant hulk of kryptonite . . . the star had fallen. [**81**, pp. 80–81]

When the star fell, he took a lot of innocent investors with him. After seven years of operation, Manhattan Fund shares sold in mid-1973 for no more than half the amount that early investors had paid for them. Investors had received only nominal income in the meantime. Kaplan notes, "It is difficult to imagine the degree of personal anguish and embarrassment Tsai must have suffered." [**81**, p. 90] Tsai "suffered" as a result of his "go-go" money management maneuvering, but such "embarrassment" cannot offset the loss of investors' assets. Anyone feeling sorry for Jerry Tsai need only recall that, in August 1968, Tsai sold his fund management company to C.N.A. Financial Corporation and became that company's largest stockholder, with personal worth then valued at approximately $30 million! To settle subsequent litigation, Tsai later agreed to pay back $1 million of this gain. Sigh!

The Other Way to Play the Game—Diversify

Many successful investors have adopted the opposite philosophy of diversification. One of the wealthiest shrewd investors to espouse a philosophy of diversification was the famous Texas wheeler-dealer, Clint Murchison, Sr. After a roaring start in wildcat oil drilling in the 1920s, Murchison started to diversify his holdings. At one point he was said to control 115 companies spread from Canada to South America. Doubtless Murchison had an awareness of industrial and national market "co-movements" and protected himself against them through diversification. His philosophy on diversification was a simple one, "Money is like manure, when it stacks up it stinks, when you spread it around it makes things grow." [190]

The premise underlying diversification is that the overall risk from owning many stocks is less than the risk of holding a few stocks. The fewer stocks you hold, the greater your injury if one does poorly. It can be shown mathematically, in fact, that when your investments are spread among several stocks—which are not related to each other—the overall risk will be reduced (see [146]). What can make this job difficult, however, is the "not related to each other" proviso. We have seen that many stocks are interdependent through common industry or economic factors. Herein lies the problem of portfolio analysis.

Modern Investment Management

The job of modern investment management consists of two quite separate parts: security analysis and portfolio analysis. Research shows that security analysis is fraught with misconceptions that render many of its techniques useless. This does not mean that investors should disassociate themselves from the stock market. Remember that an individual who has a safe 5 percent bank rate of return can actually fall behind if inflation exceeds that rate. Modern research does suggest, however, that there is merit in the science of *portfolio analysis,* which seeks to predict the collective behavior of *groups* of securities. Careful portfolio analysis is one of the most important aspects of investment management.

The Setting for Portfolio Analysis

Let's examine first, what portfolio analysis is, and secondly, how the practices of many investors are inconsistent with modern research findings. Later, we will incorporate what should be done into your investment strategy.

Portfolio analysis includes the study of:

1. The *degree* of risk in a prospective investment;
2. The *nature* of the investment's risk (that is, an understanding of intra-industry price comovements, etc.) ; and
3. The *number and dollar amounts* of separate investments which diversify that risk.

The portfolio analyst combines these ingredients with the results of individual security analysis to produce a portfolio with the highest expected return for the level of risk the investor is willing to assume.

The Degree of Risk. We have already examined the riskiness of individual stocks. Various measures of a stock's volatility can be used to measure investors' uncertainty about the stock. This historical volatility has been found to be a suitable predictor of future risk. Thus, when considering stocks for inclusion in a portfolio, it is possible to make accurate assumptions about the stock's future volatility and, hence, its inherent riskiness.

The Nature of Risk. It is possible to trace the cause of stock price movements to four components: the market as a whole, basic industry comovements, industry subgroup comovements, and the individual company. Research has shown, for example, that 49 percent of the price movement in oil stocks can be attributed to industry comovements, and another 13 percent can be attributed to the overall market's influence. For cosmetic stocks, on the other hand, only 11 percent of price variations can be attributed to either market or industry influences. The degree of diversification obtained from adding a cosmetic stock exceeds that of another oil stock, whose fate is closely tied to its industry and the economy. Little diversification is achieved when a portfolio manager selects two stocks which respond in the same way to changes in the economy, or to changes in the industry's outlook. For this reason, *diversification requires the grouping of securities which have a minimum amount of comovement.*

With appropriate diversification an investor can minimize the risk inherent in any one company's stock, while preserving the rate of return expectation for the overall portfolio. Harry Markowitz, who is considered the dean of portfolio analysis and is the author of the first, and certainly one of the most comprehensive, books on the subject, wrote:

In discharging his function of selecting securities to enter the analysis, the analyst should keep in mind the properties of a security which may make it a worthwhile addition to a portfolio. Not only should promising leads with respect to expected return (and risk) be considered, but also the value of low correlations should not be forgotten. [**112**, p. 115]

Unfortunately, what Markowitz said "should not be forgotten" frequently is. Gerald Tsai and his intertwined collection of stocks ignored portfolio diversification techniques for reducing investors' risk.

The Number and Amount of Separate Investments. A third aspect of portfolio analysis is deciding on the number of different securities to hold, as well as the dollar amount to be invested in each. To establish a bench mark for diversification, suppose a portfolio analyst pays no attention to comovement and just groups stocks into portfolios. In this situation, how many stocks would you have to hold to achieve the desirable risk-reducing effects of diversification?

The Research Bombshell

The effect of diversification in reducing risk was studied extensively by Jack Gaumnitz in his doctoral dissertation at Stanford University in 1967. Gaumnitz reported that the further lowering of risk was insignificant once the number of independently chosen securities in the portfolio reached 18. Furthermore, he reported that the returns from randomly generated portfolios tended to be higher than the returns from representative mutual funds. Gaumnitz concluded that "relatively few securities [are] needed for adequate diversification and good performance compared to mutual funds. . . ." [**57**, p. 146] Thus, Gaumnitz questioned two reasons why investors buy mutual funds: diversified risk and professional performance.

In 1968, John Evans also studied the effects of diversification in his doctoral dissertation at the University of Washington. Evans randomly constructed 2,400 portfolios, which were composed of from one to sixty

FIGURE 25–1
Impact of Number of Securities Held on Risk Level of Portfolio

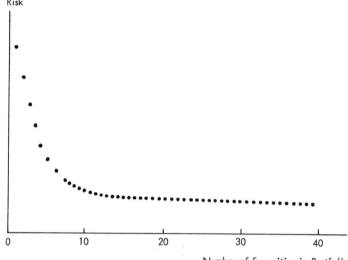

Source: Evans [39, pp. 57–58].

stocks: his results, which are summarized in Figure 25–1, are most surprising.

Evans' calculations show that a portfolio with maximum diversification (that is, equal dollar amounts in *all* stocks studied) would be expected to have a rate of return fluctuation (hence, risk) of 11.9 percent during a six-month period. Yet, if the investor held only one stock he could expect a six-month variation in his rate of return of approximately 20.5 percent. The startling part of Evans' research, however, is what happens when an investor places equal dollar amounts in portfolios consisting of two, three, four, five and ten securities. Notice in Figure 25–1 that the additional reduction in risk is relatively minor as one moves from a portfolio containing 10 securities to one containing 20 or even 40 securities. In fact, a randomly selected portfolio with equal dollar amounts in just five stocks has only slightly more risk (that is, one seventh more variation in expected return) than a portfolio with equal dollar amounts invested in *all* Evans' stocks.

Another Popular Belief Is Disproved

This evidence is clear! Holding more than a small number of unrelated stocks has a negligible impact on reducing your portfolio's risk. The importance of portfolio management lies not in the *number* of holdings, but rather in both the nature and degree of the combined risk of the underlying stocks. Brealey has shown quite dramatically what can happen when one considers both the nature and degree of risk in portfolio composition. He has reported that a portfolio containing only 11 securities, which were carefully selected for their risk-diversifying characteristics, would be less risky than a portfolio of 2,000 securities which were selected without regard to risk. Modern research shows quite conclusively "that the quality of diversification is more important than the quantity. . . ." [**12**, p. 127]

This research does not mean that large institutions should restrict themselves to a limited number of securities. In fact, the disruptive market influence of institutions' large holdings is already serious and would be compounded if they concentrated in still fewer securities. Rather, this research shows that there is a risk-reducing advantage to be had from true diversification. The importance of this research lies in its implications for the small investor. The small investor has been sold on the benefits of professional money management, such as through mutual funds, partially because of the diversification such large portfolios offer. This concept has been oversold!

Investors should realize that diversification, and the concomitant reduction of risk, pays off handsomely as holdings are increasingly diversified among two, three, four, and five unrelated stocks. *A typical portfolio with equal dollar amounts in just five stocks, selected for diverse risk characteristics, will have only slightly more risk than would be attained by placing equal dollar amounts in all stocks* (see [**39**]). The belief that small investors cannot adequately diversify their holdings is a myth!

Summary

You, as an intelligent and informed investor, can strike a happy balance between Gerald Tsai and Clint Murchison, Sr. Through proper diversification, you can achieve the same stable investment posture as Murchison, with a small fraction of the money he invested. While you will probably not enjoy Tsai's occasional performance spurts, you will be insured against concentration's double-edged sword—volatile ups *and* downs. All you need is five or six stocks, selected for their off-setting risk characteristics, to obtain stability comparable to most mutual funds, which invest hundreds of millions of dollars!

chapter
26
Winning the Investments Contest

Value Line, a widely distributed investment advisory service, has sponsored three public stock selection "contests." Although the rules and performance analyses of the three contests differ, *nonrandom* results are discernible in the myriad investment selections of the contestants. Since this conclusion appears to be counter to the efficient capital market theory, the contest results deserve special discussion.

The First Value Line Contest

According to the 1965 contest's rules, each entrant picked exactly 25 different stocks from an eligibility list of 350 stocks, 250 of which Value Line had rated "below average," with the remaining 100 rated "lowest" in terms of probable market performance. John Shelton [151], now Chairman of the Finance Department of U.C.L.A.'s Graduate School of Business Administration, published a thought-provoking analysis of the 18,565 different portfolios submitted by contestants that gives us much useful insight into our own investing contest.

Value Line's objective in running such a contest was, of course, to demonstrate the accuracy and usefulness of its ranking system. Therefore, Value Line itself entered the contest. It challenged contestants to outperform the Value Line portfolio. Unlike the other contestants, Value Line picked its portfolio from its group of highest-ranking stocks in terms of probable market performance. Value Line then published its portfolio. Six months later, the price appreciation of all portfolios was compared.

Of the 18,565 contestants, only 20 outperformed Value Line's selections. This appears at first glance to be strong evidence supporting the ability of such advisory services and an automatic refutation of efficient capital market theory. Unfortunately, though, it is impossible to say whether or not Value Line picked stocks well or if the stocks performed well *because* they were picked, published, and promoted by Value Line. Shelton very accurately noted that ". . . Value Line's good results may have arisen from the phenomena of self-fulfilling predictions. There is no way of knowing. . . ." [**151**, p. 267]

The real significance of Shelton's analysis of the first Value Line contest lies, however, not with "the competition between Value Line and the participants, but . . . with the unstated 'contest' between the total performance of the entrants and the average performance of the universe of stocks from which they made their selections." [**151**, p. 255] This "contest" can be thought of as an experiment to determine whether the contestants did better, or worse, than the market as a whole.

In terms of this experiment, Shelton concluded that "the average performance of the contestants was better than could have been expected if . . . stock prices (were) utterly unpredictable." [**151**, pp. 265–266] This much-heralded finding, arrived at by a careful and respected researcher, bolstered Wall Street's rejection of the efficient capital market theory. Shelton's conclusion that investors did a better-than-random job of stock selection is what people wanted to hear.

Unfortunately, Shelton's publicized conclusion that "the average score received by the 18,565 contestants . . . is significantly . . . greater than the expected . . . score" was not based on a risk-adjusted measure of performance. Shelton's statistical analysis assumed that contestants picked their stocks from the eligible list as if each stock had the same popularity among contestants. But, as Shelton himself clearly pointed out, the contestants favored certain stocks and neglected others. In fact, 10 percent of the stocks on the Value Line list accounted for 28 percent of the actual selections.

Warren Hausman, a member of Cornell's faculty, has shown how investors' tendencies to select particular stocks muddied the statistical waters in Shelton's study. Hausman emphasized that Shelton's conclusion that the average performance of contestants was significantly better than the performance attained by random selection was not necessarily correct. Hausman's more elaborate explanation of contestant behavior led him to conclude that it is "questionable" whether any nonrandom "skill" was demonstrated by the contestants [**70**, p. 320].

The Second Value Line Contest

In 1969, Value Line held another contest. For this contest, the rules were changed to allow contestants to select their 25-member portfolios from Value Line's entire list of 1,258 stocks. The public's response to the second contest, which is indicative of the publicity received by the 1965 contest, was overwhelming. The task of mailing entry forms to possible contestants far exceeded Value Line's estimates. Even with mail snafus, there were 65,000 on-time entrants. A separate contest was held for another 4,000 entrants who did not receive their entry forms before the filing deadline.

With such a large number of contestants, Value Line decided not to calculate the performance results for all portfolios. Instead, they provided each contestant with a list of how all 1,258 eligible stocks had performed during the six-month contest. Each entrant was asked to calculate the average return for his contest portfolio. If a contestant's actual portfolio entry exceeded the performance of all eligible stocks by 4 percent, he was instructed to submit a claim for validation and ranking. Unfortunately, this meant that nothing is known about the losers.

The data from the 1969 Value Line contest were analyzed by John Murphy, a financial analyst at American Express Investment Management Company. Murphy's conclusions, as published in the *Financial Analysts Journal,* were that "a large number of portfolio selectors did significantly better than random." [**123**, p. 99] This is a startling conclusion, especially since nothing is known about the results of people who performed poorly. Notice, too, that Murphy did not (and could not) conclude that the *average* performance of investors was better than random selection. Instead, he only wrote that "a large number of portfolio selectors did significantly better than random."

It is very likely, however, that people entering such a contest would submit undiversified portfolios of favorite stocks and industries. Indeed, this occurred! The contestants' portfolios were not well diversified and were structurally different from the random portfolios assumed by Murphy's performance comparison. Hence, the conclusion that "a large number of portfolio selectors did better than random" says no more than that the contestants' portfolios were less diversified than the random portfolios and showed more widely varying returns.

While many contestants "did better than random," it follows logically that many may have done *worse* than random. The published research on these two Value Line contests does not contradict the efficient capital market theory. The results, in fact, strongly indicate that some contestants did outperform the market—by merely adopting high risk!

The Third Value Line Contest

Value Line's third contest spanned the six-month period of August 18, 1972 to February 16, 1973. Again, the procedure was modified and Value Line supplied all contestants—nearly 90,000 this time—with a complete list of the service's rankings of the more than 1,400 eligible stocks from which each 25-stock portfolio could be chosen. As during the second contest period, the market was again for the birds and, like them, headed south for the winter. During the six-month contest, the price of the more than 1,400 stocks covered by Value Line went down an average of 6.7 percent.

The Actual Performance Results

In the three Value Line contests, substantial cash prizes were offered to those entrants whose portfolios appreciated most during the six-month period following the contest filing date. There was, of course, no penalty for loss and no risk associated with the contestants' portfolios. It was a *game*. Also, with few prizes for thousands of entrants, only the most extreme performance could win the game.

If one is to "play" such a game cleverly, *one should assume the wildest of risks*. If luck blesses the particular selections made, a prize might be won. If the high risk turns out unfavorably, so what! But, almost certainly any prudent, sound, or convervative portfolio would be buried somewhere in the middle of the performance game—winning nothing for its creator. Clearly, therefore, the way to win the game is to maximize risk by concentrating your selections in a single, volatile industry. If you hold such a high-risk portfolio, Nature's roulette wheel is more likely to toss you to the very high end (or very low end) of the performance scale than the average entrant. Without wide swings—risk taking—there would be almost no way to reach the top (or bottom) of such a large heap. With great rewards for being at the top and no penalty for being on the bottom this is the only way to play the game!

Murphy's analysis of the 1969 contest verifies that there were an extraordinarily large number of better-than-random portfolios *as measured by investment return only*. Shelton's data from the first contest showed the same effect. Yet, these results are easily explained by the fact that investors overtly chose more risky portfolios. So while many people outperformed random selection in the Value Line contests, a large group also did worse than random. Contestants chose not to diversify to the degree that the requirement of having to pick 25 different stocks would imply. Naturally or deliberately, they selected high-risk portfolios. This tendency to thwart the intent of the mandated diversification into 25 stocks is sufficient to explain the nonrandom results that were observed.

How to "Play" the Performance Contest

Many rational contestants looked at the Value Line contests as just that—a contest. The payoff opportunity came from an extremely slim chance for a large prize, coupled with no risk of personal loss for poor performance. In this situation, the best strategy is to pick an extremely risky portfolio and hope its widely swinging results will happen to be on the upside.

It is not difficult to select a portfolio that will be extremely risky. One method of increasing risk is by concentration—holding only a few issues in one's portfolio. Value Line, however, required exactly 25 issues in each contestant's portfolio. This tends to lessen the impact of any single stock's performance. Wit can easily be matched by wit. Skilled contestants sought to revoke this law of large numbers, which tends to stabilize the performance of a many-stock portfolio. How can the effect of this enforced numerical diversification be nullified?

The new science of investing holds the answer. We know that stocks in certain industries tend to move together. The risk-reducing effect of diversification comes from the fact that a loss in a stock in one industry can often be offset by gains in another industry. The risk-stabilizing effect of diversification can easily be overcome, however, if one's 25 stocks are confined to a few closely related industries.

Stock price movements within certain industries, such as metals and oils, are highly correlated. Also, the shares of companies belonging to certain industry groups, such as the extraction and mining industries, tend to act very similarly in the market. A Value Line contestant's success, or lack of it, is likely to be far more dramatic if he tries to pick a "lucky" industry than if he scatters his 25 stocks among several, often counterbalancing, industries. With such a concentration strategy, risk is high and the impact of diversification is reduced, despite the fact that the contestant is forced to hold 25 separate stocks.

Value Line's contest data reflect precisely this kind of contestant behavior. Far from selecting random stocks, the contestants showed a preference for certain stocks and for risk-accented portfolios. In effect, the contestants' results show a statistical pattern corresponding to holding fewer than 25 randomly chosen stocks. That is, the contestants avoided full diversification and encouraged risk, so that their portfolios were characterized by wider swings—both up and down—than would be expected from portfolios of 25 randomly diversified stocks.

Clearly, this investment strategy is fine for a *contest,* but few investors would entertain such a strategy when their personal capital is at stake. Far from verifying the existence of superior analysts producing better-than-random results, the Value Line contests confirm only that a game is a game. When the chances of winning are slim and there is no real penalty for losing, contestants should naturally gamble for outstanding performance. This is very rational behavior for a contest!

How to "Win" the Performance Contest—Sometimes

It is clear that high risk—concentration in the highly volatile shares of similar companies—offers the only hope of sufficiently exceptional performance to win the Value Line contest. Within this strategy of concentration in volatile companies in related industries, there are many possible portfolios from which to choose. Which portfolio has the best chance of being rare in its performance? In addition to being dependent on their industries, almost all stocks are also dependent on the market as a whole. Since all stocks tend to move together, it becomes especially difficult to pick a 25-stock portfolio likely to be significantly different (hopefully on the upside) from the thousands of other contestants' portfolios.

For the clever contestant who realizes that his chances of winning improve by adopting a wildly different strategy, there is a very logical additional step—selecting a "crisis" industry," such as the "gold crisis" or the "energy crisis," that is likely to move *counter* to the general market. For many years, stocks of firms in the extractive industries, particularly gold-mining stocks, have been havens for the bears because of their tendency to go up when the market goes down. Gold stocks represent the one industry whose "market effect" is generally in a direction opposite to that of all other groups!

Now we have the perfect strategy for the Value Line contest. First of all, assume a very risky investment posture so as to separate yourself from (hopefully above) the crowd. This is best done by concentrating your 25 selections in very volatile stocks in a single industry or closely related ones. Even with this extremely risky posture, your investments and those of the thousands of other contestants will be swept along by the market. You are gambling, in this situation, that you can outdistance the run of the market.

There is another very good gamble. You can concentrate your investments in "crisis industries" which can be expected to move most *differently* from the parade of all the rest. In short, you can gamble on a gold crisis, an energy crisis, or whatever industry is likely to move independently—and differently—from the market at large. Should the market go down (an almost 50–50 bet in any six-month period), most portfolios will go down with it. A portfolio designed for crisis speculation, however, would pay off handsomely—as long as the crisis materializes.

Such a contest makes no pretension to superior analysis. This strategy, in fact, assumes that the market is unpredictable! Working from this premise, we have merely developed the most logical *contest* portfolio. The strategy does not require skilled investment selection. It merely says that, if the crisis materializes, the portfolio will stand a good chance of winning by being concentrated in this single industry.

What happened during the 1969 and 1972–73 Value Line contests? The market went down! In the six-month period from November 15, 1968 to May 16, 1969, the average stock in the contest fell 1.51 percent during the incipient "gold crisis." Not surprisingly, virtually every winning contestant in the 1969 Value Line contest had "a heavy concentration in extractive industries, particularly gold mining." [123, p. 99] In the six-month period from August 18, 1972 to February 16, 1973, the average stock on the official contest list fell 6.7 percent during talk of an approaching "energy crisis." The latter contest's winning portfolio, reproduced in Table 26–1, is composed entirely of stocks of *oil and gas companies!*

Another "scientific" way to play the Value Line contest is to submit portfolios selected entirely on the basis of beta coefficients. You can only be certain that the market will either go up or down (or end up where it started). If the market goes up, a high-beta portfolio should amplify the upward market movement and perform better than a well-diversified portfolio. If you hold such a high-beta portfolio in a down market you would expect to amplify the drop and have a loss that is much greater than from a well-diversified portfolio. But, since there is no penalty for loss in a contest, a wise strategy would be to hold a portfolio with the

TABLE 26–1
The Value Line Contest's Winning Portfolio
(Aug. 18, 1972 to Feb. 16, 1973)

Amerada Hess	Mapco
Apco Oil	Mesa Petroleum
Ashland Oil	Mountain Fuel Supply
Atlantic Richfield	Murphy Oil
Aztec Oil & Gas	Pacific Petroleums
Belco Petroleum	Phillips Petroleum
Cities Service	Skelly Oil
Clark Oil & Refining	Standard Oil (Indiana)
Continental Oil	Standard Oil (Ohio)
El Paso Natural Gas	Sun Oil
General American Oil of Texas	Superior Oil
Getty Oil	Union Oil of California
Helmerich & Payne	

highest possible beta and hope for an upward market swing. Conversely, in anticipation that the market might go down, it would be wise to hold an extremely low-beta portfolio.

This approach to the contest was tested by Robert Kaplan and Roman Weil [83] who submitted one very high- and one very low-beta portfolio. Since the market went down during the period, our *a priori* expectation would be that their low-beta portfolio would rank high in the performance derby and their high-beta portfolio would be among the worst performers. Illustrating not only the relevance of beta coefficients, but also the importance of setting your portfolio policy in terms of an overall market forecast, the Kaplan-Weil low-beta portfolio ranked in the top 2.3 percent of all portfolios. Their high-beta portfolio, which amplified the downward movement of the market, placed them in the lowest 0.6 of one percent of all contest portfolios.

The significance of these results is that if you do not monitor your portfolio in terms of beta and industry concentration *you might also have a portfolio designed for all or nothing performance.*

The Parallel to Investment Management

The closing note of this discussion is to draw the parallel to the behavior of some investment managers. As of June 30, 1970, following a severe market drop, the best-performing mutual fund for the prior 12 months was a fund investing solely in federal government bonds. Investment in these instruments amounts to the gold or crisis industry stock strategy. By investing in government bonds with a safe, steady, modest return, if the market falls out of bed you will be a comparative winner. Investors should remember, however, that such a fund can be expected to provide poor relative performance in up markets—just as the 1970 winner did in the year *after* it received "contest" accolades.

The crux of the matter is knowing when, and when not, to take risks. Commenting on the correlation between risk and performance, Edward Zinbarg, vice president in charge of common stock investments at Prudential Insurance Company of America, told a seminar sponsored by the New York Society of Security Analysts that "You've all heard the comment, 'Well, big deal. You did very well because you took more risk.' . . . But the fact is, . . . , I did take more risk. I was smart enough to take more risk and you weren't." [**172,** p. 52] Making *your* investment decisions is the subject to which we now turn.

part II
applying the new science to personal investing

C ANALYZING ALTERNATIVE INVESTMENT INSTRUMENTS

chapter
27
You and Your Investment Alternatives

This concluding five-chapter section synthesizes what we know about investing into a practical investment strategy that can be applied by any investor with reasonable hope for above-average return. Fortunately, even though most of the research that has spawned the new science of investing tell us how *not* to invest, it also offers many clues on *how to invest*.

Investing should be a seven-step cycle:

1. Establishing realistic investment objectives and implementing an *insure, invest, spend the rest* plan which *guarantees* the required annual investment increments necessary to attain your objectives;
2. Developing a reasoned perspective on the overall market outlook;
3. Establishing a balanced portfolio policy by setting the relative size of the conservative, aggressive, and speculative layers of the asset triangle;
4. Deciding on the mix of investment instruments (stocks, bonds, puts, calls, mutual funds, and so forth) which, in combination, are most likely to enable you to achieve your objectives;
5. Determining those industries which are most likely to offer the performance sought;
6. Selecting specific investments that meet the criteria established for each layer of the asset triangle; and
7. Monitoring the performance of each layer of the asset triangle, and each underlying investment, against the established objectives.

Objectives

A prerequisite to successful investing is establishing realistic objectives. The great Roman orator and philosopher Cicero, who died in 43 B.C., wrote "It is difficult to set bounds to the price unless you first set bounds to the wish." Cicero's wisdom still applies after 2,000 years. Unfortunately, however, we hear so much about "double your money" strategies that many investors lose sight of what should be realistically expected from their investments.

To the astonishment of many businessmen, public opinion surveys repeatedly show that "the man on the street" estimates after-tax profits on sales for U.S. corporations to be in the neighborhood of 25 percent! In reality, these after-tax profit margins have averaged about 5 percent over the last quarter century. Since people grossly overestimate corporate profits, they are also susceptible to overestimating the probable returns from their own investments. As a *Business Week* editorial commented, "Unless this area of public ignorance is corrected, U.S. economic policy [and investment decisions are] . . . likely to be based on a fantastic misconception." [**181**, p. 88] To prevent such inflated expectations from clouding investment decisions, the first step toward rational investing is to establish a reasonable goal.

Chapter 3 outlined the steps necessary to translate an ill-defined need for future financial security into a specific measurable investment goal. As stated earlier, attaining this goal and its related milestones depends on

- the value of your current investments,
- the amount and timing of additional investments,
- the amount and timing of interim investment withdrawals, and
- the rate of return on your investments.

It is highly recommended that readers avail themselves of one of the computerized financial planning services offered by an ever-increasing number of banks and brokerage firms. These analyses are invaluable for projecting year-by-year portfolio returns. Barring this kind of detailed planning, however, you should at least establish a goal and estimate the approximate annual investment required to reach it.

Market Outlook

The second step of the investment cycle is to develop a reasoned perspective on the overall market outlook. Clearly, no one can purport to predict, with 100 percent accuracy, each turn of the market. Conversely, however, too many investors substitute wishful thinking for the scientific tools we discussed in Chapter 16 that can be used to attain a reasoned perspective of the future course of the market. It must be remembered that, on average, more than 30 percent of the movement in the price of a stock can be traced to sympathetic market comovements. It is our conclusion that even a cursory examination of the forecasts by monetary theorists, econometric forecasting models, leading indicators, and consumer intention surveys, while not pin-pointing every turn of the market, can give investors a useful perspective from which to approach their basic investment decisions.

Portfolio Policy

The third step to successful investing is to establish a portfolio policy by setting the size of the conservative, aggressive, and speculative layers of your asset triangle. The investments comprising each layer are distinguished by two factors: the anticipated performance (risk/return) and the anticipated holding period. Figure 27–1 illustrates these two distinguishing characteristics for speculative investments: high anticipated return (with concomitant high risk) and a relatively short-term anticipated holding period.

FIGURE 27–1
Speculative Layer of the Asset Triangle

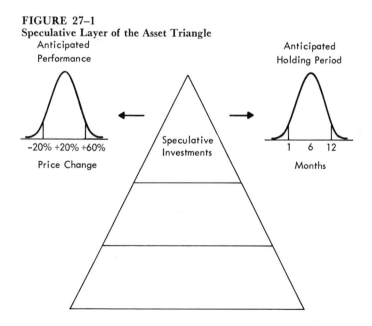

The two bell-shaped curves on either side of the triangle in Figure 27–1 show that the investment is selected because it is *expected* to return *as much as* 20 percent in 6 months. The bell-shaped (so-called "normal") curve is used by statisticians to show normal variations from expectations: As drawn in Figure 27–1, these curves show that you might expect 90 percent of the investment instruments selected for this category to provide a return of between −20 percent and +60 percent sometime within the next 1 to 12 months.

The distinguishing features of aggressive-level investments are shown in Figure 27–2. An investment in the aggressive layer of the triangle would be expected to return, on average, as much as 15 percent in 12 months. Such investments would be expected to be less volatile than those in the top layer and, consequently, could be purchased with a longer anticipated holding period in mind.

FIGURE 27–2
Aggressive Layer of the Asset Triangle

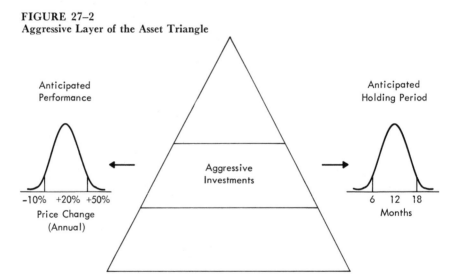

The bell-shaped curve to the left of the asset triangle illustrates that 90 percent of these investments might have returns between −15 percent and +45 percent and that the anticipated price changes are expected to occur in 12 months, though the potential span over which they could take place is set at 6 to 18 months. Hence, in comparison with those investments held in the speculative layer, the aggressive investments are expected to fluctuate less and be held over a longer period.

The conservative layer of the asset triangle is depicted in Figure 27–3. Investments in this layer are selected because they are expected to offer

FIGURE 27–3
Conservative Layer of the Asset Triangle

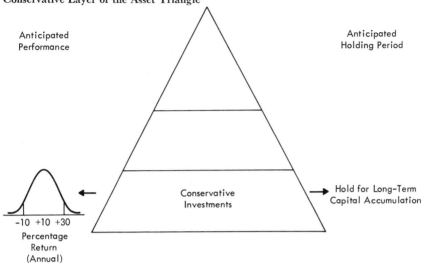

an average return of 10 percent per year. Another extremely important feature of conservative investments is that they are viewed as quality holdings that are *purchased with the intention that they will be held for long-term capital accumulation.* These investments should be carefully selected to protect against downside risk and, as shown in Figure 27–3, should rarely provide a total annual rate of return (including dividends) that falls below −10 percent.

The necessity to categorize investments that seem to belong *between* these definitions of speculative, aggressive, or conservative should not blur the conceptual importance of having a profit and time expectation for every investment. The "in-between" classification problem can be readily handled by establishing the admittedly cautious convention that anything even modestly above the percentage return guidelines for a particular layer should be categorized in the next higher, hence more speculative, layer of the triangle.

Investments that purportedly offer more return than that represented by the highest layer of the triangle can be handled by the same convention. They can be shifted to the next higher risk level of the triangle—*the one that does not exist as part of a rationally designed investment portfolio.* When an investment does not fit into one of the three classification levels because one feels the possible downside loss is "nowhere near," let's say, —20 percent, we politely remind the reader that risk is a dou-ble-edged sword and that can cut both ways!

The relative size of the speculative, aggressive, and conservative layers of each individual's asset triangle depends on

- the certainty with which we foresee the future health of the over-all market, and
- the individual's proclivity for risk.

In investing, knowing the market's future can be profitable no matter what the direction of security prices. In the words of Ralph Waldo Emerson, "this time, like all other times, is a very good one, if we but know what to do with it." Indeed, if we are certain the market is going down, we can profit just as surely as when we know that the market is going up. For this reason, the proportion of your assets that is allocated to a particular level of the asset triangle does not depend on the direction in which you believe the overall market to be heading, but instead on your *certainty about that forecast!*

The other important ingredient in establishing the relative size of the various levels of your asset triangle is your willingness to take bigger risks in the hope of securing extra returns. The interrelationship between your certainty about the future and your preference for risk, and how these variables translate into various asset triangles, appears in Figure 27–4.

Most people want protected growth and, most of the time, we have only a normal degree of confidence in our market predictions. In this case, which includes most of the people most of the time, the 15–35–50 asset triangle depicted in the upper-left corner of Figure 27–4 might be an appropriate distribution of one's investment dollars.

Two things can happen to make us assume a more risky posture. We can, by individual preference, prefer a triangle that reflects a more risky posture. Or, if we were more confident about the future, we might also rationally opt for more speculative assets. For example, the individual whose objective is protected growth of assets could, with increased confidence in the future, move to the more speculative 25–35–40 triangle shown in the lower-left corner of Figure 27–4. Similarly, a speculator with only normal confidence in the future course of the market could reasonably allocate his investment dollars according to the 25–35–40 tri-angle depicted in the upper-right corner. A more extreme case, the com-bination of prudent speculation coupled with increased confidence about

FIGURE 27–4
Translating Your Confidence About the Future into the Appropriately Proportioned Asset Triangle

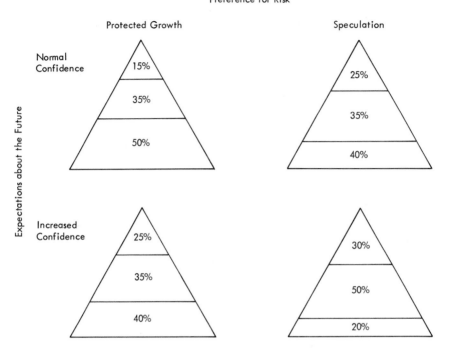

the future, could justify the 30–50–20 triangle shown in the lower-right corner.

Mix of Investment Instruments

Having defined the characteristics of the investments that go into each layer of the triangle in terms of both expected total return and holding period, and having examined guidelines for determining the proportions of your assets that belong in each layer, we must select investment *instruments* that meet our expected appreciation and holding-period criteria. Successful investing demands that you reorient your thinking to the broad spectrum of investment instruments and select those best suited to your personal needs at a given point in time. Besides stocks and bonds, there are puts, calls, warrants, commodity futures, and shares of mutual funds—to name only a few. Many alternatives are also available within each general instrument category. Bonds, for example, include tax-free municipals, convertible debentures, speculative discount bonds, triple A corporates, a host of government issues, and so forth. Even in the seemingly high-priced area of real estate, for as little as $25 you can buy a share of a Real Estate Investment Trust (called an REIT), which allows you to participate in the growth of selected real estate.

It has been said that, because of the large number of options available on today's automobiles, and the consequently far greater number of option combinations available, it would be possible for a manufacturer to produce cars all year without making two autos which were exactly the same. The same statistical phenomenon applies to how investment instruments can be combined into portfolios. Considering investment *instruments* alone, without regard to underlying companies, investors have more than 25 different alternatives. Suppose that you decided to own only 5 instruments. Five instruments could be selected from 25 available alternatives in 53,130 different ways. Thus, with 25 choices, 53,130 people can each hold a different combination of 5 instruments!

Why, then, do most investors just buy stock or mutual fund shares? The answer is that the average investor has failed to define measurable financial objectives and then analyze the many available alternatives to determine the *combination of instruments that is best suited to his specific goals and objectives.*

One point that occurs again and again in the new science of investing is that owning "good stocks" at the wrong time can cause disappointing losses. Hence, the kinds of investments that go into a particular layer of the triangle must depend on one's market outlook. We have examined econometric and, more importantly, marketometric forecasting based on monetary, Keynesian, and leading indicator analysis. We can conclude that the *consensus* of these forecasts, at any point in time, permits an investor to make a reasoned judgment about the future.

If we were to start today and take a monthly consensus of marketometric forecasts and expert opinions, the distribution of such forecasts several years hence would probably look something like the one depicted in Figure 27–5. Much of the time, such an exercise would be expected to show that the prevailing consensus, say for a time six months in the future, is "neutral or undecided." Such a projection, however, is far from cause for despair. If almost everyone is undecided, the odds are that the market is undecided. Without a changed consensus, the odds are that the market will neither fall out of bed nor take off like a rocket. Similarly, while the near-term consensus remains optimistic, it is unlikely that you could suddenly find yourself in a serious bear market.

FIGURE 27–5
Distribution of Five Possible States of Market Anticipation about Some Designated
Future Time as Derived from a Consensus of Marketometric Forecasts and Expert
Opinions

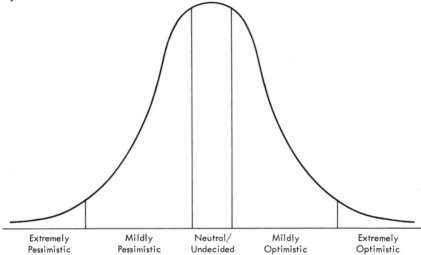

| Extremely Pessimistic | Mildly Pessimistic | Neutral/ Undecided | Mildly Optimistic | Extremely Optimistic |

Hence, with at least some assurance that extreme misestimates are
unlikely, you can select investment instruments for the three layers of
your asset triangle that are keyed to your near-, intermediate-, and long-
term market expectations. If this kind of careful market assessment pre-
cedes stock analysis, it is less likely for you to find yourself in "good"
stocks when the odds are that even "bad" bonds would be a better investment *instrument* in the forthcoming market! In the words of Professor
James Lorie, the astute and acclaimed author-professor of finance at
the University of Chicago, *"the most important investment decision is
not the selection of particular stocks, but the choice of an investment
strategy—the selection of the kinds and types of assets in their relative
proportions in a diversified portfolio* [italics added]." [**182**, p. 111]

Figure 27–6 summarizes *guidelines* that can be used to select investment instruments and strategies that will provide the combinations of
risk-reward expectations and holding periods that we have designated
for each level of the asset triangle. In looking at Figure 27–6, it is important to remember that, at a given point in time, our expectations may
be different for different time horizons. The consensus could, for example,
be neutral about the near-term, but mildly optimistic about the market's
medium- and long-term prospects.

FIGURE 27–6
Selection of Investment Instruments from Consensus of Market Forecasts

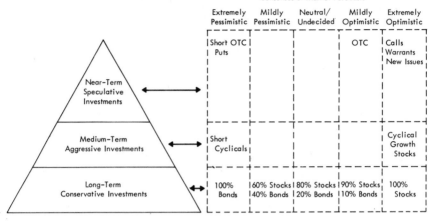

Consensus of Market Forecasts

	Extremely Pessimistic	Mildly Pessimistic	Neutral/ Undecided	Mildly Optimistic	Extremely Optimistic
Near-Term Speculative Investments	Short OTC Puts			OTC	Calls Warrants New Issues
Medium-Term Aggressive Investments	Short Cyclicals				Cyclical Growth Stocks
Long-Term Conservative Investments	100% Bonds	60% Stocks 40% Bonds	80% Stocks 20% Bonds	90% Stocks 10% Bonds	100% Stocks

Armed with a consensus of market forecasts, Figure 27–6 can be used as a guide to selecting the most appropriate instruments. If, for example, your near-term market forecast could be classified as "extremely optimistic," the appropriate instruments might be calls, warrants, new issues, and so on.

The lower level of Figure 27–6 requires special explanation. Remember that the conservative investment layer of the asset triangle is made up of high-quality investments that are held for long-term capital accumulation. The assets in this layer of the asset triangle are *not* trading vehicles which you have purchased in hopes of catching the market moving in the right direction. The only problem with the "hold-quality-stocks-forever" approach is that the winds of market adversity cannot only topple a poorly constructed triangle, but they can also literally blow away the pieces.

Consider, for example, the individuals who held "quality" stocks through the 1969–73 bear markets. By 1973, some of these "quality" stocks were still approximately half of their early 1969 value. Unfortunate investors who held steadfastly to their convictions or, even worse, bought more of these stocks on the way down, found themselves in a position where they needed a *doubling in value in a "conservative" investment to get back where they were four years before!*

To prevent such losses one should, when his market forecast so dictates, *alter the mix of investment instruments in the conservative layer of the triangle.* For example, it is irrational to hold stocks as a conservative investment if you are pessimistic about long-term market performance. An *approximate guide* for putting together the appropriate mixture of stocks and bonds, given various long-term expectations, appears in the lower level of Figure 27–6. These numbers should not be rigidly construed. What is rigid is the principle that rational investing demands that you prevent or curtail losses!

Sitting by, watching the price of quality stocks tumble, does not make sense. Nor, in this author's judgment, does buying quality stocks at a lower price in a bear market make sense. Unfortunately, however, most Wall Street research comes from analysts who follow *stocks*. These analysts frequently become so enamored with the stock they recommended at $40 that they reason it is a better buy if it is at $30, and better still at $25. Maybe it is, but the important point is not to look at the trees before you look at the forest. If the forest burns, all the trees go with it. Stated another way, *first make your market forecast and* then *decide on the appropriate instrument.* And caution yourself to remember that many Wall Street analysts recommend purchasing stocks in every market!

Industry Analysis

One conclusion we can draw from the new science of investing is that *it is more important (and easier) to be in the "right" industry than in the "right" stock.* This has been confirmed by research as well as the most recent Value Line investment contest. Of the almost 90,000 portfolio's entered in this contest, those with the best performance did not reflect the skillful selection of the "right" stocks. As expected, the winning portfolios in this contest reflected the skillful selection of the "right" industry.

Much progress is being made in industry forecasting techniques. The most modern and fruitful approach to industry forecasting is to attempt to translate various economic, fiscal, and attitude forecasts into predictions of key industry variables. The problem faced by modern industry analysts thus becomes one of translating the forecasts of general economic variables into forecasts of interest in a particular industry. A generalized economic forecast might, for example, estimate future costs of raw materials, wage rates, consumer spending power, credit availability, and so forth. In an industry, such as automobiles, a security analyst is concerned with more specific industry-related information such as unit sales of automobiles and price levels. By using sophisticated equations, researchers are now taking the information produced by the general economic forecast and using it to forecast specific industry variables, such as automobile demand and prices. In turn, these are then used to forecast company-level and profitability and stock performance.

Selecting Specific Investments

The essential differences among investments selected for each layer of the asset triangle are, as we have mentioned, determined by expected performance, potential downside risk, and anticipated holding period. Earlier chapters also examined the double-edged sword of risk and return. Our conclusion was that, contrary to the mistaken intuition of naïve investors, the potential for extraordinary gain is accompanied by the unavoidable potential for extraordinary loss. The fortune-cookie philosophy of "temptation resisted is pleasure lost" does not hold in the area of investments. The "sure thing" just does not exist. Even the seemingly riskless insured savings accounts of banks and savings institutions have the subtle risk of being eroded by inflation.

The important point to remember about risk is not that it can somehow be erased, but that it can, through proper diversification, be controlled. The new science of investing uses the concept of beta to measure this risk. As discussed in Chapter 20, beta is a quantification of two fundamental tenets of the new science:

- Most price movements bear a close relationship to the overall market, and
- Stocks offering higher rewards inflict disproportionately higher risks.

The beta measurement thus reflects a stock's (or a portfolio's) sensitivity to the overall market, which is designated as having a beta of 1.0.

When selecting investments for the speculative layer of the asset triangle, you *seek* high-beta stocks which are expected to amplify the overall market's movements. Conversely, for the conservative layer you should seek investment vehicles with a combined beta value that is below the market so as to dampen the impact of the market's overall movements. This concept is shown graphically in Figure 27–7.

Monitoring Investment Performance

Will Rogers' investment advice was "take your savings and buy some good stock and hold it till it goes up, then sell it. If it don't go up, don't buy it." Everyone expects his investments to increase in value. One

FIGURE 27-7
Comparative Volatility of Selected Investments

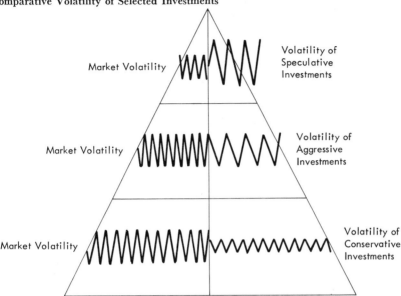

Market Volatility — Volatility of Speculative Investments

Market Volatility — Volatility of Aggressive Investments

Market Volatility — Volatility of Conservative Investments

of the most difficult things about rational investing, however, is knowing when you have been wrong. The need to know this emphasizes the importance of setting risk and reward limits on each investment. Suppose, for example, that you buy a stock at $42 for the aggressive layer of your asset triangle. For a stock in this category you expect, by definition of the layer, to realize a profit of 15 percent in approximately 12 months. You also expect that investments selected for this layer of the triangle will probably confine 90 percent of their price fluctuations within a range from −15 percent to +45 percent. With these expectations established when you buy the stock, you know when you have been *wrong*. You can, of course, be wrong two ways. The stock might fall more than 15 percent, or, more happily, it might go up more than 45 percent. The big question is what to do when you realize you were *wrong*.

When an investment's performance has *exceeded* your expectation, there are two schools of thought about what you should do. Some reason that you have so surpassed your expectation that you should be content with the gain and liquidate the position. The opposing school of thought holds that you should always let your profits run. The latter position is essentially the philosophy of Gerald M. Loeb, author of *The Battle for Investment Survival* [102] (also see [103]). Basically, Loeb espouses an investment philosophy whereby an investor places 10 percent of his assets in a single, listed security that is speculative, yet liquid. (Note that the speculative layer of the triangle that we propose is more diversified.) Upon investing 10 percent in one security, Loeb advises the investor to set a short-term investment objective. If the objective is not realized, he encourages him to move to a more suitable investment. In this way, Loeb contends the investor can move quickly out of situations that do not work out as planned and, in so doing, can gain by "losing less" in bad situations.

There are opposing points of view about what action to take when your expectations were wrong and you have a known loss and fear an even larger loss. On the one hand, some contend that the surest way to protect against "big" losses is to take them when they are still "little." On the other hand, the advocates of dollar averaging take the position that "if it was a good quality buy at 40, it is twice as good a buy at 20."

In a nutshell, the problem with all these approaches is that there have been times when each would have been incorrect. The answer lies *not* in developing hard-and-fast strategies, but in knowing when to apply one strategy or the other. The key to this seemingly complex puzzle of putting together a profitable investment monitoring system, which will *protect assets* while insuring growth, rests in the accuracy with which one can predict overall market swings.

The new science of investing is almost unanimous in its acceptance of efficient capital market theory. This theory raises serious doubts about the usefulness of traditional forms of security analysis. As discussed earlier, traditional security analysis has failed most tests of theoretical soundness, empirical investigation, and real-world performance. Three strikes are enough in any game—especially when there is an alternative game. The "keep-swinging-and-you-are-bound-to-hit-a-few" approach of the past has scored in the good years but erased the gains in bad years.

The new science of investing has shown that the common denominator in the performance equation is *risk*. If you structure your assets with a high degree of risk, your performance will amplify the market's movements—up and down. Logically, then, the route to successful asset management is to scale portfolio risk according to the overall market outlook.

To operationalize this strategy you should have, at all times, an opinion on the future course of the market derived from the econometric and marketometric forecasts we discussed in Chapter 16. You must remember, however, that such forecasts are not infallible. They are intended as a guide to avoiding the classic mistake of being in the wrong instrument or industry at the wrong time. Also, while the accuracy of marketometric analysis is continually improving through more sophisticated forecasting techniques, such analysis should not be construed as a method of short-term market timing. The planning horizon of marketometric forecasts is seldom less than three months.

The new science of investing has shown that innumerable trading strategies, when properly adjusted for risk, have failed to outperform a simple buy-and-hold policy. Two important points should be emphasized, however, to guard against misinterpretation of these findings. First, the research carries the proviso that the comparative performances are "properly adjusted for risk." There are, obviously, performance differences, but the research shows that these differences can be *explained* by *risk* and *chance variations*. Thus, if an investment performs significantly better than the market, the explanation may lie less in the skillful selection of a particular company than in being either in the right risk category at the right time or in just being lucky. Since we cannot control luck, superior investment performance boils down to knowing when to take risks and knowing when to be defensive.

The second important point about the research demonstrating the superiority of buy-and-hold investment strategies is that such studies contrast buying and holding investments in one risk category with strategies designed to select the "best" investments *in that risk category*. Expressed metaphorically, these studies contrast the performance of people who buy and hold apples with that of people who continually trade their apples *for seemingly "better" apples*. Such apple-for-apple traders feel intuitively that they can select better apples, or more appropriately, better stocks. Yet, the wealth of evidence supporting the efficient capital market theory questions the profitability of trading a stock in one risk category for another with the same degree and kinds of risk.[1]

We know from the new science of investing that, when you restrict yourself to a particular investment instrument, say speculative stocks, it is unlikely that trading investments *within that category* can improve your long-run results over those obtainable from a buy-and-hold strategy. This seemingly dour conclusion tells us what one must do to develop a successful investing strategy. Quite simply, you need to avoid downside losses and be in the right instrument at the right time. This means that you must move out of bad investments before losses become serious, but

---

[1] Realizing capital losses for tax purposes may justify a switch to a similar investment.

in so doing, *you must be careful not to sell one investment merely to buy another with almost identical risk and comovement characteristics.*

To implement such a strategy you must establish an explicit performance expectation and anticipated holding period for *each* investment. Such an expectation should be thought of as the midpoint in a range of expected fluctuations. In this way, by explicitly designating your expectations about the performance and holding period when the investment is made, you can monitor the performance against your expectations and avoid significant downside losses. But remember, the *only rational reason to switch an investment is to invest in something in a "significantly" different risk category!* Something that, in addition to being the best in its category, is going to rise, bob and float, or sink differently in the waves of the overall market!

Conclusion

One of the most startling conclusions of the new science of investing is that selecting individual stocks is *not* your most important investment decision. This almost revolutionary conclusion emphasizes *objectives and the market, portfolio, industry, instrument, and industry factors.* Unfortunately, however, the current ritual practiced by thousands of security analysts continues to focus on the selection of individual stocks. Yet, in an already efficient market, this approach has not successfully discerned, and cannot successfully discern, undervalued securities. Furthermore, analysis which concentrates on company-level information, such as forecasting earnings, can be overshadowed by investors' attitudes toward the company's industry and the market in general. Similarly, information on the stock's risk, as measured by its historical price volatility, affects portfolio composition and hence demand for that stock.

The energy myopically focused on stock selection, and the need to rechannel this analysis, is brought into clear focus by the research supporting the efficient capital market theory. This theory holds that when a large number of buyers and sellers with access to the same information actively compete, the market will become economically efficient. In such a market, *a stock's price, at any point in time, is a risk-adjusted measure of its true value and fully reflects all available information.*

While some investors may be unaware of the efficient capital market theory, the experience of most investment professionals, as well as the existing statistical research, supports its conclusion. In practice, many investors are becoming increasingly skeptical about any analysis which countermands the message of the market itself by saying that a stock's price is currently too high or too low.

Practically speaking, when many people study the same company, two things happen. First, its price at any moment is an accurate, risk-adjusted measure of value that reflects the composite opinion of numerous analysts. Second, it is very difficult for any one analyst to be consistently better than the best opinion of all other analysts and investors. James Lorie and Mary Hamilton recently noted the failure of most security analysis ". . . to determine or even consider whether the price of the stock already reflects the substance of the analysis." [107, p. 100]

Among investors, as well as analysts, there is a great temptation to project opinion and hope into their decision making. For example, concluding that the long-term earnings prospects for Eastman Kodak exceed those of U.S. Steel is only part of the story. The market *already* believes this is so. As a result, investors have typically valued Kodak's current earnings more highly than those of U.S. Steel. In the environment of an efficient stock market, the proper approach to investing involves the seven-step sequence described in this chapter. This approach focuses on those elements of investing which you can control and which account for the majority of your performance. Additional investment instruments—other than stock—are analyzed next.

chapter
28
Mutual Funds

In 1940, mutual funds managed less than $500 million of investors' assets. By 1970, in the relatively short span of 30 years, mutual fund assets increased by over one hundredfold to $50 billion spread among some 12 million shareholder accounts. Yet, for the first years in history, mutual funds subsequently experienced net redemptions—more customers' money coming out than flowing in.

Mutual funds seem, intuitively, an easy way for the small, or even the large, investor to own securities. By pooling investors' assets into one diversified portfolio, mutual funds relieve their shareholders of responsibility for investment monitoring and decision making. Brokerage commissions paid by mutual funds on their large block transactions are also proportionately less than those charged for small, individual orders. In addition, mutual funds simplify personal tax reporting by giving each shareholder an annual statement consolidating the investment results of many transactions involving different securities. Mutual funds are a *good* idea. This chapter explains how to use them.

Owning Your Share of American Business

During the 1960s, stock ownership grew in vogue. The psychology of growth was pervasive and brokers persuasive. As the public became convinced of the merit of owning stocks, mutual funds capitalized on this feeling, as well as helping to create it. Unhappily, in the bear markets of 1966, 1969–70 and 1973, over the decade stocks generally did not afford good returns relative to their risks and relative to other investment alternatives.

Mutual funds are an often recommended way for the "little investor" to own stocks. Through a mutual fund, separate investors share a common portfolio and can tap the professional management and protective diversification that large size can buy. Mutual funds, however, are not restricted to stocks, and many seek income through bonds and other instruments, sometimes balanced by stocks. Also, special-purpose funds exist for investing in a particular objective (growth), a specialized instrument (tax-exempt bonds), a philosophy (smaller growth stocks), an industry (financial services), a science (oceanography), a moral philosophy (peace), leverage (in income or capital gain), real property (real estate investment trusts), venture capital (closed-end and private placement funds), and so forth.

It is likely that Mr. Sai ("Small Average Investor," pronounced "Sigh," not Tsai!) is presold on investment in the great American stock market. It is true that a low-expense, diversified fund can effectively provide Mr. Sai with the general rate of return attainable from stocks, minus a modest overhead cost for participation. Mutual funds offer certain pivotal advantages—diversification, professional investment management, and lower commissions due to larger trades—over the do-it-yourself method.

Numerous research studies by unbiased investigators conclude, however, that professional money managers, despite a myriad of techniques and research, have failed to provide above-average investment results. In fact, some evidence identifies such management as a source of expense rather than profit. Furthermore, we have seen that diversification, which *is* desirable in reducing risk while maintaining expected return, is easily achieved even in moderate-sized portfolios. The funds' advantage of lower commission costs is to some extent tempered by the fact that the funds typically buy and sell more frequently than individual investors. So, on three counts—expert management, diversified holdings, and reduced commission charges—mutual funds may overstate their advantages to prospective shareholders.

How, then, *do* mutual funds help their clients? Clearly, mutual funds do provide a vehicle for small investors to benefit from the general level of investment returns attainable from the securities markets. They also provide reasonably efficient administration of smaller accounts and generally offset the risks of rash investments. Explained below, however, are the seven ways mutual funds *impair* their clients' investment results. We then discuss how to minimize these costs, if and when mutual funds are a logical and wise investment for you. Finally, this chapter reviews several specialized funds.

The Sales Load

The sales load on a mutual fund is a special commission charge that the investor pays in order to buy the fund's shares. Not all funds charge a sales load, but most do. Suppose, for example, that you wish to invest $1,000 in a mutual fund. After consulting with your broker or mutual fund salesman regarding the selection of a fund, you would mail him a check for $1,000. In turn, he remits this sum to the fund—less his sales commission.

Most of the largest mutual funds charge a sales load in order to induce a broker or mutual fund salesman to sign up investors. A fund distributor, acting as a wholesaler, typically takes a portion of this sales commission. The maximum sales charge, usually levied on all investments under $5,000 or $10,000, is shown in Table 28–1 for 65 of the largest mutual funds. These funds manage about 70 percent of all mutual fund assets, even though there are over 800 funds altogether. Notice that, while most of these large funds charge about an 8.5 percent sales load, some funds make no sales charges at all.

The maximum mutual fund sales commission, which most fund buyers pay, is stated in Table 28–1 as a percentage of the purchase price. Typically, 8.5 percent is charged. Hence, for our hypothetical $1,000 purchase, the commission charge is $85. Therefore, only $915 of the original $1,000 purchase price finds its way into the fund. Thus, restated as a percentage of the actual investment, the sales load is $85 on a $915 investment, or 9.3 percent.

Some mutual funds are sold under periodic investment plans. The effective sales load on these so-called "front-end load" plans is substantially higher than the average charge. Under these plans an investor makes contractual installment payments into the fund. The salesman receives his commission on an accelerated schedule. Thus, commissions during the first few years typically run substantially more than 9.3 percent of investment. Until recent legislation, such commissions ran *up to 50 percent,* but now they are generally limited to 20 percent at most and less when the installment payments extend over a long period. A proposed *maximum* load of 8.5 percent of gross investment is under consideration at the SEC.

Investors must realize that not all mutual funds have sales loads. It is somewhat incredible that a large market for mutual funds with sales loads persists in the face of alternative "no-load" funds, which are sold

TABLE 28–1
Maximum Sales Charge for 65 Large Mutual Funds

Mutual Fund	Assets (in millions of $) (6/30/73)	Maximum Sales Charge (percent of purchase price)
Affiliated Fund	$1,391	7.5%
American Express Capital Fund	154	8.5
American Express Investment Fund	154	8.5
American Investors Fund	146	none
American Mutual Fund	332	8.5
Anchor Growth Fund	316	8.75
Axe-Houghton Fund B	214	8.0
Broad Street Investing Corp.	389	8.5
Channing Growth Fund	215	8.5
Chemical Fund	897	8.5
The Colonial Fund	169	8.5
Decatur Income Fund	226	8.5
Delaware Fund	386	8.5
Dividend Shares	361	8.67
Dreyfus Fund	1,721	8.75
Dreyfus Leverage Fund	293	8.75
Eaton & Howard Stock Fund	196	8.5
Enterprise Fund	278	8.5
Fidelity Capital Fund	497	8.5
Fidelity Fund	742	8.5
Fidelity Trend Fund	804	8.5
Financial Industrial Fund	283	none
Founders Mutual Fund	175	8.5
Fundamental Investors	817	8.75
Group Securities Common Stock Fund	279	8.5
Hamilton Funds Series H-DA	497	8.5
Harbor Fund	156	8.5
The Investment Company of America	1,322	8.5
Investors Mutual	2,636	8.0
Investors Stock Fund	2,323	8.0
Investors Variable Payment Fund	917	8.0
ISI Trust Fund	365	8.5
Ivest Fund	255	8.5
The Johnston Mutual Fund	288	none
Keystone Custodian K-2 (Growth Fund)	252	8.75
Keystone Custodian S-4 (Lower Priced)	478	8.75
Loomis-Sayles Mutual Fund	159	none
Massachusetts Fund	250	8.75
Mass. Income Development Fund	241	8.5
Mass. Investors Growth Stock Fund	1,372	8.5
Mass. Investors Trust	1,726	8.5
MIF Fund	205	7.5
National Investors Corp.	895	8.5
National Securities–Growth	198	8.5
National Securities–Stock	265	8.5
The One William Street Fund	279	none
Oppenheimer Fund	468	8.5

TABLE 28–1 *(Continued)*

Mutual Fund	Assets (in millions of $) (6/30/73)	Maximum Sales Charge (percent of purchase price)
Pioneer Fund	$ 239	8.5%
T. Rowe Price Growth Stock Fund	1,163	none
Rowe Price New Horizons Fund	340	none
Puritan Fund	734	8.5
George Putnam Fund of Boston	415	8.5
Putnam Growth Fund	733	8.5
Putnam Investors Fund	496	8.5
Scudder Special Fund	150	none
Selected American Shares	150	none
Stein Roe and Farnham Balanced Fund	178	none
Stein Roe and Farnham Stock Fund	174	none
Technology Fund	492	8.75
United Accumulative Fund	862	8.75
United Income Fund	776	8.75
United Science Fund	304	8.75
Washington Mutual Investors	292	8.5
Wellington Fund	1,015	8.5
Windsor Fund	410	8.5

Source: *Forbes*, August 15, 1973.

via mail or direct advertisement with no salesman involved and therefore no commission. With the absence of commissions and compensation for personal selling of shares in no-load funds, the investor must sell himself on the merits of the fund. The initiative to send for its prospectus must come from within. One's broker cannot reasonably be expected to sell mutual funds without sales loads.

In recent years, the no-load funds have attracted increasing numbers of investors—those who decided to sell themselves. During the three-year period from 1968 through 1970, no-load shareholder accounts more than tripled. Yet, investors as a whole are still not sufficiently aware of no-load mutual funds. In 1970, the Investment Company Institute, a mutual fund trade association, analyzed investor familiarity with no-loads. Of families who had heard of mutual funds in general, only 17 percent of those with income under $12,500 had heard of no-loads. Even among families with income over $20,000, only 40 percent of those aware of mutual funds also knew about no-loads. An education job remains to be done. (Congratulations, you are now in the sophisticated minority).

Aggregate mutual fund sales went into net redemptions (dropping out exceeding joining in) during mid-1971 for the first time in history. No-load fund sales, however, have exceeded redemptions throughout this net redemption crisis, which has adversely affected the load funds. Furthermore, it should be noted that much "mutual-fund-type-money" has recently been channeled into other similar vehicles. For instance, nearly $4 billion has gone into real estate investment trusts (REITs) and private-placement income funds in the past three years. (These vehicles are discussed later in this chapter). No-loads represent only about 10 percent of all mutual fund assets, reflecting the fact that funds are still *sold* more than *bought*.

Comparing Performance After the Sales Load

Clearly, any salesman tends to sell products that provide commissions. There is no evidence, however, of any performance difference between load and no-load funds on assets actually invested. Professor Irwin Friend, at the Wharton School of Finance and Commerce has, over the past ten years, spearheaded penetrating research on the mutual fund industry. His analyses of funds' performance published with colleagues in 1963 and 1970 revealed the absence of any significant relationships between performance and sales charges [55, p. 18]. Since these computations were based on the assets actually invested by each type of mutual fund, any sales loads reduce returns on investors' full outlays. Since, if you buy $1,000 of a load fund, only $915 is invested, the overall comparison favors the no-loads. The issue was succinctly summarized in *Forbes* magazine: "After all, salesmen and sales commissions really have nothing to do with investment results." [185, p. 69]

Turnover—and Over and Over

Mutual fund managers have a well-documented proclivity for changing their minds. Portfolio turnover is measured as the portion of total assets switched from one security to another in a given period of time. Such turnover is markedly higher for mutual funds than for the market as a whole, as shown in Figure 28–1. Many market professionals believe in the tenet that high performance calls for higher-than-average investment turnover. But turnover can be a second way that mutual funds impair fundholder returns.

The very livelihood of investment advisers depends on the belief that,

FIGURE 28–1
Turnover Rates: Mutual Funds versus All NYSE Stocks
Percent

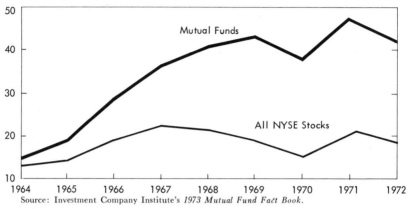

Source: Investment Company Institute's *1973 Mutual Fund Fact Book.*

through diligent, careful analysis, one can outperform the market. The efficient capital market theory, on the other hand, holds this belief to be highly suspect. Efficient markets continually digest information on securities and adjust prices accordingly. Only action taken on the basis of inside information, which is illegal, or good luck, which is unpredictable, can outperform efficient markets.

With efficient markets, even the experts stand only a statistical chance, say 50–50, of being correct. What would you do if, after much diligent and careful analysis, half of your investments turned relatively sour? You would probably switch them! But, in addition to what you might have lost in the stock, turnover generates commission expenses. These commissions, for transactions which the fund management decides to make, are paid out of the assets of the fund and therefore lower the returns available to fund shareholders.

Institutional investors, including the mutual funds, account for about 70 percent of all NYSE transactions, while individuals own a majority of total stock held. Separating these two groups discloses that institutions trade nearly *three times as frequently* as noninstitutional stockholders. Reporting on this astounding difference, Professor Friend commented:

Up to this time the SEC has devoted less attention than might have been warranted to the problem of substantially increased fund portfolio turnover rates. . . . In the first quarter of 1969 it amounted to close to three times the nonmember turnover on the New York Stock Exchange as a whole. Such adjusted fund turnover is about 2½ times the corresponding stock turnover rate of pension funds, a group of institutional investors with which the mutual funds might be compared. Fund turnover is roughly five times the turnover rate for small (odd-lot) public investors in NYSE stocks and seven times the redemption rate by purchasers of mutual fund shares. [55, p. 107]

The existence and recent growth of such inordinately high turnover raises two fundamental questions: What causes it? Does it result in improved performance? Obviously, the high turnover recorded by mutual funds cannot be traced to a single determinant. We have facetiously hypothesized that turnover is the way a fund manager corrects his mistakes. Or, we might suppose that all that electronic gadgetry and up-to-the-second information excites money managers, or at least itches their trigger fingers. It is amusing to note that the increase in mutual fund turnover coincided not only with the performance craze of the late 1960s, but also with the availability of instant, computerized data dispensed by desk-top, push-button display units.

On the more critical issue of the performance impact of turnover, Friend and his colleagues, after an exhaustive study of long-term mutual fund performance, reported that "no consistent relationship was found between [portfolio turnover] and investment performance properly adjusted for risk." [55, p. 21] While they found some evidence that higher trading activity in 1964–68 was associated with better performance, the reverse was true in 1960–64 and 1968–69. Friend's 1963 study, which examined data from the 1953–58 period, also found turnover and performance to be unrelated. Other research by Hoff Stauffer, Jr. and Robert Vogel [160] at Wesleyan University examined the relationship between turnover and performance between 1955 and 1964 and reported some tendency for performance to be inversely related to turnover. Hence, *no comprehensive evidence shows that high portfolio turnover aids mutual fund performance.*

Management Fees

Mutual funds pay a fee to their management companies for rendering certain services, primarily investment decisions. The management fee is the third way in which mutual funds typically impair the returns that flow through to fundholders. This fee is part of the investment advisory contract between the fund's shareholders and the fund's management company. Each fund must furnish potential or existing investors with a prospectus or annual report. The size of a fund's management fee, often one half of 1 percent of assets per year, is disclosed in these reports.

The Performance Fee

A minority of mutual funds also levy an additional charge—a performance fee—which constitutes a fourth impairment to fundholder returns. It is meant to motivate the fund's management to outstanding results. Under a performance fee formula, the fund's manager is paid an incremental fee if the fund "performs." The definition of performance must now be in comparison with a representative market index, and performance fees must be a double-edged sword, becoming penalties for nonperformance. These current rules were not always the case. In the latter 1960s, abuses arose from unfair definitions of performance and biased incentives for producing it. Legislation which took effect on December 14, 1970 has largely stemmed the use and abuse of performance fees.

Perhaps the paramount example of these measurement abuses occurred when Bernard Cornfeld, promoter of the Fund of Funds in Europe during the 1960s, published sales literature containing elaborate comparisons between the Dow Jones Industrial Average and his fund's performance. Cornfeld, however, showed his fund's results with dividends reinvested; the Dow Jones Average does not include reinvested dividends. This point was a key argument of the SEC in its feud with Cornfeld's fund, and he agreed in late 1966 to correct the practice with appropriate footnotes. One should be similarly careful in gauging the capital appreciation of "growth" mutual funds, which pay little or no dividends. In essence, such funds select stocks of companies which retain and reinvest profits—profits from which other companies pay dividends. Basing performance judgments or incentive compensation on growth in comparison with a price index of stocks paying high dividends may not be cricket.

Administrative Expenses

A fifth cost of owning mutual fund shares is a charge for certain administrative expenses borne by the fund and thus by its shareholders. Typically, this cost ranges from 0.25 percent to 0.5 percent per year of the fund's assets. For smaller funds it sometimes runs higher. Although varying from fund to fund, certain legal, accounting, directors', clerical, printing, and office expenses are covered by this charge.

The Liquidity Trap

The sixth impediment to fund performance is a subtle structural weakness which is seldom revealed to potential fundholders. This aspect concerns the potential illiquidity of the fund's holdings. Liquidity is the ease of converting an investment into cash *at a price representing fair value*. The liquidity of a valuable diamond ring or antique is quite different from the generally good liquidity of NYSE stocks. While everyone might acknowledge the value or replacement cost of your diamond or your antique, it is more difficult to convert such assets into cash quickly at a price representing fair value.

Mutual funds do a good job of standing ready to convert any individual investor's fund shares into cash. Such liquidity is an important part of a mutual fund's sales appeal, particularly when an interest in the fund is contrasted with nonstock investments such as real estate or works of art.

Most mutual funds are of the "open-end" type. They stand ready to redeem the funds' shares at "net asset value" within a week's time. Funds which do not buy back their fund shares are called "closed-end." However, a market commonly exists for sales to others (rather than the fund itself) of closed-end fund shares. Consequently, these fund shares may trade at a price other than net asset value, typically at a discount. Similarly, at any given time, a load fund returns a lesser amount than it charges, in view of the spread caused by the sales charge.

Ironically, while protecting fundholder liquidity, mutual funds themselves often face liquidity problems in trading for their own account. Their large size and the recent innovations of volume discounts and negotiated commissions on large orders dictate that mutual funds buy and sell stock in large blocks. On the NYSE alone, over one hundred blocks of 10,000 shares or more will usually trade on a typical business day. A few blocks with over 100,000 shares will likely trade as well. It takes great finesse and often some sacrifice to get into or out of such large blocks of stock at a price representing fair (that is, recently quoted) value.

The extent of a fund's liquidity problem is affected by many of the investment policies of its management. A fund's liquidity is *decreased* if:

1. it tends to invest in smaller companies whose shares have low trading volume;
2. it concentrates its holdings in relatively few companies;

3. it is very large in size;
4. it has high portfolio turnover;
5. it invests in low-priced or over-the-counter stocks for which the percentage commission cost or dealer spread tends to be higher;
6. it makes relatively more fund transactions during periods of volatile changes in stock prices; or
7. it invests in restricted securities that are not freely tradable.

The Enterprise Fund is a case in point. In the late 1960s, Enterprise invested in "emerging growth stocks," which were usually small companies and often were traded over-the-counter. In making large and continuing purchases of such stocks, it has been noted in the business press, the Enterprise Fund may have created some of the very performance which brought it continued new capital for continued stock purchases. But when or if Enterprise sought to sell its position, liquidity was inadequate. Enterprise was locked in by illiquidity during much of the 1969–70 decline in speculative stocks, even when it didn't want to be.

Forbes cites another example. An unidentified growth stock manager is quoted as saying: We tried to get out of a fair-sized, over-the-counter stock at $15. We got off 1000 shares at $13, and then they found out who was doing the selling. Before we knew it the stock was at $5. As soon as the traders smelled a big sale order, you were dead.

Although NYSE-listed shares are the largest aggregation of ownership wealth anywhere, large blocks of stock can strain even this market's liquidity. Trades of the typical NYSE stock total about 10,000 shares on an average day. This may represent something like a third of a million dollars of market value. If a ten-million-dollar fund has money spread equally in thirty issues, then it has a third of a million dollars in each. Its position in a typical company is equal to an average day's trading in the stock—there is essentially no liquidity problem here. Suppose, however, that a large fund decides to concentrate its holdings in order to increase its chances for achieving above-average results.

Jerry Tsai of the Manhattan Fund was famous for this concentration strategy. For example, a fund with $400 million spread among only 40 issues has holdings averaging $10 million in each—more than a month of normal trading for an average NYSE stock. The Manhattan Fund, newly formed in early 1966 by and around Mr. Tsai, adopted concentration as its investment philosophy. Another star of those days, Fred Alger, realized that Tsai's largest-ever bundle for a new fund would be used heavily to buy airlines and other Tsai-favored glamour stocks. Alger, therefore, bought airlines while the Manhattan Fund was being underwritten and before its money could be invested. He claims later to have happily sold his airlines into the face of Tsai's subsequent heavy demand. (Then, even Howard Hughes sold out his $500 million of TWA stock). Several grim years later in the 1970s, the airlines were down to a fraction of their early 1966 prices. Being able to sell large blocks at currently quoted prices is not an assured event.

Michael Milken of Drexel Burnham has developed the concept that liquidity is the third dimension of investment analysis, along with risk and return. The evidence shows that the funds *have* had problems with the liquidity of their portfolio holdings, especially in times of market volatility. Some fund managers even estimate privately the portion of their securities that they could get out of in a hurry with *only* a 5 percent or 10 percent liquidation sacrifice. Like an elephant tiptoeing through the flower garden, big blocks of stock are not good for the owner's "tulips!"

The Tax Trap

The seventh and final impediment to fundholders' returns also results from the management policy of funds. This impediment is a tax rate that may be needlessly high during the years when an individual holds shares of the fund. Mutual funds themselves do not pay taxes. They are allowed to flow through to their shareholders the taxes due on any *realized* income and capital gains. The fundholders then pay income and capital gains taxes at their appropriate individual rates.

Mutual fund managers tend to sell stocks fairly frequently. The sale of a stock in which the fund has a capital gain *realizes* that gain. Almost all net gains are distributed to fund shareholders in the year the gain is realized. Such distributions of capital gain to individuals are taxed at the appropriate rates. If the fund manager's trigger finger is too itchy, his excessive trading realizes any gains or losses. Thus, fundholders may be forced to pay the taxes at that time, rather than having their capital continue to be invested, untaxed, in a profitable situation.

How to Use Mutual Funds

Despite the loads, commissions, fees, expenses, and possible liquidity or taxation impairments, mutual funds are a good idea. They permit investors, small or large, to participate in the general returns of the securities markets. Professional management, diversification and lowered trading commissions are the selling points. Yet, each of these alleged advantages may be overemphasized. What should the investor do? As with any investment instrument, mutual funds should be bought only when they fit into your personal financial objectives and needs. For many, they are a suitable, moderate-risk, acceptable-expense vehicle for investing. If so, which fund should you choose?

The past records of mutual funds are widely reported and analyzed. *Forbes* magazine, which publishes its annual survey at mid-year, grades fund results for both up and down markets. *Institutional Investor* reports fund rankings various and year-to-date comparisons. Current prices are posted daily in newspaper financial pages. But, as the funds themselves must specify in most advertisements, past performance is no guarantee of the future. Up in good markets and down in bad ones is the rule. Thus, the type of fund one selects and its investment philosophy are more reliable indicators than past performance. Indeed, in the *Forbes* ratings of mid-1971 only one fund ranked A in both up and down markets—Japan Fund, which invests in an entirely different economy!

No-Load Funds—A Partial Solution

As we have seen, no-load funds are attracting an increasing share of the mutual fund market. No-load shares are purchased directly from the fund without sales commissions. Like other mutual funds, however, they do charge their shareholders a management fee and certain expenses, usually at about the same rates as charged by the load funds. Thus, no-load funds offer definite advantages over traditional load funds, but they are only a partial solution to the problem of choice.

Special Types of Funds

Several special types of funds exist to serve the varying needs of investors. Fund selection should be based on a knowledge of these different vehicles. A fund's objective is perhaps its most distinguishing aspect. Most stock funds seek growth, although some seek high, current income. Other funds are "balanced" between growth and income, using preferred stock or bond investments for the latter purpose. Of late, bond funds have had a resurgence of popularity, reflecting rising interest rates and investor caution following the 1969–70 debacle of the "go-go" funds. Perhaps this verifies the definition of a cautious investor as a "speculator who lost."

Real estate investment trusts (REITs) have also been a recently popular investment. These portfolios are based on investments in real property, as opposed to stocks. Thus, high income and inflation-protection are their hallmarks. REITs may specialize in short- or long-term mortgage loans, equity ownership, or a combination of these vehicles. Typically, shares in the REITs are underwritten (for a selling commission) and then traded on a closed-end basis. Frequently, warrants to buy more shares, or bonds convertible into shares, are also offered from time to time. Their securities are usually listed on national exchanges and nearly 100 REITs currently exist.

Private-placement income funds are another recent phenomenon. Again, these are underwritten funds (sold at one time rather than continuously). Their attraction includes high-income potential through active bond trading to exploit subtle shifts in yields and through participation in securities offered privately. The latter are spared the expense of public registration and thus usually carry a higher yield or other advantages, such as equity kickers. Also, some funds distribute income monthly, which gives a reassuring feeling to many fundholders.

Still another type of fund specializes in tax-free bonds, an instrument cited in the next chapter. Industry funds, such as in insurance or chemicals, have also been marketed. Here, the advantage of diversification is significantly thwarted, but the chances for extraordinary swings are increased. One further group of funds deserves explanation, as they offer an unusually attractive opportunity—the dual funds.

Dual Funds

A group of eight, dual-purpose mutual funds were marketed in early 1967. These unusual vehicles had been tried earlier in England and arrived here with great fanfare. None has been introduced since that flurry, however, because their interim performance has been spotty to downright poor. Herein lies the current opportunity.

The dual funds satisfy one of two objectives—growth *or* income. Half of the shares are designed to receive all of the fund's capital gains, while the other half receives all income from dividends or interest. In effect, these shares are leveraged in one objective or the other. Most are listed on the NYSE.

To keep the number of shares evenly matched, these funds are of the closed-end type. As a consequence, they sell for what a buyer will pay and not for net asset value like open-end funds. Perhaps because of their unconventional structure or their less-than-satisfactory past achievements, these funds typically sell at handsome discounts. This becomes attractive because, unlike in the case of most closed-end funds, their shares must rise to net asset value by expiration (ranging from 1979 to 1985), when they can be redeemed for their underlying value. A 25 percent to 50 percent price rise is built into some of the capital shares, *above* whatever appreciation the portfolio may achieve. The latter is, itself, leveraged in reflecting market gains—or losses. Percentage players should sharpen their pencils and review these instruments.

Developing a "Better Idea"

In summary, mutual funds offer interesting opportunities. Surprising and disconcerting facts about fund performance, however, apply to both the load and no-load funds. These research findings, noted below, raise serious doubts about the benefits added by the funds' professional managers.

- Historically, one could have attained performance equivalent to that of the average mutual fund, or better, from equal investment in all NYSE stocks.
- When properly adjusted for risk, there has been no historical relationship shown between fund performance and either the size, sales charge, management fee, portfolio turnover, or investment objective of funds.
- There is no evidence of performance consistency by the same fund in successive periods.

The rational investor should ask himself which would be more beneficial:

- performance derived from managed assets with standard commissions, fees, expenses and taxation or,
- performance derived from unmanaged assets of comparable risk, but with lower commissions, fees and expenses—plus *deferred* taxation.

Friend, et al. noted that unmanaged portfolios with no turnover and consisting of all NYSE stocks provided returns at least equal to those of the average mutual fund. Indeed, *a mutual fund in effect composed of all NYSE stocks* is an interesting concept. Low expenses, including no sales load, minimum turnover, and a modest "management" fee, accompany such "index" funds. Shareholder benefits, beyond those of investment in the stock market and ultra-diversification, also include lowered fees and expenses, nearly nonexistent liquidity problems, and maximum possible tax deferral. No less an independent authority than Paul Samuelson, the Nobel Prize winning economist, has advocated this concept [189].

The Economy Fund—A Better Idea

Imagine a deliberately low-expense, low-turnover, broadly diversified, no-load mutual fund which holds equal amounts of all NYSE stocks (or some similarly broad list). It might be called *The Economy Fund* to emphasize its low cost and comprehensive holdings. Such a fund would prove very effective at minimizing the seven factors noted earlier which impair fundholder returns. We have calculated the 20-year performance of a hypothetical Economy Fund and compared it to the average performances of a load and a no-load fund, based on *the same underlying market risks and returns*. The after-tax performance differences, stemming from initial $1,000 investments in each fund, are dramatic.

- Average load fund $3,544
- Average no-load fund $4,060
- *The Economy Fund* $4,639

chapter
29
Bonds and Hedges

Among Wall Streeters, portfolio managers hold the glamour spotlight. Their game is performance—the weekly, quarterly, or annual casting of rank among their ranks. But "return" must be trotted around the ring with its companion horse "risk." This approach contrasts with the go-go philosophy that "there is no risk in the past, only results." The credo of some money managers is "the best way to protect capital is to double it." This performance mania is alarming in light of research evidence showing that the quest for performance is consistently associated with inordinate risk.

Today, many investors persist in playing only one game—the stock market—in spite of overwhelming evidence favoring diversification into various instruments. Many methods by which even professional money managers select stocks are no better than throwing darts at a list of stocks with the same historical risk! It often follows that the more these professionals spend on selecting stocks, the worse they perform. Equally serious, they usually push for performance by investing only in *stocks* to the exclusion of other investment instruments.

The Forgotten Markets

Research confirms that diversification is good. But we found stock portfolio diversification easy to obtain. Several stocks, well-chosen for their risk interactions, can diversify away the major risks not associated with the stock market itself. But, the risk of the *stock market* is no small matter. Since World War II, 12 stock market declines have exceeded 10 percent. They averaged 7 months in duration and a 19.3 percent loss in value—and these market losses do not include the vanished opportunities to add to holdings by collecting bank interest or other safe returns.

Money managers tend to be "stock pickers." Bonds, some observers say, Average stumbled to 631.16 on May 26, 1970. The miserable performance records tallied by mutual funds during the entire 1969–70 downturn stands as proof of their inability to divorce themselves from overall stock market performance. How can they? Stocks move heavily together, as on November 23, 1971, a day when 357 NYSE stocks hit new yearly lows while exactly one reached a new high—and it was a utility company preferred stock!

Investing in the stock market is not the only way to manage money. Real estate, for instance, is an even bigger market than that of NYSE listed stocks. Commodities, the basic physical goods of our economy such as wheat, corn, eggs, silver, scrap iron, or lumber, form another investment market. One can invest, or speculate, in these markets via commodity futures without ever intending to be the final user of the commodity purchased. These other money management opportunities, and investment possibilities in foreign securities markets, oil and mineral rights, cattle feeding, equipment leasing, art, antiques, jewels, coins, stamps, and so on, demonstrate that the American stock market is only *part* of the money management spectrum, albeit a large part.

The Forgotten Instruments—Bonds

Money managers tend to be "stock pickers." Bonds, some observers say, have been forgotten instruments. Bonds represent the debts of the issuer. By owning a bond you become a creditor of that organization. If a bond-issuing company collapses, whatever assets can be liquidated must be used to satisfy debts, including obligations to the company's bondholders. To purchasers of these comparatively low-risk instruments, the issuer promises a regular interest payment and, upon maturity of the bond, repayment of principal. Bonds, reflecting the organization underlying securities issued, are not all of uniform quality or yield. Corporate bonds, however, are less risky for the investor than common stock ownership in the same company.

Insurance companies, with their long-term, actuarially predictable cash inflows and outflows, have been, owing to their inherent nature, convention, logic, and legal requirements, heavily committed to bonds and mortgages. Practically to the extent the law allows, however, they have shifted into stock ownership and real estate equity participations. Bank trusts, pension funds, and university endowment funds have made substantial shifts into stocks from bonds. Most mutual funds are heavily oriented toward stocks. Bonds are often forgotten—bonds are dull!

The potential return from bond investments, however, may be attractive. Indeed, many astute investors, eschewing lower-yielding savings accounts or the risks of volatile stock markets, have shifted their assets into bonds. In the summer of 1970, yields on long-term bonds reached 100-year highs followed, in summer 1973, by short-term rates—each twice the returns of several years earlier. Long-term bond rates, typified by high-grade utilities, have since settled into the area of approximately 8 percent returns, as shown in Figure 29–1. Such returns approach the long-term rate of return historically available from the stock market. The inherently lower risk of bonds in conjunction with such high returns certainly merits the attention of investors.

FIGURE 29–1
Historical Yields on Newly Issued Aa Public Utility Bonds

Source: Data in Moody's *Public Utility Manual*.

What Investors Should Know About Bonds

Bonds, while not free of risk, are considered more predictable than stocks. A bond contract has three principal features—its quality, yield, and maturity. Quality reflects the financial position and prospects of the issuer. The federal government, with seemingly endless taxing authority, is the highest-quality issuer. Major blue-chip corporations also issue bonds of high quality. Excepting railroads, such large corporations have very seldom defaulted on payments. Yield is the ratio of annual interest to the bond's price. Since a bond's interest payment is fixed, yields fluctuate inversely with the bond's price. Maturity is the scheduled date of repayment of principal. Some bonds mature in five years, while others do not reach maturity for thirty years or longer. Bonds fluctuate in price as interest rates or quality change, since such changes alter the relative desirability of a given bond's fixed interest payments. Longer-maturity bonds fluctuate more in price since more interest is at stake.

There are many types of bonds, each suitable for different kinds of investors. Short-maturity bonds provide the greater certainty and liquidity of an early payback. They generally carry a lower yield as a result. Government bonds, because of their quality, generally yield less than corporates. Municipal bonds are exempt from federal income taxes. Convertible bonds have the right to participate in corporate growth through their convertibility into stock. Some bonds are subordinated in credit standing to other debts of the issuer.

What does research reveal about the profitability of bond investing? First, bonds have historically returned less than common stocks. Second, bond yields have recently become almost competitive with returns from stocks, including price appreciation as well as dividends. Third, lower-quality bonds yield more than high-quality ones, even *after* adjustment for risk. Fourth, the lower the quality, the more diversification is helpful. Fifth, active and wise bond trading may improve returns. Sixth, and perhaps most important, many medium-grade and speculative companies whose stocks often appear in individual or institutional portfolios have bonds outstanding with risk-return characteristics surpassing those of the common stock. In 1970–73, many of these bonds were sold at such discounts in price that their return amounted to 10 percent, 12 percent, or even 15 percent annually, *guaranteed* by the issuer for periods extending to 15 years and longer.

Levered Lings versus Unlevered Levins

In 1970, Ling-Temco-Vought, Inc. (now LTV) and Levin-Townsend Computer (now Rockwood Computer) were two, out-of-favor former darlings. Both of these companies—to cite examples for comparative analysis—have suffered huge losses and have undergone top management shake-ups. Each has speculative bonds outstanding with comparable maturity dates. At 1970–73 bond market prices, these speculative bonds offered high current income and built-in capital appreciation—provided, of course, that the companies stay in business to meet their obligations.

An investor seeking above-average returns might consider such speculative investments. For instance, during much of 1973, the approximate price of a $1,000 face-value LTV bond maturing in 1988 was $500. This bond is listed in newspapers (NYSE Bonds) as LTV 5s of 88. It obligates the company on each January 1 and July 1 to pay half of the $50.00 annual interest per bond. In addition, the bond must be repaid in full ($1,000 per bond) on its maturity date in 1988. It is this stream of LTV-guaranteed payments that cost an investor around $500 during mid-1973.

The definition of just what constitutes return from a bond is often simplified by computing the bond's "current yield," as published in daily financial newspapers. The annual interest of $50.00, when divided by the price of $500, results in a 10.0 percent current yield. A capital gain, however, is also built into this bond's price, since it must be redeemed for $1,000 in 1988. Therefore, it must double from $500 to $1,000 by 1988, if the company remains solvent. A doubling from 1973 to 1988 represents capital gains of nearly 5 percent compounded annually. Thus, the investor averages this annual capital gain in addition to the current yield of 10 percent from interest payments.

Another bond priced for high return during most of 1973 was the Rockwood Computer 5½s of 87. These convertible bonds pay $55 per year interest and $1,000 at maturity on April 15, 1987, subject, of course, to the beleaguered company's financial survival. During much of 1973, these bonds were quoted around 33, meaning $330 per bond. Thus, their current yield, if bought in 1973, was 16.7 percent a year, and the tripling in price within 14 years would provide an additional return of 8.1 percent compounded annually. The use of leverage, or investing in these speculative bonds partially on borrowed money, increases their return still further, but also increases the risk of holding either of them.

The foregoing analysis should not be anything new to investment professionals. Nonetheless, the high interest level and long duration of these expected investment returns are likely to surprise most readers. The particular bonds cited above are risky compared to most bonds, although they are less risky than the stock of each of the respective companies. Furthermore, the recent prices of over 100 bonds of exchange-listed companies, with each issue containing over $25 million in outstanding bonds, were priced so low as to afford returns to maturity of over 10 percent. Their average return was about *12 percent* compounded, and their risk was low in comparison to that of stock portfolios offering the promise of roughly equivalent returns. A diversified portfolio of such medium- to low-quality bonds provide investors with protection against the potential financial misfortune that might befall one or a few of such companies. Moreover, either employing leverage or confining selections to a few dozen of the highest-returning bonds permitted expected returns approaching 15 percent compounded annually for a span of nearly 15 years!

More Forgotten Strategies

Still other investment philosophies permit desirable returns at acceptable levels of risk. Some strategies deliberately seek not to depend on skillful security selection. One such example of this approach was the published success story *Beat the Market*. It revealed the strategy of Sheen T. Kassouf and Edward O. Thorp, whose earlier book, *Beat the Dealer,* had sent Las Vegas "Twenty-one" odds-makers back to their abacuses and card-shuffling machines.

In *Beat the Market,* Thorp and Kassouf [166] explained the risk-reward structure of a specific type of stock-warrant hedge. A hedge involves holding two related instruments whose *combined* action is deemed desirable or risk lowering. The stock-warrant hedge devised by Kassouf and Thorp involved selling warrants short, close to their expiration, while simultaneously holding a long position in the corresponding stock. A warrant is a right to buy a stock for a specified price. Recognizing that warrants are more volatile than their underlying stock, Thorp and Kassouf experimented with various ratios of short and long positions to alter their combined investment outcome. By hedging a warrant against its stock in this manner, Thorp and Kassouf demonstrated results which were highly predictable, were often *independent* of the stock's price changes, and were nearly always profitable.

Why such a profitable strategy can persist is perhaps explained by a favorite story involving a former student. Upon joining a Wall Street firm, this enlightened newcomer used every available opportunity to ask people he met if they had read either Brealey's *An Introduction to Risk and Return from Common Stocks* or Thorp's and Kassouf's *Beat the Market*. The reply generally involved a lecture that "people on the Street learn from experience." After *eight months* he found *one person*—a partner in his firm—who had read both books. Amusingly, as the partner started to discuss these books, *he nervously arose and closed his office door*. In the sanctity of his office, the partner then advised his young charge that, even though he found the books fascinating, discussions of the "random-walk model and so forth" tended to alienate "people in 'the business" and that, in the interest of his career, he should "learn from experience."

Hedging—Another Experience

Once upon a time, a man named Alfred Winslow Jones had a great investment idea. As long as Jones kept the idea to himself, he prospered. Once his idea leaked out, the scheme was destroyed by ubiquitous imitators. There is a hazard in extrapolating such "once upon a time" success stories. Obviously, something that works for a few investors can be destroyed by imitating masses. It does not follow, however, that merely because someone won't tell you what he's doing, that it works!

When someone genuinely has a good idea on Wall Street, it is doubtful he can keep the secret. Word spreads fast on Wall Street. One day a few years ago, Frances Gottlieb walked out of the Chemical Bank Building. A couple of ardent girl watchers "recommended" the view of her sweater-enveloped 53-inch bust. Within three days, several thousand people—all getting the same tips—were lined ten deep on Wall Street to watch her daily stroll.

Having been forewarned, the parable of Alfred Winslow Jones and his hedging secret continues. Hedge investment strategies are designed to assure a sufficient return regardless of the future market. Basically, hedging plays one investment against another so that if one goes down the other is likely to go up. The problem, of course, is to combine investments in such a way that this canceling effect is still profitable.

Jones' strategy, popularized as the hedge-fund concept, involved both buying stocks long and selling short. A short sale is selling borrowed stock for repurchase *later*. When an investor sells short, his results are the opposite of those that ensue from owning the stock, called "being long." He makes a profit if the stock price declines and the shares can be bought cheaper later. Obviously, hedge strategists do not select two *identical* investments for holding both long and short. Instead, hedging is normally practiced by shorting stocks expected to perform worse than average, while holding long those stocks expected to perform better than average. In addition, to get more money invested, many hedged portfolios borrow to the limit, achieving leverage which might surprise even Archimedes.

The hedge fund genre was spawned by Jones, who still reigns as patriarch of the tribe. His first limited partnership was A. W. Jones and Co., formed in 1952. During the nine years until 1961, Jones compounded his investors' money at a phenomenal 21 percent annual rate. Even so, the public had little knowledge of Jones' achievements on behalf of his wealthy clients. Finally, in its April 1966 issue *Fortune* published an article entitled "The Jones Nobody Keeps Up With." The article pointed out that, in the long term, Jones not only had outperformed the mutual funds, but also had survived the 1962 market collapse virtually unscathed.

What *really* attracted the attention of money managers, however, was mention that under the private, limited-partnership form of organization money managers could take as compensation[1] 20 percent of any profits earned on their limited partners' money. To quote Carol Loomis writing in *Fortune,* "These items of news were enough to create overnight a raft of would-be hedge-fund managers, most of whom were convinced that Jones had discovered the millennium." [188]

In the early years, when he alone was "playing the game," Jones did attain remarkable performance. But in terms of supply and demand, many players make a market efficient. In a nutshell, with everyone trying to outguess everyone else, no one can predict better than the market, which reflects the combined judgment of all who participate in it. Worse still, many hedgers were caught "in their shorts" by the Johnson peace rally of April 1968. In the words of Gilbert Kaplan, "the biggest problem facing the hedge funds is the constant pressure to find good shorts, principally because the host of imitators that Jones has spawned

---

[1] In an income-tax sense this is not "compensation," but the general partner's share of gains or losses.

has narrowed down the opportunities." [**81,** p. 120] An efficient, continually adjusting market makes this Jones-style hedging difficult.

Hedging Revisited

The hedge opportunity cited below, unlike the investments of hedge funds, involves two securities of the *same issuer*. By playing the stock of one company against a short sale in another, hedge funds were often scissored by these unrelated holdings. Securities with a defined relationship to each other, however, *can* be hedged predictably. One striking hedge example, practiced by this author, was available during 1972 using American Telephone and Telegraph securities. Prices for various AT&T securities at the time were approximately:

Common stock	$42 (then a $2.60 dividend)
Convertible preferred stock	$57 ($4.00 dividend)
Warrant	$8 (right to buy a common share at $52)
Bond	$110 (8¾ to 2000)

As always, the investment question is what to do with these opportunities. A stock-warrant hedge strategy of buying 100 AT&T common shares and short selling 100 AT&T warrants would have the results shown in Table 29–1, if the investment were held until May 1975, when the warrants expire.

TABLE 29–1
Capital Gains Results of AT&T Stock-Warrant Hedge*

Final AT&T Price (May 1975)	1975 Value of 100 Warrants	Gain in Value of 100 Common Shares	Gain from Short Sale of 100 Warrants	Total Capital Gain on Combination
$35.	$ 0	−$ 700	$ 800	$ 100
40.	0	− 200	800	600
45.	0	+ 300	800	1,100
50.	0	+ 800	800	1,600
52.	0	+ 1,000	800	1,800
60.	800	+ 1,800	0	1,800
70.	1,800	+ 2,800	− 1,000	1,800
80.	2,800	+ 3,800	− 2,000	1,800

* Strategy: Buy 100 shares of AT&T common @ $42; sell 100 warrants short @ $8. Total investment = $5,000.

FIGURE 29–2
Profit Graph for Stock-Warrant Hedge Held to May 1975
Annual Rate of Return

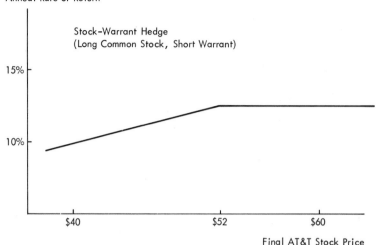

Final AT&T Stock Price

A "profit graph" is a diagram of the annual rate of return at various possible prices of the security under consideration. One is drawn above for this hedge, including dividends as well as the capital gains noted in Table 29–1.

The profit graph for the AT&T stock-warrant hedge is very flat. This means that the rate of return on the hedge is not especially sensitive to the final AT&T stock price. Such a strategy *hedges* one's stake in the stock's price fluctuations. Thus, risk is very low. The stock-warrant hedge, however, offers a significantly higher return than expected from the bond or preferred stock. Moreover, by using leverage, a very handsome return might be realized.

Fallacy of the Short Run

Sound investing via bonds and hedges may seem dull. It is a game of patience and percentages, yet it can be nicely, if not wildly, rewarding. Some investors, unfortunately, refuse to assume anything but a short-run horizon. Indeed, in the words of some, "the deals begin again at 10 A.M. tomorrow" and "long-range planning is after lunch." But, trying to succeed consistently in the short run proves difficult. On Wall Street they say that short-term traders don't get rich, but their brokers do. Nonetheless, there is a powerful *intuitive* appeal in the quick performance possible from a sequence of parlayed successes. For instance, what would a year's subscription to *tomorrow's* newspaper be worth?

Suppose an investor begins the year with $1,000. Further imagine that he is able to pick *tomorrow's best-performing NYSE stock* each day for a year. If he could buy unlimited amounts at the day's open and sell at the day's close, at year-end even with commissions our investor would *own the world!* No one has come close yet. Getting rich gradually in the market is more certain, if less exciting, than getting rich quickly.

chapter
30
Puts and Calls

Puts and calls have been resurrected from the tombs of the forgotten instruments. Over the last two decades, the volume of dealings in such option contracts has grown and, as of March 1973, they are quoted and traded regularly on a national exchange (The Chicago Board Options Exchange, or CBOE). What they are, and how these investment instruments can be used, should be known to today's investor.

Readers of the *Wall Street Journal,* or other financial newspapers, are probably aware of the existence of puts and calls. Ironically, while we hear a lot about baseball players' options or real estate options, relatively few people really understand the mechanisms of trading in stock options. Still fewer, either in or out of the investments business, understand the potentially desirable risk-reward possibilities of these instruments.

Put and Call Options

A put option is a contractual agreement which allows the holder of the option to sell, if he so desires, a specific number of shares of stock at a fixed price at any time within the contract period. Similarly, a call option is an agreement which gives the holder of the option the right to buy a specific number of shares at a fixed price at any time during the contract period. The agreed-upon contract price is called the "striking price." The seller, or "writer," of the option must stand ready to make good on his promise to the option buyer. Option contracts are endorsed by an exchange or member firm to assure that the promise is carried out.

Option contracts generally span periods ranging from 35 days to one year. Before the CBOE, options were for a little over six months (that is, six months and ten days). This permits long-term capital gain possibilities by sale of the option itself after a six-month holding period. Options for three-, six-, or nine-month periods with a standard striking price and expiration date are now prevalent.

The strict definition of the word "option" is synonymous with "choice." It follows then, that in option transactions the choice belongs to the person who buys the option contract. This buyer can choose to exercise his option at any time during the period specified by the contract, and does so only if it is to his advantage. The future right to make such a choice, in the face of uncertainty, is acquired by paying a "premium" to the option writer at the time the contract is established. Conversely, the option seller has no choice. He *must* buy (if he has sold a put) or sell (if he has sold a call) the specified number of shares at the contract price at the election of the option holder.

There are at least two reasons why option contracts are not used more often. First of all, option investing had a rather bad beginning. The second, and more pervasive, reason that "complicated" instruments like options are not used more often is that they are not widely understood. Kermit Zieg, Jr. [179] has shown that only 15 percent of the registered representatives surveyed could correctly define various types of options. Fewer than one in ten could estimate the proper selling price for an option. Another researcher who was less quantitative on this point, but more blunt in his conclusion, stated that "customers' men that understand Puts and Calls are few and far between." [94, p. 46]

Many investment professionals are, in the words of one option specialist, "habit controlled" and haven't sufficiently investigated options. The public, furthermore, is even less informed about option opportunities. Herbert Filer, dean of option traders and founder of Filer, Schmidt & Co., Inc., an option broker-dealer, estimated that only one investor in a thousand had "more than a smattering of knowledge of Put and Call options." [47, p. 16]

While the concept of option writing has been traced to biblical times, the first organized trading of options took place during the legendary tulip-bulb craze in Holland in the early 1630s. This was the tainted beginning. As the Dutch became enchanted with tulip bulbs, the demand for bulbs far outstripped the ability of the industry to supply them, and prices for the bulbs started a whirlwind rise. Dealers who were committed to supplying a fixed number of tulip bulbs at some future date found that they could insure themselves against inflation by purchasing a call option. Thus, if the bulb prices continued to rise, the dealers could exercise their call options and obtain bulbs at a fixed price. If the prices fell, they could supply their customers by buying bulbs on the open market. Dealers then and now are able to insure against price uncertainties by holding options. The tulip bulb growers could be assured of selling their crops at a fixed price by purchasing put options. If prices fell, growers could exercise these puts and sell their crops at the agreed-upon price, above the then-depressed market price. If prices rose, the growers would not exercise their puts, instead choosing to sell their bulbs on the open market. Thus, for the price of a put, a grower could insure against the uncertainties of a declining market price.

Enter the Speculator

Speculators soon realized that, as long as tulip bulb prices continued to rise, they could leverage their money by purchasing call options instead of investing directly in tulip bulbs. Leverage implies that one small change causes a large change elsewhere. A speculator can leverage his gains, or losses, by holding options. For the relatively small cost of a call, tulip speculators could own an option to buy bulbs at some future date for a fixed price. If bulb prices rose during this period, as they were accustomed to doing, the speculator could exercise his call, buy bulbs at the predetermined price, and immediately sell them, realizing a profit equal to the price increase less his cost for the call option. The only required capital investment is the money expended to buy the option.

In the early 1630s, tulip bulb trading became so profitable that virtually everyone in Holland, rich and poor, became involved in this speculation. In fact, many people left their traditional jobs to join the tulip bulb industry. Everything worked well for all concerned until 1636, when the Dutch found themselves "up to their windmills" in tulip bulbs and the demand stopped! The rest is history—sad history. As prices fell, the economy of Holland faltered. The life savings of a broad spectrum of the Dutch population vanished as a prolonged economic depression ensued.

For many years, the idea of option trading was thought by many to be synonymous with gambling—a word inconsistent with Wall Street's desired image. In fact, legislation proposed after the 1929 stock market debacle called for an outright ban on all stock options. But, due to the persistent testimony of Herbert Filer, representing the option dealers in this country, the Securities Act of 1934 did not forbid option writing. Since then, option trading has grown. Traditionally, most trading was done through firms belonging to the Put and Call Brokers and Dealers Association (PCBDA) before the CBOE also began trading options, or "stock futures."

Role of Options

Options are useful to investors because of two properties—their insurance value and their leverage value. Probably, the more useful function of options is to insure against risk. Most homeowners insure against the risk of fire. Yet in 1973, how many investors considered insuring their "paper" stock profits against excessive losses? There are several theories about how investors can best insure their positions. One such theory popularized by Nicholas Darvas in his early 1960s best seller *How I Made $2,000,000 in the Stock Market* [35] states that all an investor need do to insure profits is automatically sell the stock he owns if the price decreases to an "insurance" level. Under this theory a "stop-loss" order is placed with the investor's broker so that the stock will be sold if the price drops by some predetermined amount. Then, if the market moves up, the stop-loss price should also be moved up. When the market moves down, the stock is sold out. The theory has appeal for those who believe in price trends.

Options can also be used for this kind of insurance. The "standing stop-loss" strategy involves keeping a stop-loss order in effect at some predetermined point, such as 10 percent below the stock's recent high. In theory, stocks that rise steadily will not be sold and will continue to accrue profits. Similarly, stocks that decline sufficiently will be sold immediately for a minor loss, at worst. This intuitively appealing strategy is not consistent with the random-walk model of stock price behavior because the "trends" required for its successful implementation turn out to be nonexistent. Hence, it is not surprising that the technique has been statistically rejected.

Assuming the validity of the random-walk model, put-option contracts can be used by investors who want to insure their positions and confine possible losses to known limits. The various outcomes of such a strategy can be illustrated on profit graphs similar to that used in the prior chapter. For example, suppose a stock is selling at $50. An investor could choose to buy a six-month put on the stock for about a 10 percent premium on his investment. Unlike the investor who tries to insure with

FIGURE 30–1
Profit Graph for Stock Purchase with Put Option*

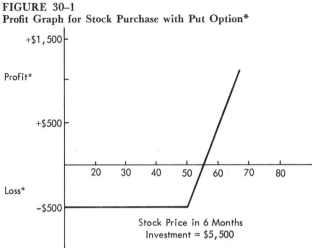

* Commission omitted.

a stop-loss order, a put holder will benefit from any ultimately higher price regardless of interim swings during the option period. On the other hand, he cannot raise his selling price, as can be done with a stop-loss order, without buying another put at the higher striking price. The profit graph in Figure 30–1 shows the possible outcomes that could result from buying 100 shares at $50 combined with a six-month put purchased for $500.

Regardless of the final stock price after six months, the maximum loss is $500. The potential gain is unrestricted. If, after six months, the stock price is below $50, the holder of the put would exercise his option to sell the stock at the option striking price of $50. He would have no loss on the stock sale, but would bear the $500 cost of his option. If the stock were above $50, he would let the put expire because he could sell his stock more favorably in the market. As shown in Figure 30–1, the maximum loss of $500 (plus commissions, of course) occurs if the stock's price does not rise above the striking price. Lesser losses occur if the stock's price rises, but not enough to recover the $500 put premium. A put option used in this manner acts as an insurance policy to limit financial exposure to an uncertain future.

The second major use of options is to obtain leverage. Here, the option buyer seeks to magnify the rate of return on his capital when stock prices move favorably. Purchasing a three-month call on our hypothetical $50 stock might also cost about $500, and resulting in a profit graph as shown in Figure 30–2.

FIGURE 30–2
Profit Graph for Stock Purchase with Call Option*

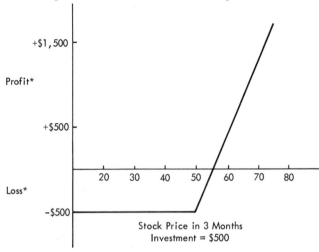

* Commission omitted.

The result is the same as that experienced by the putholder-stockholder over a six-month period. In this case, however, the leveraged call buyer has employed only $500 of capital instead of the $5,500 used by the insuring putholder-stockholder. For the leveraged call buyer, the maximum loss is still limited to $500. Now, however, this equals 100 percent of his investment! The potential for gain is again unlimited. Thus, the call buyer has leveraged the effect of the $500 risked. In truth, the price of the stock is not likely to rise as far in the three months of the call option as it might in six months. But by comparison, the call buyer has gotten most of the play obtained by the stock-and-put "insurance" investor on only one eleventh of the capital—that's leverage.

Tax Implications

Still another feature of option contracts involves their usage for tax considerations. Favorable strategies are possible in certain instances, but this advantage is less universal than insurance and leverage advantages. It is more a property of our tax system than of the option. For instance, puts provide the only means by which an investor can convert a decline in stock prices into a long-term capital gain for tax purposes. Short sales held for any length of time are taxable as income. Furthermore, options can be used to lock in the profits of a trade while postponing the realization of it until after a six-month holding period, thus achieving long-term tax status or deferring taxes into the following calendar year. Options are also used to generate large, long-term gains on successful risks, while probable unsuccessful purchases can be sold early enough to chalk up losses in the more desirable short-term category.

Option Strategies

Having discussed the uses of options for a buyer, we can investigate the position of the option writer. Again, we can use profit graphs to analyze the possible outcomes. The option writer must be prepared to sell stock (if he wrote a call) or buy stock (if he wrote a put). He must therefore have an assured reserve of capital to make good his promise. A call writer must guarantee his contract either by holding the stock or sufficient cash to buy the necessary stock at the prevailing price. Backing an option with cash rather than stock is called writing "naked."

Profit graphs for option writers tend to be, but are not always, the reverse of those of the option buyer. Generally, therefore, the option writer is seeking a small, fixed gain and risking a larger loss. But whether risk is taken on the upside or downside depends on whether cash or stock is chosen as backing for the option. The writer can also magnify his investment results by leveraging with borrowed money, up to margin-rule limits. The profit graph shown in Figure 30–3 contrasts the results of the two common ways call writers back their contracts.

Not that we need more pigeon tracks across our profit graphs, but

FIGURE 30–3
Profit Graph for Call Writer

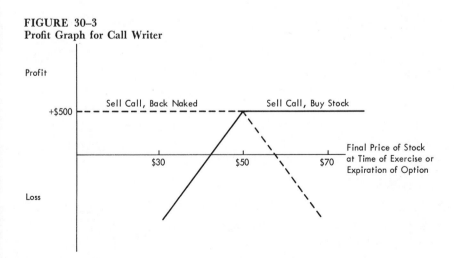

still other strategies exist. A "straddle" is an option contract that combines both a put and a call. Each option has the same striking price and expiration date, but they are exercisable separately. Straddles can also be backed naked or with stock, usually held long (backing the call) rather than short (backing the put).

A straddle premium represents the sum of a put premium and a call premium. This package is attractive to option writers. A 95-day straddle on our $50 stock would cost about $800, with the price comprised of a call premium of $500 plus a put premium of about $300. When the straddle is backed with 100 shares of the stock, the profit graph for the straddle writer would appear as shown in Figure 30-4.

FIGURE 30-4
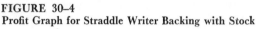
Profit Graph for Straddle Writer Backing with Stock

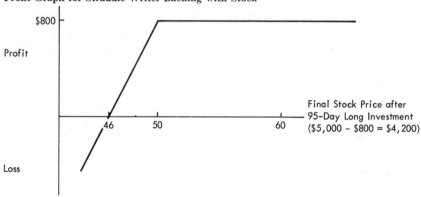

The maximum gain for the straddle writer in Figure 30-4 is $800. This is larger than the premium gain from just writing a call. The loss portion of the graph, however, descends twice as steeply as in the profit graph for the call writer, because both the stock and the put subject the writer to losses if the stock declines. The more daring way to back straddles is naked, just as it sounds. Margin requirements permit collateral deposits with less than full backing. This permits the option writer to leverage as well. The profit graph for a straddle writer with no offsetting position in the stock (backing naked) is shown in Figure 30-5.

Profitability of Options

The research investigating the actual profitability of option investing has increased in recent years, but it is still scanty and of mixed quality.

FIGURE 30–5
Profit Graph for Straddle Writer Backing Naked

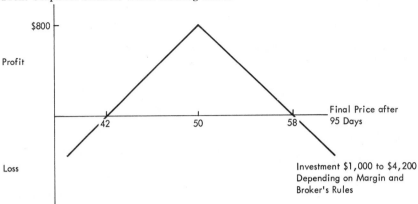

For a long time, the major piece of published evidence was an SEC staff report which compiled the outcome of every option written during June 1959. That study obviously was limited by not reflecting both up and down markets. It generated about as many misconceptions as it did pregnant understandings.

Papers published in Cootner [24], a doctoral dissertation by Gup [66] and popular books by Zieg [179] Filer [47] and Dadekian [33], and computerized simulations by Malkiel and Quandt [108] and Lederman [94] have not produced consistent results. Certain of these studies have flaws of experimental technique or statistical analysis, or their findings lack comprehensiveness. However, the more recent, complete, and technically correct studies have indicated a substantial investment role for *both* option buying and option writing in the portfolios of various types of investors. Some unpublished studies point to a 15 percent or more return at moderate risk for option writers who properly back their options. Still higher returns and risks have been reported for option buyers who concentrate on more volatile stocks.

Malkiel and Quandt [108], both respected economists on the faculty at Princeton, tested the various uses of options in computer simulations of 16 different investment strategies. Their conclusions, although stemming from hypothetical rather than historical stock price data, left *no doubt* that a large role for options exists in optimal management of investment portfolios. Depending on one's forecast for securities prices, it appeared quite likely from the results of the simulations that some type and amount of option activity produced the best portfolio outcome from the standpoint of both risk and return. Either the insurance or leverage advantages of options were worth exploiting in many cases.

Advanced Option Strategies

Still other investment strategies exist utilizing still other option instruments. Strips, straps and spreads are further contractual combinations of puts and calls whose analysis is beyond our purpose here. The technique of profit graphs, however, can be applied to understanding their results. Options provide useful opportunities, yet investment professionals themselves are too often unaware of their uses and benefits. If the "best" investment strategy in a given situation were to "strap your strip to a straddle," most Wall Streeters would not know what you were talking about.

A prior serious deficiency was the structure of the put and call market itself. This market appears to be broadening and becoming more efficient and less costly. However, the traditional weakness in option markets has been the need for a customer to deal with put and call option dealers *and* regular brokers. Most brokers cannot, themselves, deliver the option "merchandise" a specific customer wants, such as a three-month call on American Airlines at the current market price. They place option orders with put and call dealers, who specialize in such merchandise. Much like dealers in the over-the-counter market, these dealers function as market makers, but in options. They also increase the cost of doing business within this market system. The CBOE is a more efficient market structure for widespread dissemination of option prices and availability and should improve the usefulness of option investing.

chapter
31
A Few Words of Caution

It takes time to change the traditional and generally accepted ways of doing things. The concept of the rotary engine, for example, is not new. Felix Wankel conceived its basic design in 1926. Yet, today, some herald the Wankel engine as the invention of the decade.

The new science of investing has also evolved from early discoveries. Bachelier's work in 1900 preceded Einstein in the use of a key scientific equation. Since the early discoveries, however, modern investment research has made quantum jumps in our understanding of the random-walk model, the efficient capital market theory, and risk. In the next decade, much as the "newly discovered" Wankel engine may change the traditional automobile, scientific investment knowledge is destined to *revolutionize traditional investment practices.*

As the new science of investing attracts increased attention, it is imperative to evaluate it correctly. The scientific studies reported here have been conducted according to the high canons of academic objectivity and methodological excellence. In the spirit of educational interchange, these conclusions are being continually reassessed in the light of new theories and evidence. Taken together, this impartial research offers an unbiased, and not easily refutable, guide to correctly assessing the odds of various investment instruments and strategies.

The point of *assessing the odds* is important. Many people mistakenly assume that a single exception can invalidate the findings reported here. Consider, for example, the highly controversial conclusions by Irwin Friend, et al. that "when funds were classified by fund size, sales charges, management expenses, portfolio turnover, and investment objectives, no consistent relationship was found between these factors and investment

309

performance properly adjusted for risk." [55, p. 21] Many practitioners erroneously think that they can refute such studies by merely citing one or two examples which contradict these conclusions. When hearing such rebuttals, the reader should remember that such scientific findings are derived from the study of many investment portfolios. They are the odds of the overall game. We expect to find exceptions.

The words of caution are that the often-cited *exceptions neither make nor break the rules.* Moreover, knowing the odds is far more important than being misled by the stories of the exceptions. A parallel with gambling can confirm this point. A passline bet on a crap table has an expected loss of 1.4 percent of one's "investment." These are the odds of the game. If you make 1,000 one-dollar bets, you should expect to lose 1.4 percent, or $14. The more you play, the more predictable the results become. Indeed, the average loss on all bets of this type over a given day, month, or year, increasingly approaches this percentage. We do not expect, however, that every individual will have precisely this result. Some will lose a greater or lesser percentage of the total amount they wager, while others will win. Legend has it, for example, that a returning GI once won on 27 consecutive craps bets. It makes a great story—but it does not change the odds.

Similarly, one can say that in 1972 the M.I.T. Fund had one of the lowest management expense ratios and was also one of the worst performers. This is an interesting observation, but it should not be construed as revealing a cause-and-effect relationship. The important fact is that, after studying the performance of *many* mutual funds over *many* periods, Friend concluded that the level of management expenses is not correlated with fund performance!

The reader should be cautioned against using intuition or a few exceptions to reject scientific conclusions meant to reflect the *overall* odds of various investment instruments and strategies. While we anticipate exceptions, there is no reason to expect that *you* will be the exception.

The fragmented asset management and impulse buying that has characterized "investing" during the past decade has been based on intuition and stories. Over the next decade, rational investment planning and execution will be based on knowing the scientifically derived odds and using them to achieve well-planned objectives. This is the message of *The New Science of Investing.*

bibliography

Bibliography

References

1. Adams, D. F. "The Effect on Stock Price from Listing on the New York Stock Exchange." M.B.A. Thesis, New York University, 1965.

2. Alexander, Sidney S. "Price Movements in Speculative Markets: Trends or Random Walks," *Industrial Management Review*, vol. 2, no. 2 (May, 1961), pp. 7–26. Reprinted in Paul H. Cootner, ed., *The Random Character of Stock Market Prices*, Cambridge: Massachusetts Institute of Technology Press, 1964, pp. 199–218.

3. Arditti, Fred D. "Risk and the Required Return on Equity," *Journal of Finance*, vol. 22, no. 1 (March, 1967), pp. 19–36.

4. Bachelier, Louis. *Théorie de la speculation*. Paris: Gauthier-Villars, 1900. Translation by A. James Boness, reprinted in Paul H. Cootner, ed., *The Random Character of Stock Market Prices*, Cambridge: Massachusetts Institute of Technology Press, 1964, pp. 17–78.

5. Ball, Philip, and John W. Kennelly. "The Informational Content of Quarterly Earnings: An Extension and Some Further Evidence," *Journal of Business*, vol. 45, no. 3 (July, 1972), pp. 403–15.

6. Barker, C. Austin. "Effective Stock Splits," *Harvard Business Review*, vol. 34, no. 1 (January–February, 1956), pp. 101–06.

7. ———. "Stock Splits in a Bull Market," *Harvard Business Review*, vol. 35, no. 3 (May–June, 1957), pp. 72–79. Reprinted in E. Bruce Fredrikson, ed., *Frontiers of Investment Analysis*, Scranton: International Textbook Co., 1965, pp. 540–51.

313

8. Barney, Walter F. "An Investigation of Parametric Variation in a Moving Average Investment Rule." Unpublished Master's Thesis, Massachusetts Institute of Technology, Cambridge, 1964.

9. Bauer, John. "A Diffusion Index as Applied to Price Movements in the Stock Market." Unpublished Master's Thesis, Massachusetts Institute of Technology, Cambridge, 1964.

10. Blume, Marshall E. "The Assessment of Portfolio Performance—An Application to Portfolio Theory." Unpublished Ph.D. Dissertation, University of Chicago, 1968.

11. Bowyer, John W. *Investment Analysis and Management.* 4th ed. Homewood (Ill.) : Richard D. Irwin, Inc., 1972.

12. Brealey, Richard A. *An Introduction to Risk and Return from Common Stock Prices.* Cambridge: Massachusetts Institute of Technology Press, 1969.

13. ———. *Security Prices in a Competitive Market.* Cambridge: Massachusetts Institute of Technology Press, 1971.

14. Brown, Philip, and Ray Ball. "An Empirical Evaluation of Accounting Income Numbers," *Journal of Accounting Research,* vol. 6, no. 3 (Autumn, 1968), pp. 159–78.

15. Brown, Philip, and Victor Niederhoffer. "The Predictive Content of Quarterly Earnings," *Journal of Business,* vol. 41, no. 4 (October, 1968), pp. 488–97.

16. Cheney, H. L. "How Good Are Investment Advisory Services?" *Financial Executive,* vol. 37, no. 11 (November, 1969), pp. 30–35.

17. Clark, Lindley H. "Speaking of Business: Future Tense," *The Wall Street Journal,* vol. 181, no. 50 (March 13, 1973), p. 22.

18. Cohen, A. W. *The Chartcraft Method of Point and Figure Trading.* Larchmont (N.Y.) : Chartcraft, Inc., 1963.

19. ———. *Technical Indicator Analysis by Point and Figure Technique.* Larchmont (N.Y.) : Chartcraft, Inc., 1963.

20. Cohen, Jerome B., and Edward D. Zinbarg. *Investment Analysis and Portfolio Management,* Homewood (Ill.) : Richard D. Irwin, Inc., 1967.

21. Cohen, Kalman J., and Jerry A. Pogue. "An Empirical Evaluation of Alternative Portfolio Selection Models," *Journal of Business,* vol. 40, no. 2 (April, 1967), pp. 166–93.

22. ———. "Some Comments Concerning Mutual Fund Versus Random Portfolio Performance," *Journal of Business,* vol. 41, no. 2 (April, 1968), pp. 180–90.

23. Colker, S. S. "An Analysis of Security Recommendations by Broker-

age Houses," *Quarterly Review of Economics and Business,* vol. 3, no. 2 (Summer, 1963), pp. 19–28.

24. Cootner, Paul H., (ed.). *The Random Character of Stock Market Prices.* Cambridge: Massachusetts Institute of Technology Press, 1964.

25. ———. "Stock Prices: Random vs. Systematic Changes," *Industrial Management Review,* vol. 3, no. 2 (Spring, 1962), pp. 24–45. Reprinted in Paul H. Cootner, ed., *The Random Character of Stock Market Prices,* Cambridge: Massachusetts Institute of Technology Press, 1964. Reprinted in E. Bruce Fredrikson, ed., *Frontiers of Investment Analysis,* Scranton: International Textbook Co., 1965, pp. 489–510.

26. Copeland, R. M., and R. J. Marioni. "Executives' Forecasts of Earnings per Share vs. Forecasts of Naive Models," *Journal of Business,* vol. 45, no. 4 (October, 1972), pp. 497–512.

27. Cowles, Alfred. "Can Stock Market Forecasters Forecast?" *Econometrica,* vol. 1, no. 3 (July, 1933), pp. 309–24.

28. ———. "A Revision of Previous Conclusions Regarding Stock Price Behavior," *Econometrica,* vol. 28, no. 4 (October, 1960), pp. 909–15. Reprinted in Paul H. Cootner, ed., *The Random Character of Stock Market Prices,* Cambridge: Massachusetts Institute of Technology Press, 1964, pp. 132–38.

29. Cowles, Alfred, and Herbert F. Jones. "Some A Posteriori Probabilities in Stock Market Action," *Econometrica,* vol. 5, no. 3 (July, 1937), pp. 280–94.

30. Cragg, J. G., and Burton G. Malkiel. "The Consensus and Accuracy of Some Predictions of the Growth of Corporate Earnings," *Journal of Finance,* vol. 23, no. 1 (March, 1968), pp. 67–84.

31. Crowell, Richard. "Earnings Expectations, Security Valuation and the Cost of Equity Capital." Unpublished Ph.D. Dissertation, Massachusetts Institute of Technology, 1967.

32. Cushing, Barry. "The Effects of Accounting Policy Decision on Trends in Reported Corporate Earnings per Share." Ph.D. Dissertation, Michigan State University, 1969.

33. Dadekian, Zaven A. *The Strategy of Puts and Calls.* New York: Corinthian Editions, 1968.

34. Darling, P. G. "The Influence of Expectations and Liquidity on Dividend Policy," *Journal of Political Economy,* vol. 65, no. 3 (June, 1957), pp. 209–24.

35. Darvas, Nicholas. *How I Made $2,000,000 in the Stock Market.* Larchmont (N.Y.): American Research Council, 1960.

36. Douglas, George W. "Risk in the Equity Market: An Empirical Appraisal of Market Efficiency." Unpublished Ph.D. Dissertation, Yale University, 1967.

37. Driscoll, T. E. "Some Aspects of Corporate Insider Stock Holdings and Trading under Section 16 (b) of the Securities Exchange Act." M.B.A. Thesis, University of Pennsylvania, 1956.

38. Edwards, Robert D., and John Magee. *Technical Analysis of Stock Trends.* 4th ed. Springfield (Mass.): John Magee, 1962.

39. Evans, John Leslie. "Diversification and the Reduction of Dispersion: An Empirical Analysis." Unpublished Ph.D. Thesis, University of Washington, 1968.

40. Fama, Eugene F. "The Behavior of Stock Market Prices," *Journal of Business,* vol. 38, no. 1 (January, 1965), pp. 34–105.

41. Fama, Eugene F., and Marshall E. Blume. "Filter Rules and Stock Market Trading," *Journal of Business,* vol. 39, no. 1, part 2 (January, 1966), pp. 226–41.

42. Fama, Eugene F., and H. Babiak. "Dividend Policy: An Empirical Analysis," *Journal of the American Statistical Association,* vol. 63, no. 12 (December, 1968), pp. 1132–61.

43. Fama, Eugene F., L. Fisher, M. C. Jensen, and R. Roll. "The Adjustment of Stock Prices to New Information," *International Economic Review,* vol. 10, no. 2 (February, 1969), pp. 1–21.

44. Fama, Eugene F. "Efficient Capital Markets: A Review of Theory and Empirical Work," *Journal of Finance,* vol. 25, no. 2 (May, 1970), pp. 383–423.

45. Farrar, Donald Eugene. *The Investment Decision Under Uncertainty.* Englewood Cliffs (N.J.): Prentice-Hall, Inc., 1962.

46. Ferber, Robert. "Short-run Effects on Stock Market Services on Stock Prices," *Journal of Finance,* vol. 13, no. 1 (March, 1958), pp. 80–95.

47. Filer, Herbert. *Understanding Put and Call Options.* New York: Crown Publishers, Inc., 1959.

48. Fisher, Lawrence. "Outcomes for 'Random' Investments in Common Stocks Listed on the New York Stock Exchange," *Journal of Business,* vol. 3, no. 4 (April, 1965), pp. 149–61.

49. Fisher, Lawrence, and James H. Lorie. "Rates of Return on Investments in Common Stocks," *Journal of Business,* vol. 37, no. 1 (January, 1964), pp. 1–21. Reprinted (in part) in E. Bruce Fredrikson, ed., *Frontiers of Investment Analysis,* Scranton: International Textbook Co., 1965, pp. 159–76.

50. Francis, Jack Clark. "Do Some Stocks Consistently Lead or Lag the Market?" Working Paper No. 5–12. Rodney L. White Center for Financial Research, University of Pennsylvania, n.d.

51. Friedman, Milton, and Anna J. Schwartz. *Monetary History of the United States, 1867–1960.* New Jersey: Princeton University Press, 1963.

52. Friend, Irwin, et al., *A Study of Mutual Funds.* Prepared for the Securities and Exchange Commission by the Securities Research Unit, Wharton School of Finance and Commerce, University of Pennsylvania. Washington, D.C.: U.S. Government Printing Office, 1962.

53. Friend, Irwin, and Douglas Vickers. "Portfolio Selection and Investment Performance," *Journal of Finance,* vol. 20, no. 2 (September, 1965), pp. 391–415.

54. Friend, Irwin, James Longstreet, Ervin Miller, and Arleigh Hess. *Investment Banking and the New Issues Market.* New York: New York World Publishing Company, 1967.

55. Friend, Irwin, Marshall Blume, and Jean Crockett. *Mutual Funds and Other Institutional Investors: A New Perspective.* New York: McGraw-Hill Book Company, Inc., 1970.

56. Furst, R. W. "Does Listing Increase the Market Price of Common Stock?" *Journal of Business,* vol. 43, no. 4 (April, 1970), pp. 174–80.

57. Gaumnitz, Jack E. "Investment Diversification Under Uncertainty: An Examination of the Number of Securities in a Diversified Portfolio." Unpublished Ph.D. Dissertation, Stanford University, 1967.

58. Godfrey, Michael D., Clive W. J. Granger, and Oskar Morgenstern. "The Random-Walk Hypothesis of Stock Market Behavior," *Kyklos,* vol. 17, fasc. 1 (1964), pp. 1–30.

59. Graham, Benjamin, David L. Dodd, and Sidney Cottle. *Security Analysis.* 4th ed. New York: McGraw-Hill Book Company, Inc., 1951.

60. Granger, Clive W. J. "What the Random-Walk Model Does Not Say," *Financial Analysts Journal,* vol. 26, no. 3 (May–June, 1970), pp. 91–93.

61. Granger, Clive W. J., and Oskar Morgenstern. "Spectral Analysis of New York Stock Market Prices," *Kyklos,* vol. 16 (1963), pp. 1–27. Reprinted in Paul H. Cootner, ed., *The Random Character of Stock Market Prices,* Cambridge: Massachusetts Institute of Technology Press, 1964.

62. Green, David, Jr., and Joel Segall. "The Predictive Power of First Quarter Earnings Reports," *Journal of Business,* vol. 40, no. 1 (January, 1967), pp. 44–55.

63. ———. "Brickbats and Straw Men: A Reply to Brown and Niederhoffer," *Journal of Business,* vol. 41, no. 4 (October, 1968), pp. 498–502.

64. ———. "Return of Straw Man," *Journal of Business,* vol. 43, no. 1 (January, 1970), pp. 63–65.

65. Greenfield, Samuel C. *The High-Low Theory of Investment.* New York: Coward-McCann, Inc., 1968. Reprinted (in part) in Bill Adler, ed., *The Wall Street Reader,* New York: The World Publishing Company, 1970.

66. Gup, Benton E. "The Economics of the Security Option Markets." Unpublished Ph.D. Dissertation, University of Cincinnati, 1966.

67. Hagin, Robert L. "An Empirical Evaluation of Selected Hypotheses Related to Price Changes in the Stock Market." Unpublished Ph.D. Dissertation, University of California (Los Angeles), 1966.

68. Hamanda, R. S. "An Analysis of Diffusion Indices of Insiders' Transactions." Unpublished S.M. Thesis, Massachusetts Institute of Technology, 1961.

69. Hanna, M. "Short Interest: Bullish or Bearish?—Comment," *Journal of Finance,* vol. 23, no. 6 (June, 1968), pp. 520–23.

70. Hausman, Warren H. "A Note on the Value Line Contest: A Test of the Predictability of Stock-Price Changes," *Journal of Business,* vol. 42, no. 3 (July, 1969), pp. 317–20.

71. Hausman, Warren H., R. R. West, and J. A. Largay. "Stock Splits, Price Changes, and Trading Profits: A Synthesis." *Journal of Business,* vol. 44, no. 1 (January, 1971), pp. 69–77.

72. Homa, Kenneth E., and Dwight M. Jaffee. "The Supply of Money and Common Stock Prices," *Journal of Finance,* vol. 26, no. 5 (December, 1971), pp. 1045–66.

73. Houthakker, Hendrik S. "Systematic and Random Elements in Short-term Price Movements," *American Economic Review,* vol. 51, no. 2 (May, 1961), pp. 164–72.

74. James, F. E., Jr. "Monthly Moving Averages—An Effective Investment Tool?," *Journal of Financial and Quantitative Analysis,* vol. 3, no. 3 (September, 1968), pp. 315–26.

75. Jensen, Michael C. "Random Walks: Reality or Myth—Comment," *Financial Analysts Journal,* vol. 23, no. 6 (November–December, 1967), pp. 77–85.

76. ———. "The Performance of Mutual Funds in the Period 1945–

1964," *Journal of Finance,* vol. 23, no. 5 (May, 1968), pp. 389–416.

77. Jensen, Michael C., and George A. Benington. "Random Walks and Technical Theories: Some Additional Evidence," *Journal of Finance,* vol. 25, no. 2 (May, 1970), pp. 469–81.

78. Jiler, William L. *How Charts Can Help You In The Stock Market.* New York: Commodity Research Publication Corp. 1962. Reprinted (in part) in Bill Alder, ed., *The Wall Street Reader,* New York: The World Publishing Co., 1970. pp. 15–23.

79. Johnson, Paul R., and H. Marchman. "Moving Averages and Exponential Smoothing Applied to Common Stock Prices," Mimeographed, n.d.

80. Kaish, S. "Odd-Lot Profit and Loss Performance," *Financial Analysts Journal,* vol. 25, no. 9 (September–October, 1969), pp. 83–92.

81. Kaplan, Gilbert Edmund, and Chris Welles. *The Money Managers.* New York: Random House, 1969.

82. Kaplan, Robert S., and Richard Roll. "Investor Evaluation of Accounting Information: Some Empirical Evidence," *Journal of Business,* vol. 45, no. 2 (April, 1972), pp. 225–57.

83. Kaplan, Robert S., and Roman L. Weil. "Risk and the Value Line Contest," *Financial Analysts Journal,* vol. 29, no. 4 (July–August, 1973), pp. 56–62.

84. Kendall, Maurice George. *The Advanced Theory of Statistics.* London: Griffin, 1943.

85. ———. "The Analysis of Economic Time Series—Part I: Prices," *Journal of the Royal Statistical Society,* Series A (General), vol. 116, pt. 1 (1953), pp. 11–25. Reprinted in Paul H. Cootner, ed., *The Random Character of Stock Market Prices,* Cambridge: Massachusetts Institute of Technology Press, 1964, pp. 85–99.

86. Kewley, T. J., and R. A. Stevenson. "The Odd-Lot Theory as Revealed by Purchase and Sales Statistics for Individual Stocks," *Financial Analysts Journal,* vol. 23, no. 5 (September–October), 1967, pp. 103–06.

87. ———. "The Odd-Lot Theory for Individual Stocks: A Reply," *Financial Analysts Journal,* vol. 25, no. 1 (January–February, 1969), pp. 99–104.

88. King, Benjamin F. "The Latent Statistical Structure of Security Price Changes." Unpublished Ph.D. Thesis, University of Chicago, 1964.

89. Kisor, Manown, Jr., and Van A. Messner. "The Filter Approach

and Earnings Forecasts," *Financial Analysts Journal,* vol. 25, no. 1 (January, 1969), pp. 109–15.

90. Kisor, Manown, Jr., and Victor Niederhoffer. "Odd-Lot Short Sales Ratio: It Signals a Market Rise." *Barron's,* (September 1, 1969), p. 8.

91. Klein, D. J. "The Odd-Lot Stock Trading Theory." Ph.D. Thesis, Michigan State University, 1964.

92. Kolin, Alexander. *Physics: Its Laws, Ideas and Methods.* New York: McGraw-Hill Book Company, Inc., 1950.

93. Latané, Henry Allen, and Donald L. Tuttle. "An Analysis of Common Stock Price Ratios," *Southern Economic Journal,* vol. 33, no. 1 (January, 1967), pp. 343–54.

94. Lederman, David. "Put and Call Options with Special Emphasis on Option Portfolios." Unpublished Master's Thesis, Stanford University, 1969.

95. Levin, Jesse. "Prophetic Leaders," *Financial Analysts Journal,* vol. 26, no. 4 (July–August, 1970), pp. 87–90.

96. Levine, Sidney. "Heuristic Determination of Optimum Filter for Use in a Rule of Speculative Market Action." Unpublished Master's Thesis, Massachusetts Institute of Technology, Cambridge, 1962.

97. Levy, Robert A. "An Evaluation of Selected Applications of Stock Market Timing Techniques, Trading Tactics and Trend Analysis." Unpublished Ph.D. Thesis, The American University, Washington, D.C., 1966.

98. ———. "Random Walks: Reality or Myth," *Financial Analysts Journal,* vol. 23, no. 6 (November–December, 1967), pp. 129–32.

99. ———. "Random Walks: Reality or Myth—Reply," *Financial Analysts Journal,* vol. 23, no. 1 (January–February, 1968), pp. 129–32.

100. Lintner, John. "Distribution of Incomes of Corporations among Dividends, Retained Earnings and Taxes," *American Economic Review,* vol. 46, no. 5 (May, 1956), pp. 97–113.

101. Lintner, John, and Robert Glauber. "Higgledy Piggledy Growth in America." Unpublished paper prepared for the Seminar on the Analysis of Security Prices, University of Chicago, (May, 1967).

102. Loeb, Gerald M. *The Battle for Investment Survival.* New York: Simon and Schuster, 1957.

103. ———. *The Battle for Stock Market Profits,* New York: Simon and Schuster, 1971.

104. Logue, Dennis Emhardt. "An Empirical Appraisal of the Market for First Public Offerings of Common Stock." Unpublished Ph.D. Dissertation, Cornell University, 1971.

105. Loll, Leo M., Jr., and Julian G. Buckley. *Questions and Answers on Securities Markets.* Englewood Cliffs, New Jersey: Prentice Hall, Inc., 1968.

106. Lorie, James H., and Victor Niederhoffer. "Predictive and Statistical Properties of Insider Trading," *Journal of Law and Economics,* vol. 11, no. 4 (April, 1968), pp. 35–53.

107. Lorie, James H., and Mary T. Hamilton. *The Stock Market: Theories and Evidence.* Homewood (Ill.): Richard D. Irwin, Inc., 1973.

108. Malkiel, Burton G., and Richard E. Quandt. *Strategies and Rational Decisions in the Securities Options Market.* Cambridge, Mass.: Massachusetts Institute of Technology Press, 1969.

109. Mandelbrot, Benoit. "The Variation of Certain Speculative Prices," *Journal of Business,* vol. 36, no. 4 (October, 1962), pp. 394–419. Reprinted in Paul H. Cootner, ed., *The Random Character of Stock Market Prices,* Cambridge: Massachusetts Institute of Technology Press, 1964, pp. 307–337.

110. ———. "Forecasts of Future Prices, Unbiased Markets, and 'Martingale' Models," *Journal of Business,* vol. 39, no. 1, part 2 (January, 1966), pp. 242–55.

111. ———. "The Variation of Some Other Speculative Prices," *Journal of Business,* vol. 40, no. 4 (October, 1967), pp. 393–413.

112. Markowitz, Harry M. *Portfolio Selection: Efficient Diversification of Investments.* New York: John Wiley and Sons, Inc., 1959.

113. ———. "Portfolio Selection," *Journal of Finance,* vol. 7, no. 1 (March, 1952), pp. 77–91, Reprinted in E. Bruce Fredrikson, ed., *Frontiers of Investment Analysis,* Scranton: International Textbook Co., 1965, pp. 353–66.

114. Markstein, David L. *Practical Ways to Build a Fortune in the Stock Market.* New York: Cornerstone Library Inc., 1969. Reprinted (in part) in Bill Alder, ed., *The Wall Street Reader,* New York: The World Publishing Company, 1970, pp. 214–19.

115. May, A. Wilfred. "Current Popular Delusions About the Stock Split and Stock Dividend," *The Commercial and Financial Chronicle,* vol. 184, no. 5586 (November 15, 1956), p. 5.

116. ———. "On Stock Market Forecasting and Timing," *The Commercial and Financial Cronicle,* vol. 186, no. 5690 (Thursday, November 14, 1957), p. 5. Reprinted in Richard E. Ball, ed., *Readings In Investments,* Boston: Allyn and Bacon, Inc., pp. 380–92.

117. Mayor, T. H. "Short Trading Activities and the Price of Equities: Some Simulation and Regression Results," *Journal of Financial*

and Quantitative Analysis, vol. 3, no. 9 (September, 1968), pp. 283–98.

118. McDonald, J. G., and A. K. Fisher. "New Issue Stock Price Behavior," *Journal of Finance,* vol. 27, no. 1 (March, 1972), pp. 97–102.

119. Merjos, A. "Going on the Big Board," *Barron's,* (May 1, 1967), pp. 9–10.

120. ———. "Going on the Big Board: Stocks Act Better before Listing than Right Afterward." *Barron's,* (January 29, 1962), pp. 54 ff.

121. ———. "New Listings and Their Price Behavior." *Journal of Finance,* vol. 25, no. 9 (September, 1970), pp. 783–94.

122. Moore, Arnold B. "A Statistical Analysis of Common Stock Prices." Unpublished Ph.D. Thesis, University of Chicago, 1962.

123. Murphy, John Michael. "The Value Line Contest: 1969," *Financial Analysts Journal,* vol. 26, no. 3 (May–June, 1970), pp. 94–100.

124. Murphy, Joseph E. Jr. "Relative Growth of Earnings per Share—Past and Future," *Financial Analysts Journal,* vol. 22, no. 6 (November–December, 1966), pp. 73–76.

125. ———. "Return, Payout and Growth," *Financial Analysts Journal,* vol. 23, no. 3 (May–June, 1967), pp. 91–96.

126. Newell, Gale E. "Revisions of Reported Quarterly Earnings," *Journal of Business,* vol. 44, no. 3 (July, 1971), pp. 282–85.

127. Ney, Richard. *The Wall Street Jungle.* New York: Grove Press, Inc., 1970.

128. Niederhoffer, Victor. "Non-Randomness in Stock Prices: A New Model of Stock Price Movements." Unpublished Bachelor's Thesis, Department of Economics, Harvard, 1965.

129. ———. "Clustering of Stock Prices," *Operation Research,* vol. 13. no. 2 (March–April, 1965), pp. 258–65.

130. ———. "A New Look at Clustering of Stock Prices," *Journal of Business,* vol. 39, no. 2 (April, 1966), pp. 309–13.

131. ———. "The Predictive Content of First Quarter Earnings Reports," *Journal of Business,* vol. 43, no. 1 (January, 1970), pp. 60–62.

132. Niederhoffer, Victor, and M. F. M. Osborne. "Market Making and Reversal on the Stock Exchange," *Journal of the American Statistical Association,* vol. 61, no. 316 (December, 1966), pp. 887–916.

133. Niederhoffer, Victor, and Patrick Regan. "Earnings Changes, Analysts' Forecasts, and Stock Prices," *Financial Analysts Journal,* vol. 28, no. 3 (May–June, 1972), pp. 65–71.

134. O'Brien, John W. "How Market Theory Can Help Investors Set Goals, Select Investment Managers and Appraise Investment Performance," *Financial Analysts Journal,* vol. 26, no. 4 (July–August, 1970), pp. 91–103.

135. Osborne, M. F. M. "Brownian Motion in the Stock Market," *Operations Research,* vol. 7, no. 2 (March–April, 1959), pp. 145–73. Reprinted in Paul H. Cootner, ed., *The Random Character of Stock Market Prices,* Cambridge: Massachusetts Institute of Technology Press, 1964, pp. 100–128.

136. ———. "Periodic Structure of Brownian Motion of Stock Prices," *Operations Research,* vol. 10, no. 3 (May–June, 1962), pp. 345–79. Reprinted in Paul H. Cootner, ed., *The Random Character of Stock Market Prices,* Cambridge: Massachusetts Institute of Technology Press, 1964, pp. 262–96.

137. Pettit, Richardson R. "Dividend Announcements and Security Performance," Preliminary Working Paper, Rodney L. White Center for Financial Research, Wharton School of Finance and Commerce, University of Pennsylvania, February 19, 1971.

138. Pratt, Shannon P. "Relationship Between Risk and Rate of Return for Common Stocks." Unpublished D.B.A. Dissertation, Indiana University, 1966.

139. Pratt, Shannon P., and C. W. DeVere. "Relationship Between Insider Trading and Rates of Return for NYSE Common Stocks, 1960–1966." Unpublished paper prepared for the Seminar on the Analysis of Security Prices, University of Chicago, (May, 1968).

140. Reilly, F. K., and K. Hatfield. "Experience with New Stock Issues," *Financial Analysis Journal,* vol. 25, no. 5 (September–October, 1969), pp. 73–82.

141. Rieke, R. C. "Selling on the News," *Barron's,* vol. 44, no. 48 (November 30, 1964) p. 9.

142. Rinfret, Pierre A. "Investment Managers *Are* Worth Their Keep," *Financial Analysts Journal,* vol. 24, no. 2 (March–April, 1968), pp. 163–70.

143. Roberts, Harry V. "Stock Market 'Patterns' and Financial Analysis," *Journal of Finance,* vol. 14, no. 1 (March, 1959), pp. 1–10. Reprinted in Paul H. Cootner, ed., *The Random Character of Stock Market Prices,* Cambridge: Massachusetts Institute of Technology Press, 1964, pp. 7–16, and Reprinted in Richard E. Ball, ed., *Readings in Investments,* Boston: Allyn and Bacon, Inc., 1965, pp. 369–79.

144. Rogoff, D. L. "The Forecasting Properties of Insiders' Transactions." Unpublished Ph.D. Thesis, Michigan State University, 1964.

145. Ruff, R. T. "The Effect of Selection and Recommendation of a Stock of the Month," *Financial Analysts Journal,* vol. 19, no. 2 (March–April, 1965), pp. 41–43.

146. Samuelson, Paul A. "Proof that Properly Anticipated Prices Fluctuate Randomly," *Industrial Management Review,* vol. 6, no. 2 (Spring, 1965), pp. 41–49.

147. Scholes, Myron. "A Test of the Competitive Hypothesis: The Market for New Issues and Secondary Offerings." Unpublished Ph.D. Thesis, Graduate School of Business, University of Chicago, 1969.

148. Seneca, Joseph J. "Short Interest: Bearish or Bullish?", *Journal of Finance,* vol. 22, no. 3 (March, 1967), pp. 67–70.

149. ———. "Short Interest: Bullish or Bearish?—Reply," *Journal of Finance,* vol. 23, no. 3 (March, 1967), pp. 524–27.

150. Sharpe, William F. "Mutual Fund Performance," *Journal of Business,* vol. 39, no. 1, pt. 2 (January, 1966), pp. 119–38.

151. Shelton, John P. "The Value Line Contest: A Test of the Predictability of Stock Price Changes," *Journal of Business,* vol. 40, no. 3 (July, 1967), pp. 251–69.

152. Shenker, Israel. "Professors Top Wall Street's Stock Advice," *The New York Times,* Saturday, March 11, 1972, p. 37.

153. Shiskin, Julius. "Systematic Aspects of Stock Price Fluctuation." Unpublished paper prepared for the Seminar on the Analysis of Security Prices, University of Chicago, (May, 1967).

154. Slutsky, Eugene. "The Summation of Random Causes as the Source of Cyclic Processes," *Econometrica,* vol. 5, no. 2 (April, 1937), pp. 105–46.

155. Smith, Adam. *An Inquiry Into the Nature and Causes of the Wealth of Nations.* 2d ed., vol. 1, bk 2, London: Methuen and Company, Ltd., 1904.

156. Smith, Adam. *The Money Game.* New York: Random House, 1968.

157. Smith, Randall D. "Short Interest and Stock Market Prices," *Financial Analysts Journal* vol. 24, no. 6 (November–December, 1968), pp. 151–54.

158. Sprinkel, Beryl W. *Money and Stock Prices.* Homewood (Ill.): Richard D. Irwin, Inc., 1964.

159. ———. *Money and Markets: A Monetarist View.* Homewood (Ill.): Richard D. Irwin, Inc., 1971.

160. Stauffer, C. Hoff Jr., and Robert C. Vogel. "Parameters of Mutual Fund Performance," Wesleyan University, Middletown, Conn., 1969 (mimeographed).

161. Stern, Joel M. "The Case Against Maximizing Earnings Per Share," *Financial Analysts Journal*, vol. 26, no. 5 (September–October, 1970), pp. 107–12.

162. Stigler, George J. "Public Regulation of the Securities Markets," *Journal of Business*, vol. 37, no. 2 (April, 1964), pp. 117–42.

163. Stoffels, J. D. "Stock Recommendations by Investment Advisory Services: Immediate Effects on Market Pricing," *Financial Analysts Journal*, vol. 22, no. 3 (March, 1966), pp. 77–86.

164. Tabell, Edmund W., and Anthony W. Tabell. "The Case for Technical Analysis," *Financial Analysts Journal*, vol. 20, no. 2 (March–April, 1964), pp. 67–76.

165. Taussig, F. W. "Is Market Price Determinate." *Quarterly Journal of Economics*, vol. 35, no. 5 (May, 1921), pp. 394–411.

166. Thorp, Edward O., and Sheen T. Kassouf. *Beat The Market, A Scientific Stock Market System*. New York: Random House, 1967.

167. Treynor, Jack L. "How to Rate Management of Investment Funds," *Harvard Business Review*, vol. 43, no. 1 (January–February, 1965), pp. 63–76. Reprinted in David A. West, ed., *Readings In Investment Analysis*, Scranton: International Textbook Co., 1969, pp. 137–58.

168. Van Horne, James C. "New Listings and Their Price Behavior." *Journal of Finance*, vol. 25, no. 9 (September, 1970), pp. 783–94.

169. Van Horne, James C., and George G. C. Parker. "Technical Trading Rules: A Comment," *Financial Analysts Journal*, vol. 24, no. 4 (July–August, 1968), pp. 128–32.

170. von Neumann, John, and Oskar Morgenstern. *The Theory of Games and Economic Behavior*. New York: John Wiley and Sons, Inc., 1940.

171. Wallich, Henry C. "What Does the Random-Walk Hypothesis Mean to Security Analysis?" *Financial Analysts Journal*, vol. 24, no. 2 (March–April, 1968), pp. 159–62.

172. Welles, Chris. "The Beta Revolution: Learning to Live with Risk," *Institutional Investor*, vol. 5, no. 9 (September, 1971), pp. 21–27 ff.

173. West, Richard R. "Mutual Fund Performance and the Theory of Capital Asset Pricing: Some Comments," *Journal of Business*, vol. 41, no. 4 (April, 1968), pp. 230–34.

174. Whitbeck, Volkert S., and Manown Kisor, Jr. "A New Tool in Investment Decision Making," *Financial Analysts Journal,* vol. 19, no. 3 (May–June, 1963), pp. 55–62. Reprinted in E. Bruce Fredrickson, ed., *Frontiers of Investment Analysis,* Scranton: International Textbook Co., 1965, pp. 335–50.

175. Working, Holbrook. "A Random-Difference Series for Use in the Analysis of Time Series," *Journal of the American Statistical Association,* vol. 29, no. 185 (March, 1934), pp. 11–24.

176. ———. "New Ideas and Methods for Price Research," *Journal of Farm Economics,* vol. 38, no. 5 (December, 1956), pp. 1427–36.

177. ———. "Note on the Correlation of First Differences of Averages in a Random Chain," *Econometrica,* vol. 28, no. 4 (October, 1960), pp. 916–18. Reprinted in Paul H. Cootner, ed., *The Random Character of Stock Market Prices,* Cambridge: Massachusetts Institute of Technology Press, 1964, pp. 129–131.

178. Wu, Hsiu-Kwang. "Corporate Insider Trading, Profitability and Stock Price Movement." Unpublished Ph.D. Thesis, University of Pennsylvania, 1963.

179. Zieg, Kermit C., Jr. *The Profitability of Stock Options.* Larchmont, (N.Y.): Investors Intelligence, Inc., 1970.

Periodical References

180. *Business Week,* December 20, 1969, p. 36.
181. *Business Week,* December 18, 1971, p. 88.
182. *Business Week,* December 23, 1972, p. 111.
183. *Forbes,* Special Report 1967, p. 5.
184. *Forbes,* April 15, 1969, p. 80.
185. *Forbes,* August 15, 1971, p. 69.
186. *Forbes,* December 1, 1972, p. 37.
187. *Fortune,* July 1, 1966, p. 160.
188. *Fortune,* January, 1970, p. 101.
189. *Newsweek,* July 15, 1971, p. 46.
190. *Time,* June 27, 1969, p. 71.
191. *Wall Street Journal,* May 29, 1970, p. 5.
192. *Wall Street Journal,* June 30, 1971, p. 27.
193. *Wall Street Journal,* December 8, 1971, p. 2.
194. *Wall Street Journal,* December 11, 1972, p. 14.
195. *Wall Street Journal,* March 13, 1973, p. 5.

index

Index

329

Index